Relationship-Based Care
A Model for Transforming Practice

Relationship-Based Care

Care

A Model for Transforming Practice

MARY KOLOROUTIS, EDITOR

CREATIVE

HEALTH CARE

MANAGEMENT

ISBN-10: 1-886624-19-4
ISBN-13: 978-1-886624-19-1

Seventeenth Printing: July 2013

17 16 15 14 13   20 19 18 17

For permission and ordering information, write to:

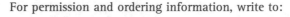

Creative Health Care Management, Inc.
5610 Rowland Road, Suite 100
Minneapolis, MN 55343-8905

chcm@chcm.com
or call: 800.728.7766 or 952.854.9015
www.chcm.com

CREATIVE
HEALTH CARE
MANAGEMENT

This book is dedicated to those health care clinicians, managers, and administrators who come to work every day and give of themselves through acts and attitudes of hope, compassion, and care. We honor you for making such a difference in the lives of the patients and families you serve.

TABLE OF
CONTENTS

Foreword • *vii*
Jean Watson

Acknowledgements • *xi*

Introduction • *1*
Mary Koloroutis

ONE — A Caring and Healing Environment • *23*
Jayne Felgen

TWO — Leadership • *53*
Mary Koloroutis

THREE — Teamwork • *91*
Donna Wright

FOUR — Professional Nursing Practice • *117*
Mary Koloroutis

FIVE — Patient Care Delivery • *159*
Colleen Person

SIX — Resource Driven Practice • *183*
Marie Manthey and Mary Koloroutis

SEVEN — Outcomes Measurement • *215*
Leah Kinnaird and Sharon Dingman

Afterword • *249*
Mary Koloroutis

Appendix A • *253*
Partners-In-Practice Overview

Appendix B • *257*
Commitment to My Co-worker Healthy Team Assessment Survey

References • *259*

Index • *263*

About the Authors • *287*

Foreword

Jean Watson

This publication marks the birth of a new era in health care. It ushers in a new consciousness of the deep dimensions of health and healing. At the core of this new consciousness are *relationships* and *caring*. What is special about this publication is that it offers practical models to guide practitioners in transforming care delivery—from the inside out.

Since the national Pew-Fetzer report (Tressolini, 1994) on health care reform and relationship-centered care, there have been myriad efforts, activities, publications, research initiatives, newsletters, and practice incentives designed to re-establish relationships and caring as the basis for transformation of health care practitioners, systems, and delivery models.

In this book, to *transform* specifically means to change the condition of what currently exists. According to the authors of this book, *transformative* change requires three things:

- Leaders at all levels of the organization who are committed to the change;

- Adoption by the organization of a methodology for the change it desires; and

- Clear communication of goals—conveyed comprehensively and persuasively enough to inspire all who are actively engaged in the process.

These three things, combined with the authors' set of 12 basic values assumptions, guide the transformation process. The twelve basic values assumptions that guide this process of internal change are:

1. The meaning and essence of care are experienced in the moment when one human being connects with another.

2. Feeling connected to one another creates harmony and healing; feeling isolated destroys spirit.

3. Each and every member of an organization, in all disciplines and departments, has a valuable contribution to make.

4. The relationship between patients and their families and members of the clinical team belongs at the heart of care delivery.

5. Care providers' knowledge of self and self-care are fundamental requirements for quality care and healthy interpersonal relationships.

6. Healthy relationships among members of the health care team lead to the delivery of quality care and result in high patient, physician, and staff satisfaction.

7. People are most satisfied when their roles and daily work practices are in alignment with their personal and professional values—when they know they are making a positive difference for patients, families, and their colleagues.

8. The value of *relationship* in patient care must be understood, valued, and agreed to by all members of the health care organization.

9. A therapeutic relationship between a patient/family and a Professional Nurse is essential to quality patient care.

10. Patient experiences improve measurably when staff members "own" their own practice and know that they are valued for their contributions.

11. People willingly change when they are *inspired* and share a common vision; when an *infrastructure* is implemented to support the new ways of working; when relevant *education* is provided for personal and professional development; and when they see *evidence* of the success of the new plan.

12. Transformational change happens one relationship at a time.

All of the elements of the practice model proposed for delivery transformation are based upon these twelve basic values. This book exists to teach readers how to bring these values to life through practice.

Relationship-Based Care: A Model for Transforming Practice was written, coordinated, and published by the consultants of Creative Health Care Management, an international health care consulting firm with an inspiring history of 25 years of excellence in transforming health care. The transformations it has overseen are all based upon existing caring theories and nursing models and have been guided by a commitment to caring relationships and the patterns of delivery that support those relationships. This collected work combines the successful leadership, experience, practice, knowledge, and expertise of its authors.

This work highlights *what really matters* in addressing both current and changing needs in health care. It is grounded in theory, research, and empirical experience. This work is a service to all health care practitioners, organizational leaders, faculty, and students who wish to survive and thrive now and in the future. This book offers a working template for sustaining caring relationships and thus transforming health care delivery. It offers lasting solutions for deepening caring and healing relationships for self and systems.

—Jean Watson, PhD, RN, FAAN, is a Distinguished Professor of Nursing at the University of Colorado Health Sciences Center in Denver, Colorado.

Acknowledgements

We extend our heartfelt appreciation to all of our clients who have invited us into their organizations and allowed us to serve them. We are privileged to work with such visionary and compassionate leaders to co-create caring and healing work environments and Relationship-Based Care. It is through our relationships with you that transformative change begins.

Thank you to Jill Bayless, CNO, Longview Medical Center (Longview, TX); Sandy Dandrinos-Smith, Healthcare Consultant (Newton, MA); Mourine Evans, Director of Staff Development and Research, Children's National Medical Center (Washington, DC); Eileen Gage, VP, Finger Lakes Health (Geneva, NY); Shirley Heintz, VP, St. Francis Medical Center (Topeka, KS); Eileen Nahigan, VP, CNO, Kaleida Health (Buffalo, NY); John Nelson, President, Nurse Environment (New Brighton, MN); Cathy North, VP, CNO, Schuyler Hospital (Montour Falls, NY); Carol Robinson, VP, University of California Davis Medical Center (Sacramento, CA); Pat Ruflin, CEO, Parma Community General Hospital (Parma, OH); Larry Savett, MD, Clinical Professor, Department of Medicine, University of Minnesota (Minneapolis, MN); Kristen Swanson, Chair, Family and Child Nursing, University of Washington (Seattle, WA); Pam Thompson, CEO, American Organization of Nurse Executives (Washington, DC); and Jean Watson, Distinguished Professor of Nursing, Murchinson-Scoville

Endowed Chair in Caring Science, University of Colorado Health Sciences Center (Denver, CO) for taking time and energy to review this manuscript in it's infancy and help us to bring it to readiness for publication. Your feedback, practical suggestions, and encouragement gave us the momentum to move forward and complete this book.

A special thank you to John Nelson for your enthusiastic support and practical assistance in the writing of this book. We appreciate your review, recommendations, and contributions particularly in the writing of the Professional Nursing Practice and Outcomes Measurement chapters. Your background in these areas and extensive knowledge of the literature are valued and recognized by all of us. Mary Jo Kreitzer, we thank you for your review and contributions to the Caring and Healing Chapter. Your work in this field is highly respected and we appreciate your assistance in this area. We also extend our deepest gratitude to Jean Watson for writing the forward to this book and encouraging our work. We have great respect for the work you do in the area of caring and therapeutic relationships. We are honored to call you colleague.

Our warmest appreciation to all the wonderful "behind the scenes" colleagues at Creative Health Care Management—with special gratitude to Beth Beaty and Chris Bjork for your proactive planning, steady guidance, assistance, creative energy, and vision. We are blessed to work with you and know that whatever we produce can only happen through the incredible teamwork we experience with you.

We thank Rebecca Smith for her art and skill in editing our manuscript. You helped us make this book "sing" through your thoughtful questions, drive for clarity, skillful challenges, and your encouragement about the importance of this work.

We extend our deepest respect and appreciation to Marie Manthey. You are our founder, mentor and wisdom keeper. We are thrilled to be able to describe the work that has evolved over the past twenty-five years through your vision and leadership. You have led the way in taking theory into practice and making it live through your no-nonsense, hands on, no-holds-barred approach. You keep us humble and honest.

We appreciate our leaders for their vision and support for this journey. Colleen Person wanted a book that would provide health care leaders with a roadmap for transforming their organizations. You are the reason this book exists. Without your "push," we would still be trying to "perfect" the product. Jayne Felgen reminds us every day that we are privileged to contribute to the field. You inspire us to keep reaching and developing ourselves and our programs and services. Brano Stankovsky supported and believed in us and this project. Your enthusiasm and commitment to creating products and services that will be useful and valuable to our clients informs all that we do.

Finally, and most important of all, we thank *you* the reader for your commitment to care and relationships and for joining with us to create more humane and compassionate health care services.

Introduction

Mary Koloroutis

We are creatures of community. Those individuals, societies, and cultures who learned to take care of each other, to love each other, and to nurture relationships with each other during the past several hundred thousand years were more likely to survive than those who did not.

Dean Ornish, MD

An organization is commonly defined as "an administrative and functional structure—as in a business." One is immediately struck by the huge disconnect between this rather technical and understated definition and what we know from experience to be true about organizations. We know that within organizations there is a complicated interplay between the needs and expectations of individuals and the needs and expectations of the organization as a whole. We know that organizations have unique cultures and pressures based on the contexts and demands of their particular environments.

We also know that *health care* organizations have a specialized and extraordinary purpose and function. Within health care organizations, profound human experiences happen every single day. Health care professionals come to work because they choose to care for people who are experiencing great vulnerability. The patients and families they come into contact with are under-

Overview

Organizations are dynamic and complex systems comprised of a diverse collection of human beings with different backgrounds and life stories.

1

going surgical interventions, facing serious or life-threatening illnesses, and/or experiencing the immense personal change associated with the joys and excitement of childbirth or the devastation of loss, grief, and death.

Just as there is a disconnect between the purely technical definition of *organization* and our knowledge and understanding of the human aspects of organizations, there is frequently the same sort of disconnect between *what drives* an organization and *what matters most* in an organization. In the past decade, health care organizations have been driven by complicated economic, political, and market forces. These forces create a chaotic environment that runs counter to much of what we value about health and healing. Health care leaders and staff often feel demoralized when they find themselves in the middle of a health care delivery system that seems to have lost touch with the very reasons they've chosen health care as their profession. Far too many report feeling like their core mission has been lost and that an unacceptable amount of their energy is spent on trying to survive the chaos.

Norman Cousins wrote *Anatomy of an Illness* about his own experience of being hospitalized for progressive paralysis, (ankylosing spondylitis) a degeneration of the connective tissue in the spine. He describes an experience of the gradual loss of control over his life and destiny in the partial list below (Cousins, 1979, p 153-154). This list, generated over 25 years ago, captures the complexity of the human response to illness and the daunting responsibility healers and health care organizations have to be conscious of the humanity of each person they serve. It magnifies the power and ethical imperative of connecting human-to-human.

There was first of all the feeling of helplessness—a serious disease in itself.

There was the subconscious fear of never being able to function normally again.

There was the reluctance to be thought a complainer.

There was the desire not to add to the already great burden of apprehension felt by one's family; this added to the isolation.

There was the conflict between the terror of loneliness and the desire to be left alone.

There was the lack of self-esteem, the subconscious feeling perhaps that our illness was a manifestation of our inadequacy.

There was the fear that decisions were being made behind our backs, that not everything was made known that we wanted to know. . . yet dreaded knowing.

There was the morbid fear of intrusive technology, fear of being metabolized by a database, never to regain our faces again.

There was resentment of strangers who came at us with needles and vials—some of which put supposedly magic substances in our veins, and others which took more of our blood than we thought we could afford to lose.

There was the distress of being wheeled through white corridors to laboratories for all sorts of strange encounters with compact machines and blinking lights and whirling discs.

And there was the utter void created by the longing—ineradicable, unremitting, pervasive—for warmth of human contact. A warm smile and an outstretched hand were valued even above the offerings of modern science, but the latter were far more accessible than the former.

Finally, in this decade, health care organizations are discovering that determining what matters most to patients, families, and staff is the most logical starting point for creating a successful organization. And not surprisingly, focusing on the value of relationships has once again come to the fore. Health care organizations exist to provide compassionate care and service to people in times of illness and suffering. This is the core of the business—the purpose of the organization and *what matters first, last, and most* in health care. Marie Manthey, CHCM's founder, goes right to the heart of the matter when she says, *"I am convinced that the chaos we are experiencing in health care will settle down when we truly focus on the patient."*

Relationship-Based Care (RBC) is comprised of three crucial relationships: care provider's relationship with patients and families, care provider's relationship with self, and care provider's relationship with colleagues.

We experience the essence of care in the moment when one human being connects to another. When compassion and care are conveyed through touch, a kind act, through competent clinical interventions, or through listening and

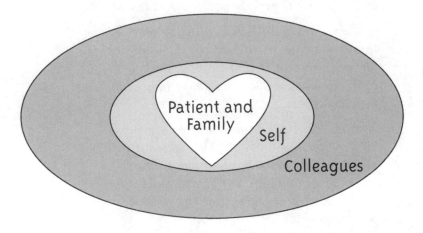

seeking to understand the other's experience, a healing relationship is created. This is the heart of Relationship-Based Care.

In RBC, the care provider-patient relationship is one in which the care provider consistently main tains the patient and family as his or her central focus. The care provider knows that each person's unique life story determines how he or she will experience an illness. The care provider conveys an unwavering respect and personal concern for the patient, strives to understand what is most important to this particular patient and family, safeguards their dignity and well-being, and actively engages them in all aspects of the patient's care.

The second crucial relationship is the care provider's relationship with *self*. This relationship is nurtured by self-knowing and self-care. Self-knowing is a prerequisite for emotional maturity, healthy interpersonal relationships, and the capacity for empathy (Goleman, 1997). Without a clear understanding of one's self, a person's emotional reactions may adversely affect their capacity for caregiving and teamwork. Effective self-care means that individuals possess the skills and knowledge to manage their own stress, articulate personal needs and values, and balance the demands of the job with their physical and emotional health and well-being. The relationship with self is fundamental to maintaining each individual's optimum health, for having empathy for the experience of others, and for being a productive member of the organization.

The third relationship is among members of the health care team. The delivery of compassionate quality care requires a commitment by all members of the organization within all clinical disciplines to accept responsibility for establishing and

Effective self-care means that individuals possess the skills and knowledge to manage their own stress, articulate personal needs and values, and balance the demands of the job with their physical and emotional health and well-being.

maintaining healthy interpersonal relationships. Quality care occurs in environments where the standard among members of the health care team is to respect and affirm each other's unique scope of practice and contribution, to work interdependently to achieve a common purpose, and to accept responsibility for creating a culture of learning, mutual support, and creative problem-solving.

We believe that the Relationship-Based Care model promotes organizational health resulting in positive outcomes in all the critical arenas that measure success: clinical safety and quality, patient and family satisfaction, physician and staff satisfaction, effective recruitment and retention of staff, and a healthy financial bottom line. This book will introduce the reader to the components of Relationship-Based Care in order to provide readers with a practical framework to create the next generation of excellent care in their organization.

The Relationship-Based Care model is designed to assist leaders within organizations to strengthen or transform these three critical relationships to achieve the quality, financial, and organizational outcomes they desire. Remember, when we speak of "transforming" we are speaking of changing the condition of what currently exists.

I_2E_2: A Formula for Leading change

Jayne Felgen developed a practical formula for change which defines four equal elements for transforming an environment of care. This formula simplifies the process of engaging individuals and groups in appreciating current successes while aspiring to a deeper integration of change within the culture of the organization. This formula for change is I_2E_2: Inspiration, Infrastructure, Education, and Evidence.

I_2 = Inspiration and Infrastructure

Inspiration promotes movement within an organization. To inspire means to "draw forth or bring out." People participate fully when they believe that what they have to offer is valued and that they are contributing to a vision they find compelling, valuable, and life-affirming. Leaders implementing the RBC model inspire others through their clarity of vision and their ability to influence others to share that vision. Successful leaders in an RBC system will maintain an unwavering focus on what matters most: *caring and healing relationships at the point of care.*

Leaders inspire others when they have clarity of vision and purpose, confidence and ability to influence others to share their vision, and a laser focus on what matters most: caring and healing relationships at the point of care.

All members of an organization become inspired by this patient-centered approach to fulfilling the purpose and mission of the organization as patient well-being is so often the basis for their own personal call to their profession. This inspired vision and purposefulness result in an organizational culture in which people are valued and respected as individuals, recruitment and retention are strong, and morale is high.

Infrastructure establishes the practices, systems, and processes through which the vision is achieved. It lays the underlying foundation that makes change possible. Infrastructure changes are necessary when we wish to implement any change in how we experience roles and relationships, operating principles and practices, communication processes, decision-making structures, and the existing tools and systems to support the work. The infrastructure must support the organization's overall vision at strategic, operational, and tactical levels.

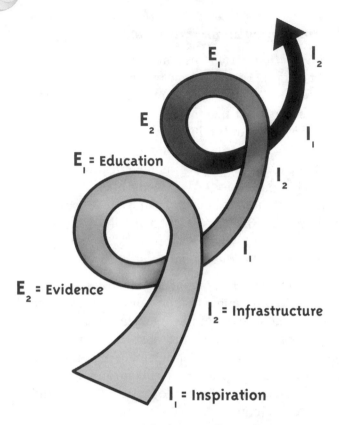

E₁ = Education

E₂ = Evidence

I₂ = Infrastructure

I₁ = Inspiration

$I_2 E_2$: Formula for Leading Change

E_2 = Education and Evidence

Education promotes competence, confidence, and personal commitment. Our commitment to education is born of the belief that people want to do a good job. Continuing education encourages and supports staff members to learn and develop to their greatest capacity, ultimately fostering in them the confidence to be more creative, productive, and satisfied with their work. Our highest priorities for educational development are in the areas of self-awareness, patient and family experience of care, developing and maintaining healthy relationships, proactive positive communication, creative thinking, critical thinking, and leadership.

In the RBC model, personal growth and professional development are viewed as an integrated whole. We believe people possess infinite potential. If the work culture is one which appreciates and promotes potential, the possibilities for growth are limitless.

Evidence demonstrates that something has indeed happened or changed. In addition, evidence demonstrates that the change *lives* within the infrastructure of the organization in its standards, position descriptions, performance evaluations, and most importantly in daily practice. Evidence of success lets people know that all their work is paying off and that progress is happening. Evidence links directly back to inspiration—as there is nothing more inspiring than seeing the fruits of our labor. In RBC, clearly defined measures based on the vision and goals of the desired change are articulated and evaluated to mark success.

Evidence of success lets people know that all their work is paying off and that progress or growth is happening.

I_2E_2 works when leaders at all levels of the organization are committed to transforming practice and understand five key conditions—*the 5 Cs*—that support people's ability to engage in change:

1. *Clarity*—When people know why the change is happening, where they are going, what the benefits are in going there, how they will know when they have succeeded, and what part they have in making it successful, they support the change. A clear understanding of the scope of their own responsibility, authority, and accountability for the work involved frees them to take action.

2. *Competency*—When individuals know what is expected of them and feel skilled in taking action, they are more able to participate in the change process. Their

competency is developed when they are provided the education to expand their knowledge and skills.

3. *Confidence*—When individuals know what they are expected to contribute, and when they have the knowledge and skills to make that contribution, they feel confident. Confidence provides the emotional foundation for exercising judgment and taking action. It enables individuals to contribute and actively collaborate with others.

4. *Collaboration*—Change requires people to work together to achieve a shared goal. When individuals understand the part they have to offer, feel competent and confident in their abilities to accomplish the work, and respect the contributions of others, collaboration and teamwork thrive.

5. *Commitment*—True commitment to accomplishing a shared goal comes from each individual's contribution, ownership for their part, and competence and confidence in accomplishing the work in collaboration with others. When these conditions are in place, progress is steady, problem-solving is creative and proactive, and desired results are achieved.

The figure below illustrates the way the 5 Cs support change. Commitment becomes the foundation upon which clarity, competency, confidence, and collaboration flourish.

Clarity + Competency ⟶ Confidence ⟶ Collaboration ⟶ **ABILITY TO ENGAGE IN CHANGE**
Commitment

The Relationship-Based Care model has evolved from CHCM's 25 years of experience in health care. Through our work in hospitals and health care settings across the United States and the United Kingdom, and through examination of evidence-based practice and research in the field, we have learned that:

- Patients and families define "caring and healing environments" as those in which they are actively involved in their own care—where they feel as though they are seen as whole people (body, mind, and spirit), and where they have established an individualized relationship withphysicians, nurses, and other care providers.

- The nurse-patient relationship is the foundation of excellent care delivery, and nurse accountability for a therapeutic relationship with a patient and the patient's family is essential to achieving quality outcomes.

- Clinical proficiency based on a sound knowledge base and understanding of the theories and science of practice, forms the foundation for the delivery of compassionate, quality care.

- Interdisciplinary communication and teamwork are vital as they promote mutual respect and role clarity.

- Patient involvement and confidence in their care is increased by positive relationships with their care providers.

- Patient safety is most effectively safeguarded when an advocate in the health care system (most practically, a nurse)

The Relationship-Based Care Model

knows the patient, the patient's family, and what matters most to all of them.

- Continuity of nurse-patient/family relationships, as well as continuity of team relationships, can be achieved through carefully designed scheduling practices and patient assignment methods. Continuity of care reduces the likelihood of medical errors.

- How an organization's leaders regard the value of the nurse-patient/family relationship within the context of a collaborative team effort determines how work is structured and what is prioritized.

- Attitudes, expectations, and structure of work practices either enhance or detract from therapeutic and healing relationships.

- The culture of care is a reflection of the people who work in that health care environment.

- Organizations with caring and healing environments and a focus on relationships have higher patient, staff, and physician satisfaction and higher productivity.

These lessons are congruent with patient satisfaction findings in which patients report that what matters most to them are the interpersonal skills of the hospital staff. Attributes such as attitude, communication, and caring behaviors are most closely correlated with patients' overall satisfaction with care and whether they would recommend an organization to others (Press and Ganey, 1997). When asked what made a difference to them in their health care experience, patients consistently respond that what matters most is being "seen as a person—not a diagnosis."

In the seminar, *Reigniting the Spirit of Caring,* patients and families talk with health care participants about what constitutes caring behaviors. They consistently say they want to be listened to, treated with respect, and cared for gently. They want to know that the people caring for them talk to each other and coordinate their activities. They want honesty, timely information, and guidance so that they can make informed decisions.

Patient satisfaction research which measured the effect of an implementation of *The Caring Model*™* (Dingman, et al, 1999) further validated that a care provider's response to requests and anticipation of needs are most significant to patients and their families, followed closely by their abilities to calm fears, communicate effectively, inform them about tests and procedures, and show concern.

The Fetzer Institute and the Pew Health Professions Commission Task Force identified the concept of relationship-centered care as key to the delivery of quality health care, recommending that *relationship* be brought back into health care (Tresolini, 1994). Their work is built on the long history of the nursing profession's emphasis on caring relationships from both practice and philosophical perspectives (Benner & Wrubel, 1989; Peplau, 1952). Despite this long history, caring relationships have not become a defining force in health care. The call of the Pew Health Professions Commission Task Force was to identify the practical infrastructure and educational support necessary to make relationship-centered care truly come alive in contemporary health care organizations.

The RBC model provides both the philosophical foundation and practical infrastructure to achieve organization-wide transformation in the

The Caring Model™ is a trademark and servicemark of Sharon K. Dingman.

way care and service are provided to patients and their families. In this model, relationships are the central focus and people from every level and area of the organization are invited to contribute to the organization's transformation. It is essential that the transformation of a health care organization be a team effort based on common vision, values, and anticipated outcomes. It truly "takes a village" to deliver world-class patient care. Everyone's work is valuable, regardless of his/her role or setting of care (Person & Marsh, 2002). Caring can occur in every relationship.

While holding in high regard the essential value of *every* individual's contribution to care, the Relationship-Based Care model also emphasizes the pivotal impact of Professional Nursing care on patient care and satisfaction. Research shows that patient reaction to and satisfaction with nursing care is the most important predictor of overall satisfaction with hospital care (Williams, 1993). Because nurses provide the greatest percentage of patient care within hospitals, a highly developed Professional Nursing Practice has the potential to distinguish one hospital from another.

The RBC model is illustrated on the following page. The six dimensions essential to the implementation of Relationship-Based Care are: leadership, teamwork, Professional Nursing Practice, patient care delivery, resource driven practice, and outcomes measurement.

Relationship-Based Care: A Model for Transforming Practice is organized around the Relationship-Based Care model on the next page, with a chapter dedicated to each dimension identified within the model. Reflecting the integrated work of Creative Health Care Management over

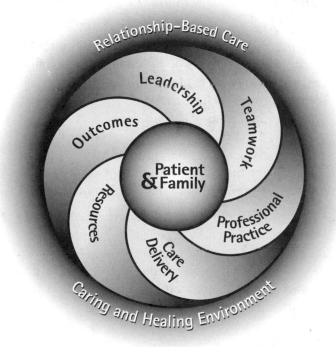

the past twenty-five years, this book taps into the deep knowledge and experience of a team of individuals within the company working with health care organizations around the world. Each chapter has been authored by members of the CHCM team.

Relationship-Based Care

The term *Relationship-Based Care* refers to both the philosophical foundation of the model and its operational framework. Health care is provided through relationships. The activities of care are organized around the needs and priorities of patients and their families. All care practices visibly demonstrate the mission and values of the organization, including those of clinicians and staff members from all disciplines, departments, and services.

Elements of the Model

Caring and Healing Environment

Jayne Felgen creates the context for Relationship-Based Care in Chapter One, by describing the essential components of a caring and healing environment. She explores caring theories and identifies ways to put those caring theories into practice. She helps care providers find ways to promote the healing power of relationships, to understand the patient's unique story, and to advocate for the active involvement of the patient and family in planning and managing patient care.

A caring and healing environment makes Relationship-Based Care possible. In a caring and healing environment, care providers respect the dignity of each patient and effectively utilize resources to accommodate the needs of the whole patient—mind, body and spirit.

Leadership

In Chapter Two, Mary Koloroutis discusses how to develop the leadership vital to creating and sustaining a *culture* that supports Relationship-Based Care. She discusses the nature and attributes of caring leaders, introduces a practical framework for leading change in daily practice, and explores the implications for roles and relationships of leaders and staff within organizations. In addition, she elucidates the concepts of *responsibility, authority, and accountability* within a decentralized decision-making structure.

Leaders create caring and healing cultures. In this book, the term *leaders* is used in its broadest sense. Here leaders are not defined by position, education, or licensure. Leaders exist at all levels in every organization. Leaders know the vision, act with purpose, remove barriers to quality care, and consistently make patients, families, and staff their highest priority. Leaders solve problems creatively to get results, and they model and support the changes they desire.

Teamwork

In Chapter Three, Donna Wright describes healthy, interdependent teamwork as one of the most statistically significant predictors of quality care. She outlines the qualities of healthy team relationships, and pays special attention to the pivotal role the physician-nurse relationship plays in the delivery of safe, high quality patient care.

Healthy teams are essential to making RBC a reality. Teamwork requires a group of diverse members from all disciplines and departments to define and embrace a shared purpose and to work together to fulfill that purpose. In healthy productive teams, members contribute their unique knowledge and skills commensurate with their established level of responsibility, authority, and accountability. Unified, collaborative interdisciplinary teams learn together and create the energy and interdependence required for well-coordinated, high quality patient care delivery and outcomes.

Professional Nursing Practice

Professional Nursing Practice is described in Chapter Four. Mary Koloroutis presents a nurse's therapeutic relationship with the patient as a privileged, sacred trust—and the cornerstone of Professional Nursing Practice. This chapter explores nursing's social responsibility, scope of practice, six professional practice roles, delegation practices, competency, and *caring* as the essence of effective Professional Nursing Practice.

Professional Nursing Practice exists to provide compassionate care to individuals and their loved ones, helping them heal, maintain health, cope during times of stress and suffering, and experience a dignified and peaceful death. Professional nurses achieve these aims through more than *clinical* knowledge and proficiency. Professional Nursing Practice requires knowledge and understanding of the human condition.

Patient Care Delivery

In Chapter Five, Colleen Person presents a patient care delivery system that has evolved from the complementary disciplines of Professional Nursing Practice and Primary Nursing. The system frames the way in which the activities of care are accomplished and is built upon the concepts, principles, and values of Professional Nursing Practice. In addition, Person outlines the four elements of care delivery and contrasts four common care delivery systems. She also discusses the ANCC's *Forces of Magnetism* as a guide for implementing this system of care delivery.

In Relationship-Based Care, the patient care delivery system provides the structure to support the professional role of the care provider, to promote collegial relationships among all members of the team, to organize work, and to effectively utilize resources. Its focus is to establish a therapeutic relationship between nurses and patients and families, create alliances between members of the health care team on behalf of patients and families, and to accomplish essential nursing interventions.

Resource Driven Practice

Resource driven practice is discussed in Chapter six by Marie Manthey and Mary Koloroutis. This chapter explores ways that clinical staff and managers share responsibility for the resources required to provide care. Manthey and Koloroutis discuss changing the nursing mindset about staffing, roles, relationships, delegation, critical thinking, reflection, and common sense decision making.

Resource driven practice requires both critical and creative thinking and is vital to the success of RBC. A resource driven practice is one which maximizes all available resources—staff, time, equipment, systems, budget—in the interest of achieving desired outcomes and safeguarding patient care. Resource decisions include determining staffing levels, skill mix, staffing schedules, and patient assignments. In resource driven practice, the use of resources at the point of care delivery is managed judiciously and authoritatively by the managers and clinical staff responsible for that care, and is based on the therapeutic relationship with the patient and family.

Outcomes Measurement

In Chapter Seven, Leah Kinnaird and Sharon Dingman present a simple, practical process for measuring outcomes to elevate standards and enhance the value of Relationship-Based Care in your organization. They begin with the premise that the RBC model has a positive impact on outcomes; the subsequent challenge is to create a meaningful representation of these outcomes on paper. They propose that data need not only be meaningful, but also motivating in order for leaders and practitioners to change the way they work.

Readers will learn strategies for capturing, processing, analyzing, and reporting relevant data that are trusted throughout the entire organization and useful from the bedside to the boardroom.

Their approach uses indicators recognized by the American Nurses Credentialing Center (ANCC), ANCC Magnet Recognition Program™, the National Center for Nursing Quality (NCNQ), Institute of Medicine (IOM), and The Joint Commission.

Achieving quality outcomes requires planning, precision and perseverance. Periodic, systematic outcome measurement assures that Relationship-Based Care stays current and relevant.

Using this Book

This book presents a fully developed model of Relationship-Based Care. Some of its readers will gain a deeper appreciation of familiar concepts, while others will encounter new concepts they may find difficult to integrate immediately. We ask this second group of readers to be patient and allow their understanding to build as concepts introduced in one chapter are elaborated upon in subsequent chapters.

Our intention with this book is to provide health care leaders *at all levels of the organization* with practical guidance in all of the key dimensions of designing and leading change in patient care delivery in their care organizations. Teamwork in interdisciplinary practice is essential. Nonetheless, readers may notice an emphasis on the role of the Professional Nurse. Within the context of interdisciplinary practice, one of our key intentions is to clarify the role of the Professional Nurse in RBC.

The nurse has a pivotal role at the point of care delivery. Subsequently, the relationship between the nurse and patient/family provides the foundation for the care experience. To be effective, this relationship must be clear to the nurse, to the

patient, to the family, and to the members of the health care team. Additionally, when all members of the interdisciplinary team understand the role of the Professional Nurse, and how that role impacts patient care, they are more able to collaborate and coordinate care on behalf of the patient and family.

Each chapter begins with an overview of the dimension. A discussion of the theory behind the dimension is followed by approaches for practical application. All chapters end with a summary of key concepts along with questions to help readers assess how this dimension is currently represented in their organization. The questions can be used for personal reflection or as discussion starters with colleagues and staff.

At the end of each chapter, exemplars are presented under the heading "A Moment of Excellence." These exemplars are authored by health care leaders in the field and describe an application of the RBC dimension in real-life examples. They have been organized based on I_2E_2.

When all members of the interdisci plinary team understand the role of the Professional Nurse, and how that role impacts patient care, they are more able to collaborate and coordinate care on behalf of the patient and family.

Inspiration (I_1): What inspired the change or strategy? What strategies were particularly effective in inspiring others toward a common vision?

Infrastructure (I_2): How does the infrastructure support the change at the strategic, operational, and tactical levels? What changes were made to assure the infrastructure supported the new vision?

Education (E_1): What initial education was provided to build skills and knowledge to enhance the changes? What education is being provided to promote and sustain the change?

Evidence (E_2): How was success defined, and which measures of evidence were helpful in tracking outcomes and leadership support?

These exemplars illustrate the theoretical aspects of the dimension as well as provide practical tips for bringing Relationship-Based Care to life.

ONE
A Caring and Healing Environment

Jayne Felgen

"When crossing a river, remove your sandals.
When crossing a border, remove your crown."

—*White Hmong Proverb*

Overview

These provocative words of wisdom, borrowed from *Healing By Heart* (Culhane-Pera, K A, 2003), a wonderful work addressing clinical and ethical case studies across cultures, were a guide for this chapter. Just as it is practical preparation to remove one's sandals before crossing a river, it is practical to prepare oneself with education and skills before providing interventions to aid the healing of those in need. Much like this proverb, however, caring for others moves us quickly beyond the practical. When a care provider crosses the threshold of a patient and family's door, he or she crosses a border, moving from the world of practical preparation into that of a personal healing relationship in which everything he or she does is in service to the patient. This border crossing brings care providers into the patient's and family's world—a world about which they know little—and within which they must tread with great humility.

I think one's feelings waste themselves in words; they ought to be distilled into actions which bring results.

—Florence Nightingale

A caring philosophy is most powerful for care providers when it is accompanied by a conscious-

23

ness of purpose, clarity about their roles and those of their colleagues, competency in managing relationships, and a commitment to touching each patient and family in ways that are meaningful to them. When nurses, allied health professionals, and their colleagues *own* their practice and consciously create environments of healing, their efforts visibly affect the practitioners, the practice, and the physical space. Initiating and sustaining a therapeutic relationship with patients and their families is central to caring and healing environments. This privileged bond between care provider and receiver has been called a "sacred space" (Wright and Syre-Adams, 2000).

If this Hmong proverb was applied to the health care environment, we might imagine that care providers would immerse themselves into the *lived* experience of patients and families. We would seek to understand their reality, and prepare to meet them where they are. And we would reach out to them with deep humility and unwavering respect.

The Proverb in Action: A Personal Story

The following story, in which my own family and I experienced extraordinary care and healing, may bring this point to life.

A few months ago my mother's thirty-five year battle with chronic illness ended in the Intensive Care Unit (ICU) of my hometown hospital in Sidney, Ohio. Her life ended where *her* mother's had ended, and where mine began. The manner of her passing and its inclusion of family provide a stark contrast to our experience when Grandma died fifty years ago. The love and the caring my Mom and our family experienced were remarkable. The staff may scoff and suggest that they were just "doing what they do," but I believe their actions, especially in Mom's last twenty-four hours, illustrate the concepts of caring and healing in a particularly compelling manner.

It was a Friday afternoon in late October, memorable because this was the 14th annual gala of the Nightingale Awards of Pennsylvania, and I was in Hershey for this black tie affair to recognize nurse exemplars. I called the hospital to check how Mom had handled her colonoscopy. After a week's hospitalization and several tests, we were hoping to learn the cause of her intense and unrelenting abdominal pain.

The capacity to watch over and guard the well-being of others is an important gift, and one that is learned with great difficulty. For it is one thing to see the situation others are in, but it is quite another to care enough about them to help, and yet another to know what to do."

—Judie Bopp

The unit clerk explained that Mom had "run into some difficulties" and she would transfer me to the nurse in ICU. However, since the physician was in the ICU, he came to the phone first. He introduced himself as new to Sidney and Mom's medical care, but not new to medicine, and he then explained the circumstances surrounding Mom's transfer to ICU.

Despite a do not resuscitate (DNR) designation, the nurses in the post anesthesia care unit responded to Mom's bradycardia with appropriate medication. She responded to this "chemical code" and was placed on a ventilator. I concurred with his judgment that the RNs had made an understandable choice to resuscitate Mom given an assumption that her consent for anesthesia temporarily overrode her DNR status. "Jayne," he said, "despite all good intentions, this situation fell into a gray zone." He and my sister, who was present and had durable health care power of attorney, agreed to continue with the ventilator for the short term, at least until I could make the nine hour drive home.

Before I departed, I received a call from the physician. He had just spoken with both of my sisters and he wanted to assure me that we were all in agreement that should Mom arrest again, the DNR would be honored, even if I had not arrived. While I desperately wanted to be with Mom in her final hours, under no circumstances did I want her to endure another resuscitation effort.

I asked the doctor if he was covering her care on the weekend and when he said he was not, he heard my disappointment and offered to be available at any time if we needed him.

The real essence of nursing is not the mechanical details of execution, but the creative imagination, the sensitive spirit, and the understanding behind these skills. Without these, the intellectual and spiritual elements are subordinated to the mechanical, and the means becomes more important than the ends.

—Isabel Stewart

After midnight I arrived in the ICU and was pleased to discover that Mom was alert and assisting the ventilator. I was so grateful to be with her! Fifty years earlier family members were not allowed to visit critically ill patients unless they also happened to be nurses, a fact that played a major role in my decision to become one. Not being permitted to see my Grandmother also has shaped how I have perceived and defined the purpose of visiting hours. It certainly increased my sensitivity to the special needs of families.

Amazingly, at 1:15AM the Vice President of Patient Care joined us. She had asked the staff to call her when I arrived. She remained with us for thirty minutes, walked me to my car and offered also to be available later that day if necessary, even though she would be out of town.

Before noon Mom was able to be extubated, and her naso-gastric tube was removed. Free at last from the paraphernalia of crisis and encumbered only by an oxygen face mask, she was able to sleep for the first time in over twenty hours. Each of Mom's children sat with her around the bed, holding her hands, and stroking her head as she began to relax. The RN and nursing supervisor decided to keep Mom in ICU rather than transfer her immediately back to the step-down unit, as typical rules regarding DNR would suggest.

All five of us children decided a break outside the hospital was in order. So, we left for a few hours to eat lunch and take a short nap while Mom dozed. At 3:50PM Karen, Mom's ICU nurse, called to summon us. When we arrived it was evident that Mom was in the process of passing. Over the next half hour we again held her, stroked her, hugged each other and said our goodbyes as she breathed her last breaths.

At one point while I was changing places with my sister, I noticed the nurse and a man standing back in the corner, silently bearing witness with all of us at this saddest of moments. Later, when Mom had passed on, he came forward, hugged every one of us, and introduced himself to me as Mom's doctor. He had advised the staff to alert him if Mom's condition changed, and had come to the hospital despite being off-duty.

In turn, every nurse in the unit offered their condolences with hugs and good wishes. Then, they wheeled in a cart—the "grieving cart." This portable tea cart was laden with fresh coffee, tea, and pop, plus warm cookies. More impressively, it came with a clear message to "take your time...as much time as you need. There is no rush. If you need to make any calls, here is a phone. Be together as long as you wish, and if you need help with any arrangements, please let us know."

I was and am at particular peace with Mom's passing for two reasons. First, Mom was surrounded by those she loved in her final moments, thus avoiding her greatest fear of passing alone and afraid. Her wishes were honored.

Second, I was so grateful that my family could experience the very best of care in the very worst of times. They are so proud of my being a nurse. And I've never been so proud to be a nurse as at that moment. The sandals were off, and the crowns were nowhere in sight.

The Environment of Care

Since the early 1980s there has been an increase in awareness among hospital leaders that the environment of care significantly impacts the way care is provided. It influences the way patients and their loved ones respond and heal. It influences the morale and subsequent efficiency of the health care team. The environment of care includes the physical layout and design of the patient's room, unit, facility as a whole, and grounds—right down to the colors, sounds, and traffic flow.

Equally important (if not *more* important than any of these tangible characteristics) is the environmental culture consistent with the principles of Relationship-Based Care (RBC). Caring and healing cultures are those in which there is palpable, visible regard for the dignity of human beings, and where relationships between the members of the health care team and the people they serve are built on mutual respect and a shared commitment to healing. There is now copious research to support our long-held common sense conclusion that environment affects well-being. This knowledge will now be put to practical use as we transform our existing health care environments.

Imagine a healing environment with relationships at its core—imagine a model of care designed by patients and their families—imagine what our environment would be like if patients were treated as if they were the Chief Executive Officers of their care. In a study done by the Picker Institute (Gerteis, 1993) patients tell us that they consider health care environments to be "healing" when care is attentive to mind, body, and spirit; when they feel they have a relationship with their healer; and when they are actively involved in decisions regarding their own care. A caring and healing environment is one that first carefully attends to the entire experience of its patients and families, then acknowledges and values its practitioners, thereby making visible the healing intention in the physical setting. Fundamentally, an intentional caring relationship between a caregiver and the patient and his or her family *is* the core of the healing environment.

Health care cannot be separated from the setting in which it's delivered. There's no doubt that the quality of the environment can enhance or retard healing.

—Jain Maikin

Practitioners

Practitioners are those people who care for the patient and family. Although a significant amount of patient interaction is with practitioners such as nurses, physicians, and allied health professionals, interaction with the patient and family by any member of the health care organization provides a valuable opportunity to promote healing. In a caring and healing environment, hospital staff members understand that each encounter is an opportunity to convey care and respect—from gathering and giving information at the time of admission, to responding to a request, to transporting patients, to stopping to offer directions in the hallway or simply acknowledging someone in need. This means that admission clerks, transport staff, dietary staff, housekeeping staff, administrative staff, business office staff—everyone—understands and demonstrates the principles of Relationship-Based Care. And *everyone* is to be acknowledged for the commitment and care he or she brings to the caring and healing environment.

The four theorists and researchers that follow outline principles and behaviors that contribute to our understanding of human caring and healing. Although their theories are based in nursing practice, their principles can be applied to anyone who is in a position to care for another person.

It is a beautiful and mysterious power that one human being can have on another through the mere act of caring...A great truth, the act of caring is the first step in the power to heal.

—Phillip Moffitt

Caring and Healing Theories: Watson

Much of what we now know about what does and does not contribute to the creation of a caring and healing environment in the world of institutional caring is the result of several decades of research by Jean Watson. Watson's *Model of Human Care* focuses on the interpersonal relationship between patient and nurse. In her theory, the patient can only change himself—healing comes from the inside out—and the nurse facilitates these changes. It is only through the understanding of patient's needs, history, and life experiences that the nurse can see the patient as a unique human being.

Watson does not believe that the common health care paradigm allows us to achieve the interpersonal relationships essential for the patient's healing. She calls for both personal and cultural transformation and describes the tenets and the significance of the paradigm shift in the table below.

The elements of Watson's framework point to the significance of a caring-healing consciousness in shaping a patient's health care experience. She asserts that the consciousness of each care provider is conveyed to the patient and family in their every interaction.

Jean Watson:
ERA II Transpersonal Caring-Healing Framework

- The whole caring-healing consciousness is contained within a single caring moment.

- The one caring and the one being cared for are interconnected.

- Human caring and healing processes (or the non-caring, non-healing consciousness of the nurse or other practitioners) are communicated to the one being cared for.

- Caring-healing consciousness is spatially extended; such consciousness exists through space.

- Caring-healing consciousness is temporally extended; such consciousness exists through time.

- Caring-healing consciousness is dominant over physical illness and treatment.

(Watson, 1999)

Watson highlights the role of the practitioner in defining the patient as a unique human being. All of her work underscores the importance of our common humanity and the connections between the care provider and patient. If we are empowered to create a caring and healing environment through each moment of caring, then we must be responsible for knowing ourselves and own an intentional way of being with patients and their families. She suggests that the manner in which care providers perceive and therefore define patients and families is a function of three filters. We must be conscious of the filters through which we perceive and therefore define or interpret the experience of others.

The first filter involves the personal and behavioral background of the care provider. These are the ways we have learned to be in the world through our families, education, and socialization, and it is essential for us to realize how individual our perceptions are, and that they are not always in alignment with the perceptions of others. The second filter includes the care provider's spiritual consciousness. The more we have attended to our own spiritual development, the more likely we are to be able to convey spiritual support to others. And, last, the care provider's belief about an individual's right and responsibility to exercise free will affects his or her perception. This is one of the most challenging filters for people in health care. Watson cautions health care workers to avoid assuming that what is available, accessible, and desirable to *us* is preferred by patients and families. Our *awareness* of our filters helps us not to impose our conditioned perceptions on others.

Along with self-awareness, Watson highlights the importance of self-care. Practitioners who are clear about who they are and seek to find balance in mind, body, and spirit are more accessible and effective in caring for others. Self-aware practitioners learn to center themselves to assure they are present to each patient and family. These practitioners may engage in personal practices such as breath-work, meditation, and imagery to intentionally shift their focus from one patient and family to another.

Caring and Healing Theories: Swanson

Kristen Swanson's *Middle Range Theory of Caring* builds on Watson's framework and brings caring theory into a pragmatic sphere by describing five caring processes as well as the practices for putting them into action. Although Swanson defines nursing as *"informed caring for the well-being of others,"* she emphasizes that the five caring processes are not unique to the nurse-patient relationship. These processes are present in any caring relationship and can be enacted throughout all levels of a caring and healing organization.

Kristen Swanson's work speaks directly to the elements of RBC. The first two processes—maintaining belief and knowing—are internal processes of providing care. The last three—being with, doing for, and enabling/informing—are action processes.

Kristen Swanson: Five Caring Processes

1. **Maintaining Belief**—Maintain a fundamental belief in persons and their capacity to make it through events and transitions and face a future with meaning. Practices include having faith, maintaining a hope-filled attitude, going the "extra mile."

2. **Knowing**—Strive to understand an event as it has meaning in the life of the other—understand the lived realities of those served. Practices include avoiding assumptions, centering on the other, thoroughly assessing, seeking cues and expertise from other colleagues.

3. **Being with**—Be emotionally present to the other. Practices include being there, enduring, listening, attending, disclosing, not burdening.

4. **Doing for**—Do for the other what they would do for themselves if it were possible. Practices include preserving dignity, protecting, comforting, and performing competently.

5. **Enabling/Informing**—Facilitate the other's passage through life transitions and unfamiliar events. Practices include explaining, informing, generating options, supporting, advocating, validating, anticipating and preparing for future needs.

(Swanson, 1993)

In Kristen Swanson's work we begin to see the integration of caring-healing consciousness with nurse behaviors that support Relationship-Based Care.

Caring and Healing Theories: Leininger

Madeline Leininger may well be the Margaret Mead of nursing. Leininger's theory of *Cultural Care Diversity and Universality* addresses care for people from a broad range of cultures. Her theory validates the natural human attachment to one's heritage, language, norms, and customs. She believes that people who emigrate to our country expect and deserve health care professionals who will be respectful and sensitive to their needs. Leininger's theory holds caring as an essential human need crossing every culture. Below, she outlines five theoretical assumptions.

Leininger purports that there are several "universal" meanings and actions that forty percent of patients representing eighty cultures identified as caring characteristics. They are:

Madeline Leininger:
Five Theoretical Assumptions on Caring

1. Care is essential for human growth and survival, and to face death.

2. There can be no curing without caring.

3. Expressions of human care vary among all cultures of the world.

4. Therapeutic nursing care can only occur when cultural care values, expressions, or practices are known and used explicitly.

5. Nursing is a transcultural care profession and discipline.

(Leininger, 1994)

- Respect

- Concern

- Helping, assisting, facilitating

- Attention to details

- Presence/being there

- Feeling a connection

- Protecting

- Touching

- Comfort measures

- Adjusting the environment to accommodate patient needs

Culturally sensitive care is important on both sides of the patient/caregiver relationship. So while the above characteristics are helpful, Leininger would admonish us to always ask the patient and family to define *in their own words,* what caring means to them.

A Model for Application of Caring Theories: Dingman

Using these and other caring theories and research as a foundation, Sharon Dingman developed *The Caring Model*™ and studied the impact of caring interactions (or the behaviors of nursing staff) on patient satisfaction. *The Caring Model*™ is a practical, customer service program that complements the professional practice principles and customer service objectives of any health care service department. The model includes processes to integrate caring behaviors and organizational learning into existing strategic and operational plans. It provides guidelines for caring behaviors that apply to every member of the care team.

In the original implementation of *The Caring Model™* Dingman measured the effects of these five caring interactions on eight patient satisfaction attributes, using a tool developed by the Gallup

---

Sharon Dingman:
Selected Elements of The Caring Model™

- Introduce yourself to the patient and family and explain your role in their care/service today.

- Call the patient by his or her preferred name.

- Use touch appropriately—a handshake, a touch on the arm, holding a hand as *prescribed* by *patient*.

- Direct caregivers sit at the bedside for at least 5 minutes each shift to plan or review care and desired outcomes. Non-direct caregivers, seated if possible or at eye level, review procedures, processes, or services involved in attaining desired outcomes.

- Reinforce the mission, vision, and value statements of the organization when planning care or service.

(Dingman, 1999)

Organization. Some of the indicators included, "Nurse helped calm my fears," "Staff communicated effectively," "Nurses demonstrated skill in providing care," and "Staff showed concern."

A descriptive design was used to evaluate the difference in patient satisfaction before and after implementing the five behaviors outlined in *The Caring Model™*. The sample size included 72 to 75 individuals per quarter from an acute care community hospital. Eighty-seven percent of the nursing staff on an inpatient medical/surgical unit and the women's center received *Caring Model™* training.

According to their patient satisfaction survey, overall satisfaction improved by 9% in the first quarter following implementation—6% in the "very satisfied" category and 3 % in the "satisfied" category. Although the sample size was small in the original study, the findings were significant, and subsequent replicated studies in four other hospitals have achieved similar results.

After *The Caring Model*™ was implemented, two of the patient satisfaction attributes scores— "Nurses anticipated needs" and "Nurses/staff responded to requests"—increased significantly. Other attributes which had been measured as "immediate priorities for improvement" before the implementation of *The Caring Model*™ became "major strengths" following implementation.

Although this research was specific to nursing care, *The Caring Model*™ has proven effective throughout a variety of health care organizations with staff members from all services and disciplines. We believe that the success of *The Caring Model*™ in increasing patient/family satisfaction demonstrates the effectiveness of integrating the basic principles of RBC into the culture of health care organizations.

Practice

Based on caring and healing theories and research in patient satisfaction, we know that caring and healing occur within some very specific conditions. We also know that many current institutional procedures that were established to standardize and routinize care do not necessarily serve the unique needs of individual patients and their families and can even run counter to caring and healing practices.

There are four general areas within practice that define how care happens: the therapeutic relationship, systems that support the therapeutic relationship, innovations in healing practices, and work process improvements. In Relationship-Based Care, the practice of each individual in every department ultimately supports the nurse-patient relationship.

1. **The Therapeutic Relationship:** A therapeutic relationship between a specific nurse and patient is established, ideally at admission, and is sustained throughout the episode of care. (Although this timing is ideal, the nurse-patient relationship can be established at any time.) Through this relationship, the patient builds trust and feels reassured that someone who understands his or her unique needs is following through on them either personally or through the plan of care, as well as through continuous, proactive communication with other team members. The nurse assures that patients' needs are met by asking them what issue regarding this episode of care is of most concern to them, and by determining how they wish to experience care.

2. **Systems that Support the Therapeutic Relationship:** In Relationship-Based Care, all systems are designed to either directly or indirectly support therapeutic relationships between nurses and patients. Principles consistent with professional practice and caring theories provide a blueprint from which unit staff take action. Systems include decision-making, staffing and scheduling, assignment-making, communications, leadership interventions, and processes that support continuity of nurse-patient relationships, coordination of care, and method of care delivery.

3. **Practice Innovations:** Innovation changes norms. In RBC, clinical and professional practices are assessed to determine how they support caring and healing interventions. When patients and their families express their care priorities, inspired visions and energy to lead change emerge from within the care team. This often prompts staff to consider changing the status quo, including the integration of complementary and alternative practices. Changes based on proven practices and research in the field shift the norms for the better.

4. **Process Improvements:** As systems and practice norms are evaluated, areas for improving work processes will emerge for change. The goal for process improvement is to maximize continuity of care and the quality of time nurses spend with patients while minimizing rework, running for supplies, redundant documentation and communication, and any other time wasters or energy drains. A primary goal is to improve processes to the point where continuity of the nurse-patient relationship is as free of obstacles as possible.

Over the past ten years, there has been tremendous growth in the field of complementary and alternative medicine. Recent surveys have estimated that close to half of the American public uses complementary approaches to healing, and annual expenditures are estimated to exceed $27 billion. (Eisenberg, 1998). This has prompted some to refer to the field of complementary and alternative therapies as "the invisible mainstream."

In her *Notes on Nursing* (Nightingale, 1860), Florence Nightingale described nursing as a holistic, integrated pursuit. In addition to advocating good hygiene and sanitation, she stressed the importance of fresh air, light, touch, diet, and spirituality. Nightingale believed that the role of the nurse was to help patients attain the best possible condition so that nature could act and self-healing could occur.

While nursing has always operated from within a holistic framework, and much of what is called complementary or alternative therapies has been within the domain of nursing for centuries, in reality, nursing education and practice over the past 35 years has more often emphasized technological aspects of care. As the nursing profession made strides to become more "scientific," the exploration and furthering of the art of nursing care was often neglected.

As consumer demand for access to complementary and alternative medicine (CAM) continues to grow, there is a tremendous need for leadership in educating health professionals; creating new clinical models; conducting research; and addressing issues of financing, credentialing, and reimbursement. The National Center for Complementary and Alternative Medicine (NCCAM) is responsible for exploring complementary and alternative healing practices through research, training researchers, and disseminating authoritative information. Information on NCCAM can be obtained from the National Institutes of Health web site: **http://nccam.nih.gov.**

Physical Space

Current research on caring and healing environments is also inspiring innovative redesign in the physical structure of health care environments. Changes are being made in hospital environments to improve ventilation (potentially reducing hospital borne infections); to expand storage capacity (removing unsightly clutter); to reduce unnecessary movement of patients (reducing disruption and conserving labor); and to create private rooms with space for families.

Gloria Bilchik describes several organizations that have redesigned their entire facilities using evidence-based principles on caring and healing environments. Bronson Methodist Hospital in Kalamazoo, Michigan, is one of her examples.

To provide a sense of control, all patients' rooms are private. Access to nature is incorporated through indoor gardens, natural light, and landscape views. Artwork, music, daylight and water sounds are built into the environment to reduce stress. Bronson is committing dollars to investigate and document its results. Its research focuses on three areas: the effect of private rooms on infection rates, an assessment of changes in the organizational culture and the impact of the physical layout on nursing productivity (Bilchik, 2002).

Roger Ulrich, professor at Texas A & M University and director of the Center for Health Systems and Design in the College of Architecture founded the field of "supportive design" through his groundbreaking study published in 1984 (Ulrich, 1984). He made the discovery that post-surgical patients whose hospital rooms offered an outdoor view recovered more quickly than those who did

The negative effects of foul odors, noise, obnoxious staff and visitors, tasteless food, dirt and hurried activity are deleterious to patient recovery.

The healing nurse-patient relationship, hospital design for good hygiene, light and air in combination with beauty and symmetry are essential to healing.

—Florence Nightingale, 1859

not have an outdoor view (Bilchik, 2002). Researchers in the field of "supportive design" (also known as "evidence-based design") are yielding results that impact economic indicators, market share, and patient and staff satisfaction indicators. Ulrich and his colleagues are working on the hypothesis that *"changing the health care environment by reducing stress factors can enhance the care-giving process, improve the delivery of medical technology, and help reduce the cost of care"* (Bilchik, 2002). Gloria Bilchik in her article, *A Better Place to Heal* (2002), highlights the following research findings:

It has been demonstrated that in all settings—not just hospitals—feeling as if we have control over our own environment reduces our stress. When we know we have options, even in the most minimal sense, we feel better. The consequences of this basic human truth are enormously important to the design of health care environments. Patients who can control the temperature and lighting in their rooms, the amount of privacy they have, the number, frequency and length of visitation, the type and volume of music, and the timing and content of meals will experience less stress and will likely heal more quickly.

Research into "positive distractions" confirms that pleasant diversions reduce stress in measurable ways. Jain Malkin, author of *Hospital Interior Architecture* (1992), which explores the relationship between the environment and healing says, *"That's why including water falls, garden views, interactive works of art and aquariums is becoming integral to health care design. These are not amenities; they're part of the healing environment."*

Although most organizations don't have the funding to start anew, existing organizational environments can be adapted and improved in alignment with research evidence and healing principles at whatever pace funding permits.

It is important to remember also, that while the physical environment promotes healing, it is the spirit and consciousness of the people providing care that are most crucial. The essence of a caring and healing environment is captured in the "moments of caring"—in the relationships between patients, families, and all members of the health care team.

- Quality care is deeply respectful of the dignity of each person, is attentive to mind, body, and spirit, and promotes the healing power of relationships.

- Practice norms, innovations in care, and system designs determine the therapeutic relationship between a specific nurse and patient.

- Practitioners and staff members throughout the organization must understand the principles of caring and apply these principles in interactions with patients and families—and with each other.

- Principles of caring and healing drive the best innovations in space and practice design.

- A caring and healing environment creates the context for relationship-based, patient-centered care.

- Existing organizational environments can be effectively adapted and improved

Summary of Key Concepts

at whatever pace funding permits, in alignment with research evidence and healing principles.

Questions for Self-Assessment

As you consider how to amplify your organization's efforts to provide caring throughout all departments and service areas, the following questions are offered as a self-assessment and to stimulate thinking regarding some of the aspects present in a caring and healing environment. Our hope is that it will support you in beginning a further exploration of the concepts at all levels of your organization. In this chapter, the questions are organized under the categories of Practitioners, Practice, and Physical Space.

Practitioners

- Are staff members in your organization aware of the significant impact each individual has on patient and family outcomes and satisfaction?

- Are staff encouraged to renew, recharge, and refocus on the important work they do?

- In what ways do practitioners demonstrate knowledge and awareness of the theories and principles for caring and healing practice?

- Are caring theories and principles currently included in recruitment, hiring, and orientation processes?

- In what ways are staff members throughout the organization trained or encouraged to interact with patients and families in a caring manner?

- Is it clear within your organization's culture that staff are expected to treat each other with respect and compassion? Are staff acknowledged for such treatment?

- In what ways do staff center themselves in order to focus with intention on patients and their families?

Practice

- Is there a standard established for timely response to call bells, (i.e. within 60 seconds)?

- How do you help patients rest while in the hospital? Is there currently a way for them to sleep for 6 or more hours without interruption?

- Are any practices from *The Caring Model*™ already an integral part of the care delivery system?

- In what ways are any of the following proactive measures, in addition to medication, used for pain management?
  - relaxation therapy
  - aromatherapy
  - guided imagery
  - massage
  - positioning the patient
  - music

- What complementary and/or alternative practices are utilized?

- How are baths perceived by staff? Are they seen as a hygiene task or as an opportunity for healing touch? Is the timing of baths routine or based on individual need, analgesia, or stress relief?

Physical Space

- Does the physical space within your unit contribute to or detract from healing?

- What are the beliefs or awareness of unit staff members toward noise?

- How would you describe the noise level in your facility? Are some units noisier than others?

- How is music used?

- Are pagers and cellular phones muted?

- Is the patient's room clutter free?

- Is the unit environment clutter-free?

- How is privacy safeguarded?

- Is the lighting soft and therapeutic?

- What control do patients and families have over lighting and temperature?

- What does staff know about the effects of lighting on healing?

- Do the colors used in the environment relate to the latest research on the healing impact of color?

- Is nature integrated into the patient's experience through art or other means?

- How do your unit's rituals of care support healing principles and attention to "mind, body, and spirit" practice innovations?

- What would it take to recreate the environment to achieve a more caring and healing setting in your organization?

Parma Community General Hospital
Parma, Ohio

Our organization had been diligently working on strengthening our culture in an effort to improve patients' satisfaction with their care. Despite all of our efforts, too often we were identifying that patients were still dissatisfied with their experience. Patients felt uncared for and nursing staff was discouraged. Nurses felt they did not have the time or opportunity to care for patients in the way they desired to. We were poised for change. After attending a seminar on contemporary nursing theories related to caring and the way these theories could affect practice, we were ready for a new model of care.

Developing and implementing a model of caring at Parma Community General Hospital (PCGH) is a work in progress. Relationship-Based Care at PCGH begins during hiring. The nurse recruiter uses a Relationship-Based Care approach in working with prospective employees. She develops a relationship with each candidate as she identifies where the candidate might best fit into the organization.

New employees are introduced to the Relationship-Base Care delivery model during the VP of Nursing's welcome to the group. She provides anecdotes on how staff has made a difference in the lives of patients and families by identifying and meeting their expressed "number one" need. On the third day of orientation, the idea of healthy interpersonal relationships with patients/families and colleagues as an expected competency is presented to the group. Subsequent departmental orientation deepens their understanding of the caring principles. Concepts that support

A Moment of Excellence: Parma Community General Hospital

intentional caring—the need be present to patients and our assertion that caring happens through the nurse in her relationship with the patient—are presented and modeled.

As a means of immersing our employees into the caring experience, we provide a values-centered three-day retreat called, "Caring Connection" which addresses care for self, patient/family, and all others. It is open to all health care providers within our organization. In addition to nurses, respiratory therapists and radiology and laboratory technicians attend the retreat. These retreats have helped us to embrace and integrate appropriate concepts of RBC into all of our patient care. We have provided this experience to over 300 employees in our organization, and we have identified a marked decrease in the turnover of the staff who have participated in this program.

The Board of Trustees at PCGH is comprised primarily of appointed members from our surrounding communities. Our initiatives and outcomes related to *The Caring Model*™ were communicated to board members with regular updates, but we wanted them to experience some of the differences we were making. We presented the model to them by inviting them to gather in a Circle of Caring. This Circle closely resembled one of our most meaningful rituals from the Caring Connection. Board members were visibly moved by this experience. When the candle used in the ceremony was extinguished, there were tears in many eyes as they congratulated us on compre-hensively and compassionately meeting the needs of our community.

Currently, we are actively searching for an educational partner to provide an associate nursing degree program on our campus. It has been our observation that there is a lack of caring elements in some of our region's nursing programs. Therefore, one of our principal criteria is that our partner's curriculum be based on caring theories. We believe that providing such a nursing program would be the best way to support us at a time when there is a diminishing supply of qualified RNs. It is our hope to be the hospital that attracts nursing graduates educated in caring theories as the basis of clinical practice. We believe that providing nurses with the opportunity to initiate their career in an organization that supports their values would be a powerful recruitment and retention strategy. Throughout our search we've spoken with people who run educational programs that currently do not have philosophies based on caring principles. After our conversations with them, however, many are giving thoughtful consideration to our assertions about the value of Relationship-Based Care to their students and to our community.

We continue to seek ways to strengthen and promote caring as our model. We have recently embarked on developing a clearly articulated philosophy of caring that would be deeply integrated into our organization. We would like it to declare who we are and who we would like to be. It will provide strong guidance for all of our organizational plans and decisions. Operations and aspects of our organization that do not support caring will become inconsistent with our declared philosophy. We believe this will be useful in areas as important as recruitment and retention, environmental design, new service decisions, the measure of personal and professional success, professional behaviors and appearance, and all aspects of care that affect the patient and family experience.

At a time when health care requires all of us to be masters in staying afloat in troubled waters, we have found an anchor in Relationship-Based Care.

Susan Sorbello, MBA, RN is the Vice President and Chief Nursing Officer and Darlene Vrotsos, RN, BSN is the Administrative Director Nursing Services at Parma Community General Hospital, a 350 bed hospital in Parma, Ohio.

A Moment of Excellence: Center for Spirituality and Healing

University of Minnesota
Minneapolis, Minnesota

As a nurse practitioner student, Louise enrolled in courses on botanical medicine and aromatherapy. She now practices in an inner city primary care clinic where she cares for people who speak 20 different languages. For many of her clients, culturally based healing traditions are every bit as important as the conventional approaches to care offered in the clinic. Louise counsels her patients on how to integrate the best of all care options.

Every Tuesday at noon, a growing number of faculty, staff and students gather to participate in a drop-in meditation hour. Gently guided by the instructor Eric, they learn how to follow their breath and to let go of the busy thoughts that race through their minds. They return to the class-room, laboratory, or patient care unit more relaxed and alert.

Linda is a nurse and epidemiologist interested in studying the use of essential oils to treat infectious diseases. After visiting colleagues in Australia, she decided to do a study on the use of tea tree oil to treat staph infected wounds.

The above scenarios describe life at the Center for Spirituality and Healing at the University of Minnesota. The Center, established in 1995, is charged with integrating complementary, cultural, and spiritual aspects of care into the education, research, and clinical programs of the University's Academic Health Center. This is accomplished by teaching health care professional students and the greater community about the interconnectedness of body-mind-spirit and the vital role that world culture and spirituality play in achieving optimal health and well-being. The vision of the Center is to transform every health care experience into one where there is a focus on caring and healing. The Center's mission focuses on various elements that are fundamental to optimal caring and healing environments including healing practices, healing relationships, the health and well-being of healers, and the physical environment in which care is provided.

In a recent survey of faculty and students (Kreitzer, et al. 2002), over 90% indicated that care should integrate conventional and complementary approaches and that content on complementary therapies should be integrated into the curriculum of health professional students. At the Center for Spirituality and Healing at the University of Minnesota, nursing, pharmacy, and medical students are exposed to content on complementary therapies throughout the course of their training. Each semester, over 250 students working on their masters or Ph.D. degree at the University enroll in courses offered through the graduate minor in complementary therapies and healing practices offered through the Center. With a choice of over 30 courses, students can choose to focus on in-depth clinical training or research. Practicing health professionals who wish to enrich or expand their practice but not necessarily earn an additional degree, have the option of completing a certificate program. On-line learning enables all students to learn wherever they are, at any time.

Over 50 faculty contribute to the research mission of the Center. Studies currently underway include the use of medicinal mushrooms to treat cancer, mindfulness meditation to alleviate symptoms in post-transplant patients, the impact of music on critically ill patients who are on ventilators, and outcomes of an eating disorder program that extensively integrates the use of complementary therapies.

Factors that have contributed to the success of the Center include:

- *A vision* for changing health care that addresses the needs of patients and families and challenges and inspires faculty, staff, and students.

- *An infrastructure* that is flexible, responsive, and supportive of interdisciplinary collaboration.

- *A commitment* to education of faculty and staff as well as students.

- A recognition that evidence, gleaned through rigorous inquiry, will lead to new discoveries that will contribute to patient care.

Mary Jo Kreitzer, PhD, RN is the founder and director of the Center for Spirituality and Healing and an associate professor in the University of Minnesota School of Nursing, Minneapolis, Minnesota.

Information on the Center for Spirituality and Healing may be found on the Center's web-site: **http://www.csh.umn.edu.**

TWO
Leadership

Mary Koloroutis

I am only one; but I am still one.
I cannot do everything, but still I can do something.
I will not refuse to do the something I can do.

—Helen Keller

Each of us has something we can do—a way to contribute that is uniquely ours. A relationship-based culture is one in which leaders understand this simple principle and set about seeding and cultivating it within themselves and within those they influence. Generally, leadership is thought to apply almost entirely to people in formal positions of authority. "*The office or position of a leader*" is, in fact, the first definition of leadership in *Webster's Collegiate Dictionary*. While it is true that people in appointed positions of authority are expected to be leaders, our definition of leadership expands to fit the second definition in Webster's— simply that "*leadership is the capacity to lead.*"

In a relationship-based culture, in which leaders encourage people to develop to their fullest capacity, leadership will emerge from people in surprising and gratifying ways throughout an organization. We believe that one of the purposes of Relationship-Based Care (RBC) is to call forth the leader within each of us, thus creating an

Overview

environment in which people take conscious ownership for their work while contributing to the mission of the organization as a whole. Leaders at all levels of the organization play a vital role in the design and implementation of the patient care delivery system and in creating and sustaining the culture to support it. Caring and compassionate service evolves from caring and compassionate leaders.

This chapter begins by exploring the nature and attributes of caring leaders as essential to transforming the environment of care. Second, a personal leadership strategy is presented as a practical way to lead change on a daily basis. In it, the roles, relationships, and critical competencies of leaders at all levels of the organization are discussed within the context of Relationship-Based Care. Finally, decentralized decision making is presented as a fundamental means for developing and empowering people throughout the organization.

Caring Leaders Transform Care

Leading for transformation requires the ability to influence people to accomplish extraordinary things. We know that the greatest leaders influence others most by embodying the change they want to see. People are highly reactive to a disconnect between what is said and what is done. You are, I am sure, familiar with the phrases, "walk the talk" and "practice what you preach." Effective leaders understand that success depends on their *living* what they believe. Thus, an important first step for strengthening Relationship-Based Care in the work environment is for leaders to align their own beliefs about care with the principles of RBC and to act in alignment with those principles at all times. Caring leaders understand that caring is not merely an emotion—caring is strong, conscious action.

I asked health care professionals who participated in our *Reigniting the Spirit of Caring*
seminar to reflect on someone they have experienced as a caring leader and to identify some of
their key attributes. Here are their comments:

*Caring leaders
understand that
caring is not merely
an emotion—caring
is strong, conscious
action.*

- "He is available and present; I get the
  feeling that I am important and that what
  concerns me matters."

- "She keeps the big picture in mind and is
  able to translate the importance of that
  for me. She helps me to stay clear about
  what matters."

- "He has great positive energy. He deals with
  the hard stuff, but I always get the feeling
  that we will get through and come out the
  other side. He has hope; it's just there."

- "She tells me the truth even when it is
  hard to hear. I feel respected and know
  she thinks I can deal with reality."

- "He 'gets it.' He listens to my perspective and asks questions. I know his work
  is different from mine, but I feel like he
  really values and respects what I do and
  really wants to understand it."

- "He gives me information so I am not
  working in the dark. It helps me deal with
  situations that would otherwise be very
  frustrating."

- "We have gone through a lot together. I
  know that she does not view my moments
  of weakness as character flaws, but rather
  what they are—simply moments of weakness. She is also vulnerable with me; I feel
  like we support each other and can get
  through a lot of tough times that way."

- "She has very clear expectations for all of us. And her standards are high, especially when it comes to patient care. She makes me want to be on her team."

- "He makes me feel like he knows what he is doing—and that in those rare instances that he doesn't, he is the first to say that he doesn't know but will find out what needs to be done and who can help us get there. I really respect that honesty and the way he models asking for help."

- "She encourages me and pays more attention to what is working (rather than what's going wrong) and how we can make more of what's positive happen. She doesn't focus on the negative. She looks at possibilities. As a result, I feel energy and hope and want to keep at it!"

- "The person who immediately comes to mind can only be described as a ferocious patient and staff advocate!"

Caring leaders create an environment in which caring relationships happen. Caring leaders directly influence caring interactions with patients and families by virtue of their own caring interactions with staff.

The attributes of caring leaders emerge from the comments of participants as:

- Emotionally present

- Able to see beyond the current problem or situation

- Possessing a positive energy

- Having a hope-filled attitude, consistently seeing possibilities

- Honest, truth-telling even when it is difficult

- Open, listening, seeking to understand

- Respecting and believing in others

- Supportive and encouraging

These attributes are highly consistent with Swanson's Five Caring Processes (1993). The caring processes were identified as key themes that emerged from interviewing patients, families, and health care providers about how they experienced giving and receiving care. While Swanson's processes refer to patient care, these processes apply to human behavior as a whole and certainly have implications for caring leadership. When leaders live these processes, they have a powerful impact on the way care is provided. Caring leaders create an environment in which caring relationships happen. Caring leaders directly influence caring interactions with patients and families by virtue of their own caring interactions with staff. Swanson's processes are adapted to caring leader behaviors in the following table.

Caring Leader Behaviors

Maintaining Belief: A caring leader has faith in others to get through difficult or challenging events. A caring leader finds meaning in challenges and participates in solutions.

- Holds and conveys a hope-filled attitude
- Sees possibilities in situations
- Respects and values all people
- Does whatever it takes to do the "right thing"
- Follows through on commitments

Knowing: A caring leader strives to understand an event as it has meaning to others.

- Seeks to understand the other person's perspective
- Avoids making assumptions
- Seeks to understand other's experiences

Being With: A caring leader is emotionally present and available to another.

- Listens
- Suspends judgment
- Promotes healthy, productive interactions
- Consciously monitors own reactions
- Models healthy personal boundaries
- Offers support

Doing For: A caring leader provides help and service to others as appropriate.

- Initiates actions to resolve problems
- Gets things done
- Models desired behaviors

Enabling and Informing: A caring leader facilitates another's development and passage through events and transitions.

- Articulates expectations
- Seeks and supports opportunities for growth and development
- Serves as teacher, coach, and/or mentor
- Leads with purpose and integrity

Caring is at the heart of leadership.

—James Kouzes and Barry Posner

A discussion of caring leadership would not be complete without including the work of James Kouzes and Barry Pozner. Their books, *The Leadership Challenge* (1995) and *Encouraging the Heart* (2003) delve deeply into the essence of leadership, confirming that not only is leadership *"everybody's business,"* but that it is about being in relationship— *"a relationship with self and personal self-development and a relationship with those being led."* Their major premise is that caring is at the heart of leadership. They say,

"Without caring, leadership has no purpose. And without showing others that you care and what you care about, other people won't care about what you say or what you know. As a relationship, leadership requires a connection between leaders and their constituents over matters, in the simplest sense, of the heart. It is personal and it is interpersonal." (Kouzes & Posner, 2003)

A key leadership responsibility is to keep hope alive and to encourage the heart. Kouzes and Pozner's leadership premises are consistent with the behaviors outlined in the *Five Caring Processes* and include: setting high standards and expectations, expressing optimism, giving feedback and publicly recognizing a job well done, letting people know their work is important, teaching and coaching, and leading by example.

The new way of leadership starts with who we are as human beings and how we show up in the world and workplace.

—Colleen Person and Bonnie Marsh

It is apparent that transformative change calls for a new model of leadership. The call for leadership is a call for a new way of thinking, being, and doing. This new model encourages leaders to emerge from all levels of the organization and it values each person for the vital contributions he or she makes in creating a life-affirming and productive work environment. In a health care environment, caring leaders engender caring and compassionate service. These leaders encourage people, instill hope, remove obstacles, and live their vision and values moment-to-moment, day-by-day.

Colleen Person and Bonnie Marsh compare the call for a new view of leadership with the old view which they say is one built on competition, expertise, and dominance. The new way of leadership is one in which "*leaders demonstrate an understanding that meaningful work is the highest motivator*" and that *"meaningful conversations are the prerequisite to bringing out the best in everyone."* The new leaders, they say, *"empower others through a fundamental respect for each individual and their capacity to be accountable for their contributions and outcomes"* (Person & Marsh, 2002).

Tranformational Leadership Cycle: A Personal Story

The famous quote by Gandhi, "Be the change you want to see in the world," has guided how I think about leadership and what is required for leading change. I learned about what it means to transform a care environment in my work as a clinical manager and director in several organizations over a span of twenty-five years. I learned that transformative change—the kind that affects each individual's way of being and doing their work—takes time and that it cannot be dictated. I learned that transformative change happens one person at a time and occurs from the inside-out. It takes vision, persistence, and modeling by leaders to inspire the change. And it takes the emergence of leaders *within* the clinical staff who embody their values and beliefs and are able to identify and boldly address the dissonance between espoused values and actual behaviors. Transformation takes action and courage.

Transformative change happens one person at a time and occurs from the inside-out.

The Transformational Leadership Cycle is a fancy label for a diagram I drew on a napkin in a hospital cafeteria after sitting through an outrageously frustrating and dysfunctional meeting. It's not like the experience of frustration was new. What was different was the flash of insight I had about *my* part and the part *my* team was playing in creating our own dysfunction.

We were caught in a "victim leader" mentality. We had been working for over a year on some key practice changes which would enhance relation-ships on the unit and improve therapeutic rela-tionships with patients and families. We were moving from a task-based focus to a relationship-based focus. Councils had been established to provide greater participation and leadership among staff members. Continuity of care, rather than geography, would now drive patient assign-ments. Some key staff members on one particular unit were highly resistant to the change. They preferred the old way and were putting a great deal of energy into maintaining the status quo.

As I listened that morning in the meeting, I heard blaming and complaining from people in leadership positions. *"If they would only ...", "They just don't get it ...", "They will never change ..."* As I watched and listened I was struck by the hope-lessness in the conversation and the diffusion of energy. I was also bothered by the lack of respect being conveyed for staff members not present. Finally, I made a time out sign with my hands and said, *"Please, step back with me and listen."* I began to wring my hands and said, *"So, what we are about here today is formalizing the helpless and hopeless method of leadership...do I have that right?"* There was a long silence. Fortunately, many others in the room felt the same way—and suddenly we began laughing at ourselves. The energy in the room changed immediately and we began to talk about how we could do things differently. We committed to going away and thinking through how *we* – not *they* – would change our way of being. How *we* – not *they* – would change our way of leading. And how *we* – not *they* – would begin to embody the change we wanted to see. We also agreed to an important first step—to hold each other accountable for leading from a basis of respect and regard for our staff colleagues and for each other.

An important first step – to hold each other accountable for leading from a basis of respect and regard for our staff colleagues and for each other.

So that is how I found myself in the cafeteria doodling on a napkin. The way I saw it, I was at a turning point. I was re-committing to lead this change and to do so with all the integrity and energy I had at my disposal. Yes, health care was chaotic and frustrating. And, yes, some people preferred to fight as hard as they could to resist new ways of thinking and working. They may have been afraid of doing things differently—worried that any changes would make their work more difficult, and perhaps worried about whether they had the knowledge and skills necessary to work from a relationship-based perspective. What was also true, was that there were other staff members who had emerged as leaders committed to transforming the practice environment, and they were eager to participate in changes that would get us there. I made two decisions that day. First, I decided that I wanted to continue the work and lead the change. Second, I decided that I would lead with intention and hope—focusing on the possibilities—every day. I laid out a set of steps in the model below and shared it with the rest of the team. The Transformational Leadership Cycle (TLC) became my roadmap for leading each day.

You get what you pay attention to.

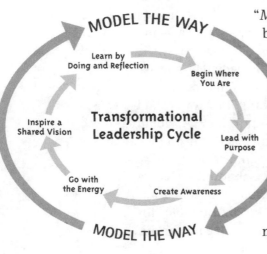

"*Model the Way*" is a term borrowed from Kouzes and Pozner (1997). It encircles the model as its meaning must find its way into the team's every action and interaction. This is another way of saying "walk your talk." What this means practically, is that my responsibility as a leader is to ensure that my actions and interactions

are consistent with the values I espouse. *I will embody the change I want to see in practice.* Our leadership team had heartfelt discussions on how we interacted with staff, what questions we asked, and what got our attention. We identified some specific changes we would make in our behavior when we made rounds. We supported each other in improving our listening skills, being fully present, and seeking to understand the experience of the staff providing care. We expanded our conversations with staff from the doing and logistics of care to the challenges and rewards of caring for people. We inquired about specific patients and their unique story. We were guided by the timeless adage, "you get what you pay attention to." We paid attention to what mattered most—the care of patients and families and support of the staff in providing that care.

Step 1: Begin where you are.

This means that as a leader I have my eyes wide open. I see and accept what is. Each day provides new opportunities and possibilities. There is no room for carrying resentments from yesterday. It means celebrating and appreciating strengths and identifying and changing what is unacceptable. To *begin where you are* means having the capacity to see and accept reality and to lead from this as a starting point. This step was a huge "aha" for our team. It meant we would no longer spend energy on conversations which begin with "We tried it before, but ...", *"They* won't ..." "I don't see how ..." Instead we would look at what is possible given our current reality. And we know that what is possible today is different from what may be possible tomorrow.

We know that what is possible today is different from what may be possible tomorrow.

Step 2. Lead with purpose.

Our purpose for existing as a health care team is to provide compassionate care and service to patients and families. As our team clarified this purpose, we also clarified what it meant to each of us in our various roles. We agreed that what was common to all of our roles was our commitment to maintaining an unshakable focus on care and service. This meant maintaining caring relationships among our team members and supporting therapeutic relationships between nurses and patients and their families. We adapted Richard Leider's (1997) definition of purpose as "*the recognition of the presence of the sacred within us and the choice of work that is consistent with that presence. Purpose defines our contribution to life.*"

Purpose defines our contribution to life.

—Richard Leider

Step 3. Create awareness.

This happens by asking the right questions and encouraging conversations that stimulate new ways of thinking and being. Our team discussed the idea of "seeding" to create greater awareness of new ways of working or being. This meant we would take opportunities in day-to-day interactions to plant the seed of an idea, and we committed to subsequent conversations to nurture and grow those ideas. We confirmed that creating awareness meant we would lift up what is important and encourage others to do the same. We reviewed our staff meetings, educational offerings, and quality review processes and made the changes necessary to assure that they were designed to focus on and reinforce what mattered most. This step requires that the leader has a clear picture of current reality and is able to identify opportunities to narrow the gap between where we are and where we want to be.

Step 4: Go with the energy.

Positive energy is inspiring, generative, and contagious. Step four is built on this premise. Too often leaders focus their energy on trying to "fix" people who are resistant to change. Our team was circling in frustration by focusing on what negative things were happening rather than what positive things were happening—or at least what positives could be encouraged. It's no wonder we were feeling "helpless and hopeless." With any major change, a small percentage of the people affected will enthusiastically engage and participate in that change; a small percentage of the people affected will want no part of the change and may actively resist it; and the majority of people will remain in a "wait and see" mode in the middle until something causes them to either embrace or resist the change. While people in all three categories must be respectfully engaged, leaders will create greater momentum by aligning their energy with people who can see the possibilities and take ownership for moving the change forward. Additionally, when energy is focused on what *can* happen, those in the middle will begin to align with the positive energy. This is also a crucial step for the emotional health and motivation of leaders. I decided I would quit trying to "swim up a waterfall" every day by trying to convince people who were not ready for change to consider a new way. I decided to go with the positive energy and seek out those people who were able to see possibilities. In doing so, I also nourished my own spirit.

Step 5: Inspire a shared vision.

Steps one through four create a solid foundation for inspiring a shared vision. These steps open up new conversations and create a new level of awareness and possibility. When people are encouraged to speak from their hearts about what is truly important in their work environments, when leaders listen, and when action is taken toward creating what people ask for, the environment transforms into one that is relationship-based. Within that structure, individuals are unified by a common purpose and direction.

Step 6: Learn by doing—and reflection.

This means putting our words and plans into action. A key barrier to effective results is the fear of making a mistake. This step "unfreezes" our fear and moves us into practical action. This step means that we take risks and have the courage to pursue what we value—even if the result is not perfect. Another barrier to change is the idea that change has to be huge to have effective results. Not true. We've learned that change happens one person at a time, and that small changes can have significant impact. Our team identified small, everyday steps we could take as leaders to change our practice for the better. We tried them out and reflected on the impact. We refined our actions based on our reflection, constantly seeking to improve. We identified and prioritized specific outcomes measures to monitor our progress and success. Step six feeds directly back into the first step—*begin where you are*. This represents the ongoing nature of the cycle. Each day, each interaction is a new opportunity to lead with intention, hope, and possibility.

Each day, each interaction is a new opportunity to lead with intention, hope, and possibility.

Role and Relationship of Executive Leaders

The role of the organization's executive leaders is to create an organizational culture in which it is possible for transformational change to occur. The role of this team is not one of "driving" the change, but rather one of inspiring and guiding the change. The traditional hierarchical model—one in which the executive level leadership made all of the decisions—is clearly extinct. Although some key decisions will be made at the top, organizational cultures are not changed through unilateral decisions. Desirable cultures evolve when executive leaders create an environment in which individual and team learning is promoted and where commitment is valued over compliance. Substantive change depends upon the commitment of each member of the organization, and this demands a new model of relationships.

Cultures evolve when executive leaders create an environment in which individual and team learning is promoted and where commit-ment is valued over compliance

According to Charlotte Roberts, co-author of *The Fifth Discipline Fieldbook* (Senge, et al., 1994), a key role for the executive team in transforming the work environment is to promote new relationships and to stimulate a culture of learning and shared leadership. One key action to accomplish this is to share relevant information—and further to educate people to comprehend the information. This is a crucial and sometimes illusive step, she says, in that many people believe their authority comes from *"holding on to"* or *"concealing"* information. If the executive team makes it clear that providing information is fundamental to empowering people in making decisions and accepting responsibility for results, the culture will begin to shift for the better. The information that the executive team chooses to share must be relevant and supportive of the team's efforts—it may even be information that was historically "privileged."

We have learned that the following leader behaviors are present in executive teams that have succeeded in leading transformational change.

Little significant change can occur if it is driven from the top...

—Peter Senge

- They inspire a commitment to a common purpose and shared vision.

- They work as champions, advocates, sponsors, and mentors for the unit leaders and staff.

- They establish overall strategies for meeting the organization's mission with prioritized and measurable results.

- They deal with systems barriers quickly and appropriately.

- They create a culture for learning, empowerment, and risk taking.

- They encourage, recognize, support, and validate progress.

- They celebrate successes and stay the course.

Role and Relationship of Unit Manager and Unit Staff

The role of the unit manager is pivotal to any successful transformation. The manager sets the tone of the unit environment. As a key leader at the point of care delivery, the manager creates the relationship-based culture whereby healthy interpersonal relationships and caring and healing practices can flourish. A successful relationship-based culture has the following essential attributes:

- The patient and family are central. There is a constant focus on the core mission of the work.

- Healthy interpersonal relationships are highly valued and expected. They are based on trust, mutual respect, consistent and visible support, and open and honest communication.

- People expect the very best from each other, listen to each other, and support each other through encouragement and teamwork.

- Learning is ongoing and expected.

- Self-awareness and self care are visible and encouraged.

The unit manager and staff members bring the RBC vision to life. They literally translate the vision into day-to-day actions and unit norms. In a relationship-based culture, staff and managers view each other as *colleagues*—not as boss or subordinates. Colleagues share a common purpose and rely on each other for the unique work they do to accomplish that purpose. They work interdependently with mutual respect and recognition for each other's work, understanding how each contributes to providing the best possible care and service to patients and families. When the relationship between manager and staff is truly collegial, leadership is shared, empowered initiative is promoted, and there is unified ownership for achieving quality results.

The table on the next page compares and contrasts the responsibilities of managers and staff members in a relationship-based culture. Many of their responsibilities overlap—the difference is in the way they are implemented and with whom.

Successful clinical managers serve as mentors and guides for transforming care. They promote the fundamental principles of RBC—most essentially that *the relationship between the nurse and the patient is vitally important and must be safeguarded*. The nurse-patient relationship is where

Responsibilities of Unit Manager	Responsibilities of Unit Staff
Leads with a purpose. Maintains a clear and unrelenting focus on care and service to patients and families.	Accepts and embodies the role of leader at the point of care delivery. Maintains a focus on care and service to patients and families.
Establishes and maintains healthy interpersonal relationships.	Establishes and maintains healthy interpersonal relationships.
Establishes clear standards and articulates expectations for performance.	Provides care based on established standards and expectations.
Continually assesses the quality of care and provides ongoing recognition and support for those exemplifying the vision and principles of Relationship-Based Care.	Provides compassionate care and encourages and recognizes colleagues who exemplify the vision and principles of Relationship-Based Care.
Inspires and encourages staff to learn and develop. Serves as coach and mentor.	Assumes accountability for his or her own ongoing learning and development. Serves as coach and mentor for less experienced colleagues.
Demonstrates respect for others in all interactions.	Demonstrates respect for others in all interactions.
Facilitates and expects timely and direct resolution of problems/conflict between individuals and teams.	Initiates direct communication to resolve problems/conflicts with individuals and teams.
Applies critical and creative thinking to resolve problems and remove barriers for care providers.	Applies critical and creative thinking to resolve problems and identifies barriers to care.
Advocates for patients, families, and staff colleagues.	Advocates for patients, families, and colleagues.
Determines and allocates resources to support the best possible care delivery.	Determines and utilizes existing resources to provide the best possible care.
Recognizes and celebrates exemplary care for patients, families, colleagues, and self.	Recognizes and celebrates exemplary care for patients, families, colleagues, and self.
Leads the way; creates the environment where the vision and principles can be lived in daily practice.	Leads the way; puts the vision and principles into daily action.

information is exchanged, decisions are generated, and therapeutic interventions occur. This relationship is a key ingredient in the formula for high levels of satisfaction for the patient, family, staff, and physicians. The clinical manager promotes this core relationship through creating the environment to support it. This is accomplished by developing and coaching staff members, educating and supporting physicians, and designing the most effective systems to support the delivery of RBC.

The unit staff members will assume various degrees of leadership based on their background, experience, and areas of expertise. The important point to emphasize is that leadership is within each of us and differing situations call forth different leaders. Within RBC, all staff members are encouraged to develop to their fullest potential, to voice their opinions, to engage in problem resolution, and to understand their full scope of responsibility, authority, and accountability for their work.

A unit-based infrastructure which engages staff in decision making at the unit level promotes shared leadership, further ensuring outcome achievement. The ideal infrastructure is one that provides a forum for communicating, reflecting on care issues, identifying quality issues, and creative problem resolution. This ideal structure involves the manager and staff working collaboratively to achieve desired results. There are numerous specific models that have been successful. Our bias is that the design of the infrastructure be simple and clear, and that it facilitate learning by action and reflection.

Staff level leadership is developed through ongoing education and coaching. Some of this is "real-time" learning. A leader/manager is continually developing these education and coaching skills within the care environment when he or she uses challenges as opportunities to engage the thinking of different staff members and to reflect on results and identify ways to improve in the future. Additionally, using current literature, on-line references, and other resources to assist in dealing with daily work and patient care challenges, promotes learning as an on-going process. Formal educational offerings in healthy communication, managing relationships, reflection, and problem-solving skills will further promote leadership skill development throughout the work environment.

Decentralization: The Infrastructure for Relationship-Based Care

In Relationship-Based Care, decision making is shared. When staff members are clear about their roles, responsibilities, authority, and accountability, they have greater confidence in their own judgments and are more willing to take ownership for decision making at the point of care. Decentralization creates the conditions in which *"authority is granted to those at the level of action—those who are in the best position to judge the adequacy and efficacy of the decisions they make"* (Manthey, 2002). Decentralization changes both *who* controls decision making and the roles and relationships of the managers and staff within the organization. While the managers are responsible for allocating resources, achieving healthy financial results, and assuring overall quality of care and service, staff members are responsible for appropriate utilization of resources, meeting financial targets, and providing, monitoring, and evaluating their care and service. Skillful interdependence of these roles and functions is core to achieving excellent results.

Within a decentralized infrastructure, organizational hierarchies do remain in place. However, decentralized approaches can be effectively

implemented even in centralized organizations. A comparison of decision making in centralized and decentralized management approaches is presented below.

Centralized		**Decentralized**
Position-based		Knowledge-based
Distant from point of care or service		At point of care or service
Hierarchical communication		Direct communication
Limited staff input		High staff input

With RBC as the goal, the question is not *whether* to move to decentralized decision making; the question is *how*. As leaders accept this challenge for change and begin moving toward the goal, they'll want to consider the following questions:

- What is our current approach to decision making?

- What beliefs and behaviors will we change in order to move to a decentralized way of working?

- How will we educate staff on accepting broader responsibility, authority, and accountability for delivering care?

Organizational hierarchies will remain; however, decentralized approaches can be effectively implemented even in centralized organizations.

Decentralization is most successful when responsibility, authority, and accountability (R+A+A) for decision making are clearly defined. This means that there is a clear and specific allocation and acceptance of *responsibilities*; that individuals have the *authority* to act in those areas where they have accepted responsibility; and that they review their judgments and decisions, demonstrating *accountability* for their own effectiveness. (Creative Health Care Management, 2003).

Responsibility, Authority and Accountability Defined
R + A + A

Responsibility: Responsibility refers to the clear and specific allocation of duties in order to achieve desired results. Assignment of responsibility is a two-way process. Responsibility is visibly given and visibly accepted. Personal ownership and aligned action are evident when one truly accepts responsibility.

Authority: Authority refers to the right to act and make decisions in the areas where one is given and accepts responsibility.

Accountability: Accountability begins when one reviews and reflects upon his own actions and decisions, and culminates with a personal assessment that helps the accountable person determine the best actions to take in the future.

Decentralization is less about structure (although structure influences communication and expectations) and more about human interaction. The fact is most organizations have a hierarchical structure. In these organizations, leadership is challenged to work in a decentralized way within a centralized system. The outcome for leaders who successfully navigate this challenge is that the authority to take action is transferred to those responsible for frontline service and decision making.

One method for increasing the level of staff participation in decision making is the formation of a staff governance structure. While specific designs may vary, all can be classified as participatory models that strengthen authority and accountability for decisions affecting work at the point of care delivery. Tim Porter-O'Grady (1987) identified three primary models of staff or professional governance:

1. The **Councilor Model** consists of councils on clinical practice, quality assurance, and education.

2. The **Congressional Model** features an elected president and cabinet of officers made up of a combination of managers and staff who oversee the operations of a department or unit. (This model may have several committees that report back to the cabinet.)

3. The **Administrative Model** has two structural units (management and clinical) which are often aligned in a hierarchical relationship.

Porter-O'Grady (1986) also identified the five conditions necessary for a professional practice environment. He theorized that the following are essential for an environment to fully promote decentralized decision making processes.

Decentralization, with its emphasis on where decisions are made and its focus on the manager-staff relationship, supports the positive evolution of care delivery.

*   Freedom to function effectively

*   Support from peers and leaders

*   Clear expectations of the work environment

*   Appropriate resources to practice effectively

*   An open organizational climate

Porter-O'Grady's milestone work on the concept of shared governance provides a practical blueprint that empowers individuals to make solid decisions at the point of care or service. Shared governance is a system that facilitates shared leadership. It creates a forum for collective wisdom. It provides us with a structure to measure practice against standards, allows individuals to evaluate the effectiveness of their decision making as a group, and further allows them to improve their processes and practice. When competent care providers are empowered to make decisions that affect patient care, work processes are carried out more efficiently and care providers have more control over the quality of their own work and their work environment.

Although decentralized processes have become increasingly commonplace in health care organization, persistent myths create barriers to maximizing decentralization. Some common myths about decentralization are:

Myth1: Decentralization always means a "flat" organization.

Fact: Actually, it is difficult to identify decentralization by analyzing the number of levels on an organizational chart. While there has been an effort to reduce the number of levels within organizations over the last decade, fewer levels do not automatically mean that decision making is decentralized or that the manager-staff relationship evolves into one that is more collegial. In a decentralized organization, the activity level of the unit and the diversity of services may require several levels. Flattening the structure does not guarantee that managers let go of control and support staff members in the decisions they make. Decentralization occurs as a result of behavioral changes within the relationships depicted on any organizational chart—whether it is flat or multi-leveled.

Myth 2: Decentralization creates inconsistency. It invites chaos!

Fact: The identification of goals and how those goals are achieved is a part of the decentralization process. Consistency is actually gained as managers clarify responsibility, authority, and accountability for themselves and in teams within the organization. Therefore, there is greater efficiency and effectiveness in a well run decentralized organization. In a fully decentralized organization, decision makers know their boundaries, as guidelines for independent action are clearly stated. In a decentralized organization, clearly articulated principles and standards that guide behavior and performance reduce chaos.

Myth 3: Decentralization means that everyone is involved in all decisions.

Fact: In a decentralized organization, decisions are made at the level where the most knowledge about that decision exists. Thus, at budget time, the size of the annual budget is determined at the board/executive level. The department manager and staff decide how to allocate and manage their part of the budget. In a decentralized organization, the unit staff decides how to meet the needs of the patients. The key to decentralization is to ask who has the most information when a decision is necessary and to move the responsibility, authority, and accountability to that level of the organization.

Myth 4: Decentralization is not achievable.

Fact: While it takes time and effort, decentralization is achievable and the results are worth the investment. A change to decentralization requires leadership and persistence by the entire management team. When an effective approach to management is coupled with leadership effectiveness, a climate of growth and a culture of empowerment exist within the organization. This transforms professional working relationships from the "superior vs. subordinate" relationships of the past. When staff members are treated like responsible adults, there is a greater potential for patients in this environment to be treated in the same way.

Decentralization provides the opportunity for managers to share authority for decision making, and requires them to support staff in developing their own competencies as decision makers. Managers who wish to create an environment for Relationship-Based Care accept the responsibility to build a repertoire of leadership behaviors to support these changes in their staff. Within this model, leadership focuses on staff growth and development. Leaders encourage judicious use of both autonomy and interdependence in team members and help staff build competence and confidence in their work and relationships. They provide the means to bring about changes needed in the environment and lead to the evolution of the care delivery system.

Summary of Key Concepts

- Transitioning to Relationship-Based Care calls for renewed leadership at all levels of the organization.

- The role of the organization's executive leaders is to create an organizational culture in which transformational change can occur. Cultures evolve when executive leaders create an organizational environment in which commitment is valued over compliance.

- Executive leaders provide information to empower people in making decisions and accepting personal responsibility for results.

- Managers at every level of the organization are leaders because they influence others.

- Unit managers support the development of RBC by moving care decisions to the staff at the bedside (creating a decentralized foundation) and by developing leadership behaviors that support the staff's ability to take responsibility, authority, and accountability for decision making for patient care.

- Leadership (unlike management) can be found at every level of an organization's structure.

- Staff members who offer support and feedback to peers are modeling positive leadership.

- Staff commitment to building healthy interpersonal relationships creates an environment of trust and respect, ultimately enhancing patient care.

- In a decentralized system where decisions about patient care are moved to the patient's bedside, the key decision makers about daily clinical practice and patient care are the staff members rather than management. This fundamentally changes the manager-staff relationship within the unit.

- Decision making at the point of care requires that the staff develop into competent, confident decision makers and that leaders actively promote and support that development.

- Leaders at all levels of the organization play a vital role in the design and implementation of RBC and in creating and sustaining the culture to support it.

- In an RBC culture, staff and managers view each other as colleagues rather than as bosses and subordinates. They work interdependently, showing mutual respect and giving recognition for each other's work, specifically acknowledging how that work contributes to creating the best possible care delivery system.

- New leaders create an environment of hope and creativity— one which replaces problems with solutions and initiates actions to achieve the RBC vision.

Questions for Self-Assessment

- What are your current beliefs about leaders and leadership? Who do you consider to be leaders?

- How do you recognize and support leaders in your organization?

- How do you develop leaders in your organization?

- What are your current strengths in leadership?

- What is the current role of your executive team? What do staff members from different parts of the organization expect from them?

- In what ways do leaders in your organization inspire staff, give voice to expectations for a caring culture, and model caring behaviors?

St. Francis Health Center
Topeka, Kansas

Recapturing the essence of nursing at St. Francis Health Center was the vision of a number of nursing staff members who felt that we had moved from "hands on" nursing to exclusively high tech nursing. We believed that time spent with patients and families had disappeared and that "me-me-me-ism" among nursing staff had eclipsed patient needs. We had survived an innovation process during which Primary Nursing, our long embraced nursing care delivery method, had become a thing of the past.

A new Vice President of Patient Care Services closely examined our nursing practice and patient care and had the foresight to commission a volunteer group of nursing staff from various work areas, shifts, and roles to address what changes would most benefit St. Francis.

The goal of the group was to rediscover what was once so prevalent in our facility: professional, dedicated, relationship-based, holistic nursing care. The group charged with resurrecting an aspect of our nursing experience that had long been in ashes was appropriately named the Phoenix Group. The group developed a purpose statement with which to provide vision for nursing practice; promote professional growth; communicate the essence of nursing; support nursing openly through empowerment, mentoring, education, collaboration, and valuing; and revitalize professionalism and accountability. Next we reviewed existing nursing literature to obtain supportive data and gain direction for our journey. As a result we fashioned our "Five Dimensions of Caring": self care, love, hope/belief, spirit, and knowledge. Each dimension would guide our work and help us to maintain alignment with the mission of the organization. Self assessments were conducted to identify why we chose to become nursing professionals in the first place and what brought us joy as caregivers, and to examine characteristics of effective caregivers.

The next leap toward the future of nursing at St. Francis was extensive, appreciative inquiry work done with larger numbers of staff members by way of CHCM's consultation. Their findings emphasized the value of strong relationships for both patients and staff. Not surprisingly, this inquiry complimented the smaller scale reflection done with Phoenix Group members, creating an enthusiastic "buzz" among personnel around the direction we were taking. It was apparent that something was changing—that hope was returning to an injured nursing staff, that we could share the great work for which we were known and of which we were so proud. This was new to us at St. Francis; we would be instrumental in directing what patient care was to become; we, *the staff,* would lead the way.

Concurrently the changes that were identified as necessary for nurses were also identified as necessary for all patient/family/visitor caregivers. This meant that all therapists, transporters, dietary staff, admission staff and so on would be included in this system change. This was beginning to take on many exciting possibilities for the entire care delivery process at St. Francis.

Self-care education was provided as an offering to all nursing staff within the hospital and the clinics. We felt strongly that if the staff did not practice self-care they could not be effective in providing care to others. Additionally, we implemented education regarding care of spirit, another important dimension of caring, and made that education available to ancillary staff. The dimension of *spirit* focuses on seeing the essential, and it emphasizes relationships and intentional presence along with knowing one's self.

Other educational programs that promoted leadership skills and strengthened our knowledge and intention in caring and healing processes for patients and families were provided for both managers and clinical staff within the facility.

The transformational work crafted at the staff level was incorporated into the structure of other concurrent organizational initiatives and became known as "Kindness Connects," its emphasis being kindness and caring in every relationship. The two main components of the endeavor were *The Caring Model™* for all staff and a principles-based patient care delivery system for all patient care areas.

The behaviors and anticipated outcomes of *The Caring Model™* provided the common expectations for caring relationships for staff from all departments and disciplines. Many Phoenix Group members were recruited to be *Caring Model™* facilitators. All employees, including staff from the clinics, were required to attend one two-hour session to become familiar with five caring behaviors of the model; these behaviors manifest focus, accountability and intention in relationships between staff, patients, families, and visitors. An unexpected outcome is that staff would meet and share stories with colleagues with whom ordinarily they would not interact. These sessions proved to be a turning point. Secondly, a principle-based Professional Nursing Practice model was recognized as a necessary part of this evolution. In line with the Phoenix Group vision, Primary Nursing principles were once again integrated into the model with unit groups developing unit-specific plans on how the principles would be accomplished in each of the nursing areas.

"The proof is in the pudding," as they say. Relationships within the organization are stronger, and patient satisfaction scores have improved right along with our employee satisfaction surveys. This truly is the beginning of something good. The *feel* of the organization is returning to what it once was—an organization where caring is palpable and genuine, where relationships thrive, and where the essence of nursing truly exists.

Shirley Heintz, MSA, RN, CNAA is the Vice President of Patient Care Services and Teresa Kellerman, MSN, RN, is a Clinical Nurse Specialist at St. Francis Health Center in Topeka, Kansas.

A Moment of Excellence: Centra Health

Centra Health
Lynchburg, Virginia

I joined the Centra Health Leadership Team in the spring of 2000. Centra Health is a two hospital organization operating 500+ beds, located in Lynchburg, Virginia. Prior to my appointment as the Chief Nursing Officer, there was not a nurse at the senior leadership level within the organization. Previously, there were two vice presidents at each hospital who reported to two different senior vice presidents. This system had worked well for the organization for a time, but in the latter part of 1999, with urging from nurses, my position was created. My first task as the new leader was to establish a trusting relationship with the staff and to raise the professional level of nursing.

I started my position with a Joint Commission visit the second week of my employment.

This Joint Commission survey provided me with the opportunity to see the organization through the eyes of the surveyor and to do my own surveying. I was very impressed by the level of nursing care I witnessed. During the survey week, nurses were observed demonstrating very caring behaviors to patients and family members. The survey was successful for the hospitals and Centra's other services. At the end of the survey week, I proceeded to complete my own comprehensive assessment of the organization.

I held Town Hall meetings on all shifts to solicit staff input. I also made rounds on all shifts and held one-on-one sessions with nurses to gain a greater understanding of the work experience through their eyes. Nurse managers and directors were assessed for learning needs. Sessions were held with new graduates to assess their orientation and introduction into work. Many issues surfaced and it was clear to me that the nursing staff wanted to be listened to, to be involved in decisions that affected them, to receive feedback when problems were presented, and they wanted a trusting relationship with hospital leaders.

As a result of the assessment, the following have been accomplished:

- **Closed staffing was implemented December, 2000.** No nursing staff member is forced to work on another unit to cover staffing needs. Sick time decreased 25% after the first year of implementing closed staffing and turnover and vacancy rates have decreased.

- **Senior Nurse Executive makes rounds and hosts meetings for staff,** frequently with the CEO in attendance. Evidence on staffing and the value of

RN staff as researched by Linda Aiken and Peter Beurhaus have been widely shared throughout the organization. The CEO goes to units and asks questions like, "How is your staffing?" Most recently, the CEO spent two days on a unit observing the administration of medications. He used his experience to implement changes in the medication administration process. Recently, one million dollars has been approved to upgrade the medication system.

- **New graduate orientation has been reviewed each year by the new nursing leadership team, and changes have been made based on feedback by new graduates.** The CEO joins the nurse executive for meetings with new graduates and has been able to support orientation needs and other programs for graduates. Additionally, the CEO, retention specialist, and I meet with new graduates at 3 months, 6 months and one year over breakfast, lunch or dinner. Our purpose is to connect with them, listen to them, learn about their experience, and find ways to improve new graduate orientation. Centra hired 60-75 new graduates per year and first year turnover has been less than 10%.

- **A Nurse Leadership Development program was established.** A management development questionnaire (MDQ) was used to assess nurse leaders' learning needs. The tool addresses skills such as planning, communication, analytical skills, resilience, etc. The tool was first administered in October, 2000, shortly after my arrival. Results were used to plan education and developmental programs to improve leadership skills. The Darden School for Business from the University of Virginia, the VHA Leadership Institute, and the Advisory Board Leadership Academy have provided programs at Centra over the past four years.

The MDQ instrument was administered a second and third time and scores have improved in all leadership categories. This same tool with a structured approach to skills development was used for shift managers. Shift managers work 3:00 PM – 11:30 PM and 11:00 PM – 7:30 AM, and they assist the managers in running the units. They have also shown improvements.

We believe that every nurse is a leader and so as we continue our leadership development, we are introducing *Leading an Empowered Organization* and *Reigniting the Spirit of Caring,* two programs from CHCM which provide education in leadership skills and knowledge and inspire and renew passion and commitment to practice.

- **We've begun holding retreats for all nursing units.** Money is budgeted annually for all nursing units to hold retreats that provide for group learning and team building. Units split staff schedules so that all may attend. These retreats help to align the organizational goals with the unit staff's goals.

- **We give regular updates to staff by email and at meetings.** Email has been a great vehicle to maintain communication with staff. Regular updates are sent to managers by the Chief Nurse Executive. In addition, written updates are provided by the CNO at each Nurse Leadership group meeting. Managers then have key points to take back to the units to share. Very often, the reports are posted for all staff to read.

- **Shared Governance was recently implemented.** The staff has embraced the concept with lots of energy and enthusiasm.

- **We've instituted a Staff Nurse-CEO-CNO Summit.** Two years ago Centra held its first staff nurse-CEO-CNO Summit to provide an opportunity for nurses at the bedside to network with CEOs and CNOs. The second one was held in 2004. These Summits have been rated very highly by all participants. National speakers such as Peter Beurhaus, Marie Manthey, Lillee Gelinas, Mary Foley and Keith Harrell have participated. In 2004, more than 600 nurses and leaders attended.

- **We hired a retention specialist.** As a new executive at Centra, after reviewing turnover rates in 2000, I decided that 70% of the time for nurse leaders would be spent on retention and 30% on recruitment. Centra has a retention specialist whose role is to promote and support nurse retention. Emphasis is placed on recognition and rewards, such as gift certificates for staff, which are given for excellence in patient care and professional practice. There is a retention budget for each nursing unit and as well as a retention budget for the nursing department as a whole. Managers at Centra have

developed a list of 101 ways to recognize and reward staff.

During my four years at Centra Health, the RN turnover rate has dropped from 14.3% (2000) to 8% (2003). The RN vacancy rate dropped from 12% to between 3%-6%. There has been no use of agency or traveler nurses in more than three years. I believe the relationship established over the years with the staff has made a difference. Nurse leaders have developed new and different skills and have improved in others. As a result, they are leading with a new level of confidence. Senior leaders listen and act. Staff want to be listened to and to be heard. The actions listed above provide you with our response to a few of the many issues presented by staff. They speak, and we listen and act.

Golden Bethune, RN, CNO, is Senior Vice President of Patient Care Services for Centra Health, a 400 bed hospital in Lynchburg, Virginia.

THREE
Teamwork

Donna Wright

Gettin' good players is easy.
Gettin' 'em to play together is the hard part.

—Casey Stengel

Overview

Casey Stengel, the hard-bitten manager of the New York Yankees, knew that putting a group of people together and giving them a common purpose did not in itself make them a team. No team wins if its members don't play together. Most leaders in health care strive to build healthy teams because statistics show time and time again that healthy teamwork produces better results.

In 1993, Jon Katzenbach and Douglas Smith examined the difference between work groups and teams. Basically, they identified that work groups are collections of individuals who come together for a joint effort, but whose outcomes depend primarily on individual efforts. In contrast, a team works together collectively to magnify the group's overall results, usually achieving higher results than what any one individual could achieve independently. (Manion, Lorimer & Leander, 1996).

Work groups differ from teams in many respects—most notably in their perceptions of individual responsibility, levels of authority, approach to work, and accountability. Here is a comparison of the differences between work groups and teams. (Manion, Lorimer, & Leander, 1996).

Teamwork is the most statistically significant predictor of quality as perceived by patients, families, staff, and doctors.

—E.C. Murphy

Work groups	Teams
Members rely on individual contributions.	Members rely on collective contributions.
Members come together to share information and solve problems to help individuals do their jobs better.	Members come together to solve problems and make decisions to improve the team's work and group performance or outcome.
Members do NOT take responsibility for results other than their own.	Members share a common purpose and goals and hold themselves mutually accountable for results.

Teamwork requires a group of diverse members to focus on a shared purpose and to work together to fulfill that purpose. In healthy and productive teams, each member contributes his or her unique knowledge and skills within a clearly defined scope of responsibility, authority, and accountability (R+A+A). Although teams are part of the infrastructure in any modern organization, the role of teamwork in health care organizations has a particular significance. The purpose of health care is to care for and serve people who are ill, suffering, giving birth, and dying—people who are experiencing profound vulnerability. *Everything* that happens to them matters. Teamwork, therefore, must focus members on assuring that safe, competent, and compassionate care is provided. In an unpublished study done by E.C. Murphy LTD., in the mid-nineties, teamwork was defined, in part, as *"proactively sharing information on behalf of the patient, and not allowing conflicts to interfere with work."* High functioning health care teams create the energy and interdependence required for well-coordinated, high quality patient care delivery and outcomes.

Sometimes, one of the biggest challenges health care professionals face is getting past the day-to-day problems, conflicts, and attitudes of its staff members, in order to rise to a level of functioning where our collective actions are in line with our care goals. Too often the focus on our collective goal of caring can be interrupted by interpersonal conflicts exacerbated by a "look" someone gave to someone else or a miscommunication from individuals on one shift to those of another. We've all experienced conflicts in which individuals end up feeling "dumped on," or where some other problem is allowed by a group's members to balloon out of proportion because no one had the skills or confidence to talk about the problem honestly. If gone untended, these conflicts can evolve into toxic patterns of behavior which can completely undermine the capacity of teams to provide effective care. If we are to be successful in reaching our care goals, we must *help* groups of people develop the skills to become teams. The skills necessary for successful teamwork include effective communication, critical and creative thinking, personal leadership, and maintaining healthy interpersonal relationships.

Successful teams also require tools to accomplish their goals. These tools may include:

- Strategies to articulate our expectations to each other and to create an environment of mutual respect and open, honest communication.

- A system or nomenclature to identify different levels of individual and group responsibility and authority.

- Processes that help individuals analyze problems and generate creative solutions.

- Interpersonal approaches for responding positively and proactively to attitudes and behaviors that might otherwise hinder a positive environment.

- Strategies and methodologies that can assist a group to achieve consensus and to support a common goal even in the heat of conflict and controversy. (Wright, 1998)

An organization's leaders are active participants in the development of successful teams. Positional leaders of successful teams will take the time to discuss team expectations and team challenges on a regular basis. Leaders will support the development of team members, providing them with the time, education, and skills to address team communication and team issues. Leaders will also expand their own skills pertaining to team participation. Team leaders must learn to surrender some control without abandoning individuals, to support individuals without micromanaging them, and to learn new and innovative techniques for keeping the collective vision alive in the whole team.

This chapter addresses three key aspects of teamwork within the Relationship-Based Care (RBC) model.

1. The unique nature of health care teams is explored with an emphasis on the patient at the center of the team as well as the value of clearly articulated expectations for the responsibilities, authority, and accountability of all individuals in the organization.

2. Approaches for understanding and building healthy team relationships are presented along with a practical tool for implementation. The concept of team

Team leaders must learn to surrender some control without abandoning individuals, to support individuals without micromanaging them, and to learn new and innovative techniques for keeping the collective vision alive in the whole team.

members as "colleagues" is discussed as key to building respectful work environments and achieving desired outcomes.

3. The physician-nurse relationship is examined as it relates to a collegial work environment and safe, coordinated patient care.

Individuals Within the Team

Health care teams exist to care for patients. As the patient and his or her family are central to RBC, the health care team incorporates patients and families as the center of its individual structure as well. In order to meet patients' needs and to effectively coordinate care, a partnership is created among the patient, family, and members of the health care team. In this partnership, patients are treated with respect and dignity, informed of their rights and responsibilities, provided information that affects their care, included in the planning of their care, and supported as primary decision makers in their care.

Healthy teamwork is always supported by a clearly defined system of care delivery. Expectations are defined for each team member's role in a way that helps delineate appropriate boundaries, while not being so exclusively defined that they preclude natural overlap, delegation, and shared responsibilities. A main building block for an effective, interdependent team is to have established areas of R+A+A, laid out explicitly by role and discipline.

In addition to the articulation of R+A+A, the required skills or competencies for each role must be clearly articulated. These competencies include all that support a team member to be successful. Among them are technical competencies,

In a care partnership that is functioning well, all parties to it will enjoy a feeling of mutual trust and respect. Each will experience the confidence that comes from working as an equal member of a healthcare team.

—Mary Dale Scheller

interpersonal competencies, and critical/creative thinking competencies. Competencies specific to personal leadership may strengthen individual performance as well as overall team function.

Team Members' Roles and Expectations:

The Manager

The manager is an important and influential team member. The role of the manager is to acquire, develop, support, and encourage staff members in the delivery of care to patients and families and to manage the overall resources necessary to provide that care. As the manager works with the direct care team from a collegial and supportive foundation, team members gain confidence in assuming individual and collective ownership for the overall quality of care.

The Registered Nurse

In an RBC system, the Professional Nursing staff set the standards for the level and quality of care. They accomplish this through establishing primary therapeutic relationships with patients and their families. The professional registered nurse (RN) has responsibility, authority, and accountability for the provision of nursing care. The RN determines what care is delegated to others and coordinates care with the patient, physician, and other members of the interdisciplinary team. The RN provides leadership to other members of the unit team by articulating expected standards of care and encouraging and supporting team members and their contributions. The success of the team is based on RNs taking responsibility and accountability, while the organization and its leadership support them in doing so.

The Licensed Practical/Licensed Vocational Nurse

The role of the licensed practical/vocational nurse (LPN/LVN) is a vital one. The LPN/LVN is licensed to provide direct care to patients and families under the supervision of a registered nurse. A partnership between the RN and LPN/LVN begins with a mutual understanding of licensure and role requirements. Such a partnership maximizes each person's contribution to patient care. This partnership is most effective when supported by a system that reflects strong team values—for example, one that implements scheduling practices that promote continuity of a specific RN and LPN/LVN consistently working together. The *Partners in Practice Model* is one method of scheduling to promote and formalize these types of strong team relationships. (See appendix A.)

The Nursing Assistant

Nursing assistants also have a critical role in meeting patient and family needs. Their care giving responsibilities involve highly intimate contact with patients over time. Often, it is the nursing assistant who provides hands-on hygienic and comfort care for patients. It is through compassionate interactions with nursing assistants (as well as LPN/LVNs) that patients experience a feeling of being cared for with dignity.

Through their care and observations, nursing assistants also have access to a significant amount of information regarding the patient. A key opportunity to practice strong team relationships is in the communication of this information among the RN, LPN/LVN, and other members of the interdisciplinary team to ensure that the patient's care needs are being addressed appropriately. The team values that have been articulated (formally and informally) to each team member will determine the success of these communication interactions. Sometimes these interactions are respectful and healthy, and sometimes these interactions are filled with negative attitudes, mistrust, and frustration. The tone of daily interactions is a strong indicator of the current reality of a team's cohesiveness, and it is a solid predictor of whether they will ultimately achieve success in their objectives.

The Housekeeping Staff

Housekeeping staff care for the patient's surroundings and often have interactions with patients and their families as well. A clean and aesthetically pleasing environment is extremely important for the patient's healing and recovery. Additionally, patients and their families tell us that when the environment is attended to, they have higher confidence that their other needs are also being addressed. To create a healing whole, all aspects matter. The role of the housekeeper, in concert with the other members of the team, is critical in creating and sustaining a caring and healing environment.

The Interdisciplinary Team

Departments within the organization that have an indirect or non-clinical impact on patients and families are also a part of the health care team. (This may not always be apparent to members of those departments *or* to members of the direct care team.) The driving principle here is that "it takes a village" to provide world class care. The work of each person in each department contributes either directly or indirectly to the care of patients and families. Every person in every department shares the common purpose of contributing to the patients' and families' experience of care; every person in every department touches patients and families in some way during their stay; every person in every department deserves to be recognized for his or her essential contribution.

The make up of the interdisciplinary team is dependent upon the care needs of each patient. Members of the health care interdisciplinary team can include professionals from pharmacy, pastoral care services, social services, physical therapy, occupational therapy, radiology services, and nutritional services. Physicians are members of the health care interdisciplinary team as well as members of a medical interdisciplinary team which includes both medical specialties and subspecialties. Effective interdisciplinary collaboration and coordination are achieved through an established system of care delivery and communication. Each team member brings distinct expertise to the patient and works with the nurse and physician to assure that their care is integrated into the overall plan. In a high functioning interdisciplinary team, collegial relationships are established, each member of the team knows his or her scope of responsibility, authority, and accountability, and everyone knows what to expect from other team members.

Healthy Team Relationships

In our extensive work with teams and team building, we have determined that healthy, productive teams have one very consistent element—they have given attention to relationship management within the team. Relationship management includes teaching team members how to interact with one another, to effectively and respectfully communicate what needs to be done, and to deal with "people problems" as they arise throughout the day. Every aspect of relationship management is essential to the success of patient care delivery. One of the best ways to create a team with strong relationship management potential is by articulating expectations within the team about how to manage relationships. One of the main reasons we have miscommunication or misunderstandings in our personal daily interactions is that we fail to articulate expectations regarding these interactions. We often assume the other person or group knows exactly what we want or that they value the same ideas we have. This is often not the case. Articulating our expectations about team interactions provides an opportunity for our team colleagues to discuss, negotiate, and commit to a common set of ideas and values. The action of articulating expectations is one of the strongest ways to prepare a group to be a successful team, ready to meet the challenges they face everyday.

Here is an example of an articulated expectation for relationship management within a team:

Each member of this team is expected to establish and maintain healthy interpersonal relationships with other members. Healthy relationships are characterized by trust, mutual respect, consistent and visible support, and open and honest communication.

An important underlying premise to this expectation is that people have the *capacity* to learn how to develop and maintain healthy interpersonal relationships. For many people, developing healthy interpersonal relationships means "unlearning" less healthy patterns of interaction. This is a significant challenge, but it is achievable. Successful change requires agreement. We have observed dramatic team improvement in

situations in which all parties accept that change is warranted, commit to personal change, identify and agree to unlearn old unhealthy patterns of relating, learn new healthy patterns of relating, support and coach each other in these new patterns of relating, and stay committed to the change. This type of change is a journey, *not* a quick fix. It is, however, one of the most satisfying investments an organization can make.

There are four basic characteristics that are the foundation for all healthy teams. When a problem arises in a team, the underlying premise of the issue is usually due to a breakdown in one of these four elements:

1. **TRUST**—This ranges from the belief that a team member can do the job that he or she was hired to do (functional trust) to the concept of trustworthiness. Trustworthy people are able to develop trusting relationships by virtue of their character (integrity, maturity, abundance mentality) and through their competence (clinical/technical, interpersonal, critical/creative thinking, leadership).

2. **MUTUAL RESPECT**—This means that people are accepted and treated with positive regard for who they are, not for what they represent by title, position, or educational level.

3. **CONSISTENT AND VISIBLE SUPPORT**—This means team members can count on each other to be there when things are going well and when a mistake occurs. This is reinforced by a mutual commitment to win-win relationships and to learning and growing together.

4. **OPEN AND HONEST COMMUNICATION** —This means being direct and truthful. It is based on the "three commandments for effective communication."
   1. Send the mail to the right address.
   2. Ask for what you need; it ups the chance you will get it.
   3. To thine own self be true.

   (Creative Health Care Management, 2003)

Developing strong teams requires the right tools. A good example of a tool to strengthen a team is the *Commitment to my Co-worker* statement, developed by Marie Manthey. It articulates practical expectations to achieve healthy interpersonal relationships within a health care team.

Commitment To My Co-workers© for Health Care Teams

As your co-worker and with our shared organizational goal of excellent patient care, I commit to the following:

- I will accept responsibility for establishing and maintaining healthy interpersonal relationships with you and every other member of this team.

- I will talk to you promptly if I am having a problem with you. The only time I will discuss it with another person is when I need advice or help in deciding how to communicate with you appropriately.

- I will establish and maintain a relationship of functional trust with you and every member of this team. My relationships with each of you will be equally respectful, regardless of job title, level of educational preparation, or any other differences that may exist.

- I will not engage in the "3B's" (Bickering, Back-biting and Blaming). I will practice the "3C's" (Caring, Commitment and Collaboration) in my relationship with you and ask you to do the same with me.

- I will not complain about another team member and ask you not to as well. If I hear you doing so, I will ask you to talk to that person.

- I will accept you as you are today, forgiving past problems and ask you to do the same with me.

- I will be committed to finding solutions to problems, rather than complaining about them or blaming someone for them, and ask you to do the same.

- I will affirm your contribution to the quality of our work.

- I will remember that neither of us is perfect, and that human errors are opportunities, not for shame or guilt, but for forgiveness and growth.

Copyright 2009, Creative Health Care Management, Inc.
Compiled by Marie Manthey

This statement addresses many of the values and behaviors embraced by successful teams, and is a useful tool for strengthening the team commitment to achieving healthy relationships. The *Commitment to my Co-worker©* statement helps us to establish what each of us will bring to the team and what we expect in return from our co-workers. It can help to improve the tone, morale, and level of personal satisfaction in your team members.

But the statement does not work by itself. It will be of little effect to put this statement in everyone's locker with a memo stating, "We will begin this on Monday!" *Commitment to my Co-worker©* is a tool to begin a team building dialogue. Here are some strategies for using the statement successfully:

1. Set aside some time for your group to discuss the current work environment—perhaps a few minutes at your next staff meeting.

2. Use the Commitment to my Co-worker© statement to introduce healthy relationship expectations. Take some time to discuss these expectations, and allow individuals time to reflect on these expectations.

3. Ask your team if they, as a group, endorse these statements, and are willing, individually, to commit to them.

4. Periodically review the statement at the beginning of meetings and group discussions. It is especially important prior to what promises to be a tense discussion.

5. Periodically evaluate team relationships as to whether they currently express the expectations articulated in the statement. (An example of an evaluation tool used to

measure team relationships, based on the *Commitment to my Co-worker©* statement, can be found in Appendix B.)

Tools like *Commitment to My Co-worker©* can be the cornerstone to building a strong team. Here is a personal story of teamwork in action—one in which members feel the need to talk to each other (or some may say, "confront each other") about a concern related to team expectations.

I remember a time when I worked as a hospital educator. I was stopped in the hallway by a staff nurse who was currently on a hospital committee with me. She stopped to ask me if I had finished the minutes from our last meeting, as it had been my turn to take minutes. I told her I had given my handwritten minutes to one of the secretaries in the secretarial pool to type up, and that I had not received them back from her yet. The staff nurse informed me that she really needed the minutes in order to follow up with each member of the committee before the next meeting. I told her that I knew how urgent it was to have the minutes, but I had given my handwritten notes to Michelle in the secretarial pool, and I said, "You know how Michelle is! I have called her several times, and I never get any response..." I started to complain about my frustrating interactions with Michelle, the secretary. Half way through my complaining, the staff nurse interrupted me and said, "Excuse me; I do not mean to interrupt your complaining, but have you had a chance to talk with Michelle directly about this issue?" I responded to her, sheepishly, "No, I haven't." The staff nurse then said, "Ok, then, I would be happy to listen to you

talk about Michelle, IF it leads you to go talk with her directly about this issue. If you do not want to do this, then I do not want to talk about Michelle. If we do so, it will just be gossip, and that is not healthy."

I was so impressed that she could do this, and in a way that was non-threatening to me. In a manner that left no doubt as to her commitment to healthy team communication, she reminded me of my *own* commitment, and showed respect for everyone on the team, including Michelle. We were able to have this interaction, because we had used *Commitment to My Co-worker©*, and had agreed as a team that we would support statements like:

I will accept responsibility for establishing and maintaining healthy interpersonal relationships with you and every member of this staff. I will talk with you promptly if I am having a problem with you. The only time I will discuss it with another person is when I need advice or help in deciding how to communicate with you appropriately.

This staff nurse held me accountable to this statement in a very supportive, respectful way. She was not intimidated by my title or position, nor inhibited by her own. In her eyes we were equally responsible to support these values for the success of the team. I do not think this would have been possible had *Commitment to my Co-workers©* not guided our prior discussion of our team values and philosophies.

Teamwork *does not* mean we always agree with each other, it *does* mean we support each other, respect each other, and help each other move toward a collective goal.

Fostering true commitment among co-workers turns disparate members of a would-be team into colleagues. As team members recognize each other as colleagues, the work paradigm evolves from a task-based focus to a focus on shared purpose and principles. Mary Koloroutis captured the essence of the concept of colleagues in poetic fashion in the following reflection:

About Colleagues

Colleagues care for each other. They understand that support, validation, and compassion for each other as people establishes the foundation to care compassionately for patients and families.

Colleagues listen to each other. They listen with an authentic and compelling desire to understand each other's perspective. Colleagues listen to learn and to discover new ways to be and work with each other.

Colleagues treat each other with respect. They honor each other as fellow human beings with unique life experiences and viewpoints. Colleagues do not compromise their respect for each other even during times of conflict.

Colleagues are "self-responsible." They understand that to function effectively and interdependently with others, they must take ownership for their choices and behaviors.

Colleagues learn from each other. They hold learning as a high and constant value and leverage interactions and experiences to learn and grow together. Mistakes and interpersonal conflicts are viewed as opportunities to learn.

(Koloroutis, 2002)

The Nurse-Physician Relationship

The Institute of Medicine (2000) identified the nurse-physician relationship as a pivotal element in the delivery of safe patient care. A recent study of a network of Veteran Health Administration (VHA) hospitals on the west coast confirmed that daily interactions between nurses and physicians strongly influence nurses' satisfaction with their work environment and their overall perceptions of their ability to provide quality patient care (Rosenstein, 2002). William Knaus and his associates evaluated patient outcomes in intensive care units in major medical centers and found that communication patterns between nurses and physicians were the most significant element associated with patient mortality—more significant, for example, than whether the ICU had a medical director or was within a teaching hospital (Shortell, et al., 1994).

Although nurses' and physicians' work is highly interdependent, the two disciplines have a long history of education and role socialization that has traditionally lent itself to a parallel and indirect, rather than a collaborative and direct, way of providing care to patients. Leonard Stein, MD described this socialization as the "doctor-nurse game" in a classic article published in 1967 and revisited again in an updated article in 1990. The role socialization in the old hierarchical doctor-nurse game called for nurses to be passive in their interactions with doctors. They were to advocate for patients without being direct or obvious. The goal of the interaction was to safeguard the patients without open disagreement with doctors' orders and to appear to respect the physicians' thinking no matter what. The physician was to be seen as *"captain of the ship"* and in charge of all decisions affecting the patient. The nurse was to go along for the ride

When information is shared and the nurse and doctor do what they each do best in a coordinated and deliberate manner, the patient can only win.

—H. Albert, MD

and to *"do her best"* to assure the ride was safe and error free without *"rocking the boat..."* (Stein, Watts, and Howell, 1990; Stein, 1967).

This old paradigm has changed dramatically over the past few decades. Although authors vary on how significant the change has been, there is agreement that attitudes are changing from a traditional hierarchical model to a collaborative model (Barrere, 2002). Both physicians and nurses are seeking more collaborative, interdependent working relationships as they know that the old hierarchical games are not in the best interest of the patients nor are they in the best interest of the nurses and physicians providing care. The following excerpt reflects one physician's thoughts on the benefits of a collaborative model of practice (Albert, et al, 1992):

> *Physicians are not with their patients all day long. Physicians cannot watch over everything that happens in the hospital nor are they necessarily qualified to do so. In this world of rapidly expanding technology and complexity, it is a miracle that patients get through an inpatient experience as well as they do. Part of this success is due to the interventions of nurses. Additionally, nurses have access to information useful to the physician about how the patient is doing and how the patient is feeling that is not available from anyone else. Likewise, the physician has information that would allow the nurses to carry out their roles smoothly and achieve their objectives more completely. When this information is shared and when each does what he or she does best in a coordinated and deliberate manner, the patient can only win.*

A collaborative model of practice between physicians and nurses requires system-wide commitment to that model at all levels of the organization. It requires an understanding of the old paradigm and a conscious decision to move into or strengthen the new way of thinking. The specifics of this transition are made explicit in the following comparison of the old and new rules adapted from the doctor-nurse game described by Stein (1990).

Doctor-Nurse Game: Comparison of the Old Rules and the New Rules

Old Rules	New Rules
Medical care is more important than nursing care.	Good health care requires both good nursing care and good medical care.
The nurse can help the doctor as long as nobody knows about it—including the doctor.	The doctor and the nurse are both there to help the patient and communicate directly and openly to accomplish this.
The doctor knows more than the nurse.	Good doctors know more medicine than good nurses; good nurses know more nursing than good doctors.
If the doctor tells the patients what to do and they don't do it, it's the patient's fault. The doctor did his best.	If a health care plan is to be carried out, it must be worked out with the patient's needs and capabilities as foremost.
Good doctors rarely make mistakes and see to it that other's don't either.	Everyone makes mistakes, but open communication between doctors and nurses minimizes them.

In order for the physician and nurse to create a care team that will positively impact patient outcomes, they must function as colleagues. Successful physician-nurse teams will embrace the characteristics of team members described throughout this chapter. The organization they work in can support this collegial, team-based relationship by encouraging and providing opportunities for open dialogue between team members and by actively participating in review of team practices through ongoing performance improvement activities.

The philosophies required to create healthy, interdependent, collegial relationships between doctors and nurses are described below. Movement from the traditional to the collaborative model requires both physicians and nurses to change their roles and belief patterns.

From:	To:
Independence	Interdependence
Hierarchical relationship	Collegial relationship
Parallel functioning	Team functioning
Medical plan	Patient's plan
Resisting change	Leading change
Competing	Partnering
Indirect communication	Direct communication

Moving from the old hierarchical practice to collaborative practice has never been more urgent. Collaborative practice is based on respect for the unique, independent functions of both physicians and nurses. The physician oversees the medical diagnosis and delegates treatment for the patient. The nurse implements these delegated medical functions based on his or her knowledge and critical thinking skills. In addition, the nurse oversees and implements the nursing assessment and plan of care.

Neither doctor nor nurse gives the other "permission" to carry out their designated professional practice. They are not independent; they are *inter*-dependent. That interdependence is the essence of true teamwork. Although the doctor-nurse relationship is being addressed in this section, these principles apply to all health team member relationships.

Alan Rosenstein, MD, in his research on the nurse-physician relationship and its impact on nurses' satisfaction and retention, summarized the following strategies for improving the relationship based on surveys completed by more than 1,200 physician and nurse respondents (2002). These strategies have implications for all disciplines involved in patient care delivery.

Rosenstein's Strategies for Improving the Nurse-Physician Relationship:

- Create more opportunities for collaboration and communication through open forums, group discussions, and collaborative workshops.

- Highlight the cause-and-effect connection between communication, collaboration, and teamwork—and improved quality, safety, error rates, and patient outcomes.

- Increase availability of training and educational programs for nurses and physicians that focus on improving teamwork and working relationships.

- Improve organizational processes by taking a more proactive approach to avoiding potential confrontations related to staffing, scheduling, and equipment.

- Establish a zero-tolerance policy for disruptive behavior, holding both nurses and physicians accountable for their actions.

- Disseminate code-of-conduct policies and reporting guidelines to both nurses and physicians, and apply policies consistently and quickly, providing feedback to all involved.

- Ensure appropriate nurse competencies.

- Have physicians sign a code-of-conduct policy when they are credentialed or re-credentialed.

- Appoint a physician who will champion and lead training and education programs.

- Provide an ongoing forum to increase physician awareness of the issues that increase nurses' stress level and enable them to gain a better understanding and appreciation of the nurses' role.

Summary of Key Concepts

- Team-focused, collegial relationships improve patient safety and outcomes, and contribute to an increased satisfaction rate among employees.

- A partnership must be created among the patient, family, and members of the health care team in order to meet the patient's needs and to effectively coordinate patient care.

- Each member of the team is expected to establish and maintain healthy interpersonal relationships with all other members.

- Healthy relationships are characterized by trust, mutual respect, consistent and visible support, and open and honest communication.

- A clear system of care delivery with roles defined by responsibility, authority, and accountability (R+A+A) provides a foundation for healthy teamwork.

- The nurse-physician relationship is pivotal to the delivery of safe patient care.

- Implementing a collaborative model of practice among interdisciplinary care teams, physicians and nurses, and non-clinical departments requires system-wide commitment to the model and leadership at all levels of the organization.

- True teamwork and collaborative practice are essential to delivering safe, ethical, efficient patient care.

Questions for Self-Assessment

- What are examples of collaboration that have resulted in positive patient outcomes in your work area? What will it take for those experiences to occur regularly?

- What examples of collaboration and teamwork across departments are most noteworthy?

- What are some examples of effective nurse-physician collaboration in your organization? What will it take for this type of collaboration to occur on a daily basis?

- How would you describe your own responsibility for contributing to colleagueship? What are the barriers that impede you from functioning as a true colleague? Do you notice any resistance in yourself to collaborating with certain team members?

- Recall an extraordinary experience of collaboration that occurred despite the normal barriers. What made this experience possible? What would it take to increase the frequency of this kind of extraordinary collaboration?

- In what ways have expectations for healthy interpersonal relationships been articulated and supported in your work area?

- How would you assess the current level of the health of your team relationships? (To assess the health of your team, use the *Commitment to My Co-worker©—Healthy Team Assessment Survey* in Appendix B)

A Moment of Excellence: Rice Memorial Hospital

Rice Memorial Hospital
Willmar, Minnesota

Rice Memorial Hospital's vision in team-building has been a journey that began many years ago. One of our key values is excellence, and we recognized long ago that you cannot provide excellent care without excellent teamwork. Health care is interdisciplinary; it's interdepartmental. In order to provide the best level of care, all of our staff need to be engaged, and all must understand the value of working together as a team.

At Rice, we've raised the bar. We want to consistently be an excellent place to work and receive care. Rice has made a commitment to do everything we can to make excellence a reality. This is not a quick fix program. Rather we want to hardwire excellence into the way we conduct business on a day-to-day basis. This is only possible when the entire team commits to excellence—and to each other.

Early on, in our commitment to team-building, our employees began to see the importance of their individual roles in delivering care. When employees truly believe in their significance, things change for the better. When employees decide to be excellent in their work, in their delivery of care, and in their commitment to the team, the organization improves.

Like many healthcare facilities, Rice is currently in a building mode, constructing a new state-of-the-art facility. However, we know that this rebuilding process is not just one of brick and mortar. Rather, we began first by building positive attitudes, empowering individuals, and encouraging teamwork. This foundation is just as important as the one beneath the building itself. Now Rice will have the facility to match its commitment to excellence.

Rice has long been visionary in terms of employee empowerment. Continuous Quality Improvement (CQI) has been an integral part of Rice for years. Staff from all levels have been involved in the CQI steering committee, along with serving on individual CQI teams. Rice has also moved to a "Shared Governance" model, again giving employees not only the responsibility to act, but the authority to do so.

Another important dimension was added two years ago when Rice developed several teams comprised of a cross-section of front line staff with specific responsibilities such as defining standards of behavior, developing a service recovery program, measuring our progress in patient and employee satisfaction, and developing innovative ways to recognize excellent performance in our people.

Open communication has also been a key component in our growth. Our CEO fosters a "transparent" environment, keeping staff abreast of pertinent information through quarterly Employee Forums. He and the rest of the administrative staff encourage questions and comments. Our staff has a voice—an essential component in building and maintaining effective teams.

Open, honest communication between administration and staff helps keep everyone educated and informed. Rice Hospital administration has an "open book" policy of sharing information with staff, including finances, patient and employee satisfaction results, board meeting agendas, and more. To further engage our staff we expanded the membership of our leadership team five-fold, to include all staff who supervise anyone or coordinate any program.

Rice recognized that if its vision was to become a reality, a conscious commitment to the continuous education of our staff was essential. That commitment included ongoing CQI training, leadership in-services, and quarterly workshops to encourage a continuous focus on our vision. All these strategies helped us to "hard-wire" our *vision* into our daily operations.

At Rice we are still under construction—building, not only a new facility, but also a culture that emphasizes the importance of individual contribution and of teamwork. In our commitment to excellence we have discovered the value and power of individual employees who, working together, can have a profound effect on the lives of our patients and their families.

Joyce Elkjer is Service Excellence Coordinator in the Education Department at Rice Memorial Hospital, a 100 bed hospital in Willmar, Minnesota.

FOUR

Professional Nursing Practice

Mary Koloroutis

"Nursing is a moral art...It involves the design and fostering of
a healing atmosphere that rests upon the creation of a therapeutic
relationship and the application of scientific knowledge and skill."

—*Author Unknown*

Overview

The nurse-patient relationship is the cornerstone
of Professional Nursing Practice and a fundamental element of Relationship-Based Care (RBC).
There is universal agreement among nurses that
their relationship with patients and patient families is a sacred, privileged trust. Nurses voice a
fierce commitment to the values of caring, advo-
cacy, collaboration, safety, and seeking what is in
the best interest of the patients and families they
serve. Despite these commitments, however, the
realities of existing care delivery systems and
today's health care environment challenge the
abilities of nurses to live their vision every day.

Marie Manthey describes the often frustrating
role of the Professional Nurse in a less-than-perfect
system as "deprofessionalization," a phenomenon
that ultimately affects not only the nursing profession but other professions as well. She says, "*In the
last two decades of the 20th century, macro political and economic changes profoundly influenced
society, health care, and nursing. The two most*

prominent drivers of change were financial and technological" (Manthey, 2002). Sandra Thomas refers to this phenomenon as the *"devastating effects of the corporatization of health services"* which has occurred over the past decade (1998).

Magnet hospitals are renowned for their capacity to recruit and retain highly qualified professional nursing staff and to promote and support Professional Nursing Practice. Magnet status is granted when hospitals meet specific criteria and are reviewed and credentialed through the American Nursing Credentialing Center. From the beginning of Magnet credentialing, the American Academy for Nursing found four consistent common characteristics in hospitals which achieved Magnet status (2003):

- Nurses have the status and autonomy to obtain necessary resources for patient care.

- There is good collaboration between nurses and physicians.

- Nurses participate in policy decisions and perceive more control over their practice.

- Primary Nursing is the established care delivery system.

Research conducted in the 1990s by Linda Aiken and her colleagues found that patients in Magnet hospitals have better outcomes than others. Magnet hospitals have higher patient satisfaction rates and lower rates of mortality, nurse burnout, and needle sticks to nurses (Aiken, 1997; Aiken and Slocane, 1997). In a groundbreaking 1988 study on Medicare mortality rates, Aiken and her team found that the Magnet hospitals had a 4.6% lower mortality rate than other hospitals they studied. This translates to between 0.9 and 9.4 fewer deaths per 1,000 discharges.

Aiken hypothesized that, *"as nurses are the only professional caregivers in hospitals who are at the bedside of hospital patients around the clock, what nurses do—or do not do (or in some circumstances are not allowed to do)—is directly related to a variety of patient outcomes, including in-hospital deaths"* (Aiken, et al., 1994). Their working assumptions were that *"hospitals that facilitate professional autonomy, control over practice, and comparatively good relations between nurses and physicians will be the ones in which nurses are able to exercise their professional judgment on a more routine basis with positive implications for the quality and outcomes of patient care"* (Aiken, et al., 1994). Their findings supported these assumptions.

A study conducted by the Department of Health and Human Services entitled, *Nurse Staffing and Patient Outcomes in Hospitals* (Needleman, 2001), found a strong and consistent relationship between the number and mix of nursing staff and five key outcomes in medical patients. The study is based on 1997 data from more than five million patient discharges from 799 hospitals in 11 states. The outcomes measured were urinary tract infection, pneumonia, shock, upper gastrointestinal bleeding, and length of stay.

The study found that when the staffing mix included a higher number of registered nurses, rates of adverse outcomes dropped 3 to 12 percent. This study quantified what many in the field have known—that the number and mix of nurses in a hospital makes a significant difference in the quality of care patients receive. According to John Eisenberg, MD, the director of the Agency for Healthcare Research and Quality (AHRQ) it also pushes further inquiry and should drive strategy. He says, *"We need to know more not only about* how nurse staffing affects quality, but also about the working conditions in which nurses provide care. Excellent nurses may have difficulty providing care if they are working in conditions that are not conducive to quality care" (HRSA News, 2001).

Organizations committed to excellence in patient care are taking action to establish or strengthen Professional Nursing Practice. They are seeking ways to integrate solid business practices with the best in care and service to patients. These organizations recognize the nurse-patient relationship as fundamental to world-class patient care delivery and are taking action to structure and promote this relationship. One chief executive officer stated it succinctly when he said, *"nurses are our main customer service."*

An important condition for promoting the nurse-patient relationship and supporting Professional Nursing Practice is to understand the nature and scope of nursing. As you will see in the excerpt below, the nature of nursing practice is definitely not *simple*, and it is mostly not *complicated*, however it is highly *complex*. The following illustrates important distinctions between simple, complicated and complex problems:

> *Baking a cake is a simple problem. Simple problems lend themselves to a recipe approach.*

> *Sending a rocket to the moon is an example of a complicated problem. Complicated problems are best dealt with using formulaic and expert-knowledge approaches. The overall problem can be mechanistically broken down into component parts . . . When surprising events do occur, we can study these, build improvements into the system, and raise the probability of future success.*

Nursing is a response to the human situation. It comes into being under certain conditions—one human being needs help and another gives it. The meaning of nursing as a living human act is in the act itself.

—Josephine Paterson and Loretta Zderad

In contrast to simple and complicated issues, a complex issue is that of raising a child. Success in raising one child is no guarantee of success in raising another. Past experience, coupled with knowledge and advice from experts can help, but we know that simply applying the formula that worked before may not lead to success . . . every child is different (Gouberman & Zimmerman, 2002).

Similar to the example of the issues surrounding child rearing, caring for human beings in a health care setting is highly complex and cannot be reduced to a simple or even complicated formula for success. Each person is unique, as are their responses to stress, illness, and a multitude of unknowns which accompany their need for care. Nursing practice is based on a broad body of knowledge and skills and it is provided within the context of a highly complex and multifaceted health care environment. A successful practice is built on the nurse's ability to continually assess patients and situations and to use critical thinking, judgment, and decisive action to achieve desired outcomes.

This chapter presents some fundamental principles to assist in thinking about what constitutes Professional Nursing Practice. It is intended to demystify professional nursing, in order to help strengthen it within health care organizations. It explores the following areas: characteristics of professional nursing practice; nursing's social responsibility; three realms of practice; scope of practice; six professional practice roles; essential functions of nursing practice; delegation; competency; and caring as the essence of nursing practice.

Characteristics of Professional Nursing Practice

A profession is characterized by extended educational preparation, a well-defined body of knowledge, and specialized skills unique to the professional role. Values, beliefs, and ethics which are integral to the profession are integrated into the educational preparation for that profession. Additionally, there is a strong identity with the role itself and its meaning within society.

As early as 1910, Abraham Flexner, a reformer of medical education in the United States and Canada, looked at the meaning of a true profession in medicine and other disciplines and identified the criteria he believed true of any profession. His work is considered seminal and continues to hold true today. Flexner asserts that a profession—

- Is basically intellectual (as opposed to physical).

- Is based on a body of knowledge that can be learned.

- Is practical rather than theoretical.

- Can be taught through the process of professional education.

- Has a strong internal organization of members.

- Has practitioners who are motivated by altruism (the desire to help others).

Marian Larisey (1996), associate professor and chair at Medical University of South Carolina contrasts a profession with an occupation in the following excerpt:

By definition a professional is autonomous in decision making and is accountable for his or her own actions. Personal identification and commitment to the profession are strong, and individuals are unlikely to change professions. In contrast, an occupation is characterized by training that may occur on the job for varying lengths of time. The training does not incorporate, as a prominent feature, the values, beliefs, and ethics of the occupation.

Nurses have worked to be seen as members of a legitimate profession for many decades. Too often in the past, they have been seen merely as members of an occupation. When health care administrators view nursing as a profession, they attract and retain talented, intelligent individuals into the field. For this reason, influential leaders in nursing and health care must maintain a strong vision of nursing as a professional discipline and do what it takes to support the Professional Nurse in his or her delivery of professional level care and service.

Professional Nursing exists to provide compassionate care to individuals and their loved ones. Nursing is a segment of a complex, interdependent health care delivery team. Nurses help patients and their families maintain health, affect healing, cope during times of stress and suffering, and—when all medical options are exhausted—to experience a dignified and peaceful death. They bring to this noble pursuit clinical knowledge and proficiency and a profound understanding of the human condition.

Nursing's Social Policy Statement (American Nurses Association [ANA], 1995) is derived from the landmark document, *Nursing: A Social Policy Statement* (ANA, 1980) which was the profession's first description of nursing's social responsibility and role in the American health care system. The intent of these documents is to *"present clinical*

Nursing's Social Responsibility and the Three Realms of Practice

nursing practice as it has evolved according to society's health needs and to set direction for the future" (ANA, 1995).

The relationship between nursing and society is defined as follows:

The authority for the practice of nursing is based on a social contract that acknowledges professional rights and responsibilities as well as mechanisms for public accountability (ANA, 2003).

Nursing is defined as:

The diagnosis and treatment of human responses to actual or potential health problems (ANA, 1980).

The social responsibility of nursing is demonstrated in each of its three distinct realms of practice. When these three realms are fully developed, patients and families receive high quality comprehensive nursing care and service. When any one of the realms is weak, quality is compromised. These three realms are Delegated Practice, Independent Practice, and Interdependent Practice.

1. **Delegated Practice** – Assessments and interventions in this realm are determined by the medical plan of care and specific physician-directed interventions. The nurse carries out these delegated functions when his or her knowledge, experience, and judgment confirm that the specific medical order is appropriate and safe for the patient being served.

2. **Independent Practice** – The nurse conducts assessments and interventions for the purpose of promoting health and healing. The focus is on the patient's response to actual or potential health problems.

3. **Interdependent Practice** — The nurse initiates communication with other members
of the health care team to assure that the
patient and family receive the full scope
of interdisciplinary expertise and services
commensurate with a coordinated and
integrated plan of care.

The challenge for the Professional Nurse is to
balance and integrate these three distinct areas or
practice. While nurses clearly accept responsibility, authority, and accountability for the *delegated* realm of practice, the independent and
interdependent realms are not implemented as
consistently and may even go undelivered. It is
also surprisingly common that some members of
the health care team do not understand that
nurses have an independent realm of practice
outside the delegated medical functions. When
this imbalance exists, patients and families do not
receive the full scope of nursing care and services,
and the quality of their care is compromised.

The Scope of Nursing Practice

The American Nurses Association has identified
a conceptual framework within which Professional Nursing Practice occurs. For a clearer
understanding of the scope of nursing practice,
the ANA invites practitioners to consider the
boundaries, intersections, core, and dimensions of
Professional Nursing Practice.

1. Boundary. . . something that indicates a limit or extent

The boundary establishes the parameters within
which decisions are made and actions are taken.
The boundary for nursing, as is true for all professions, is flexible and responsive to the changing

needs of society and the expansion of knowledge and research.

Within the context of an organization, it is important for nurses and all other members of the health care team to understand and be able to articulate their boundaries based on their practice discipline and their individual level of knowledge and skills. When boundaries are not clearly delineated, mistrust, team conflict, and misuse of resources result. If boundaries are too rigid (as may be the case in a highly centralized organization where the goals are conformity or compliance to a specific way of doing things) they can inhibit creativity, initiative, individual perspective, individualization, autonomy, and independent practice.

When boundaries are clearly defined and appropriately supportive of the practice discipline, they offer individual clinicians and teams guidance by:

- Clarifying the level of autonomy (right to act) that is being granted through licensure and role.

- Facilitating the ability to carry out one's level of authority for decision making and action.

- Encouraging creativity, individual judgment, risk-taking, assertiveness, and growth.

- Clarifying which people can be counted on to contribute.

We recommend that boundaries be defined by clarifying responsibility, levels of authority, and accountability for decisions and actions. The responsibility, authority, and accountability for Professional Nursing Practice are determined based on licensure and nurse practice acts, educational preparation and experience, professional standards, regulatory standards, and position descriptions within an organization.

2. Intersection . . . a shared common area

The intersection is where nurses connect with others on the health care team. Professional nursing practice is built on interdependent relationships. Nurses, physicians, and other health care professionals share the common purpose of caring for patients and families. A key predictor of safe, quality care is effective communication in healthy relationships. The nurse plays a key role in creating collaborative relationships among members of the health care team that promote coordinated care and service for patients and families.

3. Core . . . inner aspect or essence

Knowledge-based caring is the core or essence of nursing practice and is expressed through the therapeutic relationship between the nurse and patient/family. Knowledge-based caring is built on both the art and science of nursing practice and is conveyed through relationships and privileged intimacy. Nursing care is a "laying on of hands" practice in which nurses affect the body, mind, and spirit of another person as they assess the individual's response to a health problem and intervene to promote greater well-being.

4. Dimensions . . . elements that make up an entity

The dimensions of Professional Nursing Practice are those elements that further describe, enhance, or deepen the meaning of the profession.

Examples are: licensure, established nurse practice acts, nursing theory, statements of core values and beliefs (philosophy), codes of ethics, scientific theories, research findings, and professional and regulatory standards. These dimensions will vary to some degree based on the practice environment and the patient populations served.

Six Professional Nursing Practice Roles

The six practice roles described in this section provide us with a way to put voice to the work of nursing. This idea builds on the work of Bernice Buresh and Suzanne Gordon who wrote the book, *From Silence to Voice: What Nurses Know and Must Communicate to the Public.* The authors (who are journalists, not nurses) wrote the book to make nursing care more visible to the public. They are advocates for nurses to step up, express their value, and speak so that their voices are heard and their work understood. They implore nurses to, *"Tell the world what you do!"* They advocate for recognizing the importance of caring work and of nurses as a group as well as individuals. This is accomplished, they say, by developing a *"voice of agency."* The voice of agency means that *nurses "know that they can and do act on clinical knowledge and the exercise of clinical judgment"*–and that they say so. The voice of agency dares to say *"I'm here. I am doing something important."* Only nurses can tell the public what they do and why it is valuable.

Voice of Agency

- Recognizes the importance of caring work
- Recognizes the importance of care givers
- Knows that they act on clinical knowledge
- Exercises clinical judgment
- Dares to say, "I'm here. I am doing something important."
- Involves being able to speak for one's self
- Represents the authentic self
- Speaks from experience and observation
- Says, "I want, I think, I know, I feel, I am, I need, I will, I can, I won't"

(Buresh & Gordon, 2002)

Defining the six roles of nursing practice gives us the vocabulary to articulate the work of nursing care. The six roles are: sentry, healer, guide, teacher, collaborator, and leader. Each role is defined below along with an example of how one might communicate the service provided through the particular role.

Six Practice Roles

1. As a sentry (one who watches over and protects), the nurse continuously assesses, monitors, and intervenes for the patient to prevent complications, promote healing, and optimize safe outcomes.

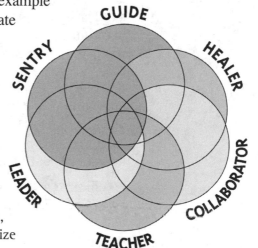

The Six Practice Roles

Voice: *"I am here to observe you and evaluate how you are responding to your care and treatment. I will monitor how you are progressing and take action to prevent complications. You can count on me to listen to you and to respond quickly when you need help. I will be talking with your physician frequently so that she is apprised of any changes and to ensure that we are all working together toward your recovery."*

2. As a healer (one who cares for another's body, mind, and spirit; one who helps others improve their level of health), the nurse establishes a therapeutic relationship with the patient and family assuring they receive physical, emotional, and spiritual care based on an assessment of their needs.

Voice: *"I am _____. I am here to care for you. I can do that best if I learn more about who you are and what is important to you. You can count on me to tell you what I am doing and thinking as I care for you. What I ask of you is to let me know what you need and what is of concern to you."*

3. As a guide (someone who leads or directs another's way through unfamiliar circumstances; one who possesses intimate knowledge of the way), the nurse helps the patient and family by translating pertinent information and processes into lay language, by clarifying and explaining procedures, and by making certain that the patient and family understand what to expect, ensuring that they are informed enough to make decisions about their care.

Voice: *"I will help you get through the treatment you have scheduled for tomorrow. My job is to make sure you understand what is going to happen, why it's happening, and to answer any questions you have on the procedure itself. There is no question you cannot ask and there should be no language that is mysterious to you. My goal is that you feel confident that you have been completely informed and know exactly what to expect."*

4. As a teacher (one who imparts knowledge; someone who helps another learn a skill), the nurse teaches the patient and family how to safely care for themselves within the health care setting and upon discharge.

Voice: *"Who in your family will be caring for you when you return home? I would like to meet him and include him in the care of your wound over the next few days; that way he will have greater understanding and practice in how to change your dressing and what to look for to prevent any complications."*

5. As a collaborator (one who works cooperatively with others to achieve a common purpose), the nurse works with each member of the health care team to assure they receive and provide pertinent information regarding the patient and family and to coordinate the patient's plan of care.

Voice: *"I will let the social worker and physician know about our conversation and your concerns about your discharge. I will ask them to meet with you and me tomorrow morning to discuss the concerns and explore alternative solutions. This afternoon I will plan some time with you so that I can assist you in clarifying your questions. I can assure you that we will be able to determine the best options by working this through together."*

6. As a leader (someone who has the authority to act on behalf of others; possesses the capacity to effect change and influence direction), the nurse advocates for the individual patient and family, provides appropriate supervision and leadership to other members of the care team, and identifies and initiates changes that will improve the quality of care for patients and families.

Voice: *"I am sorry you had to wait for your care, and I can understand how it would be upsetting to you. I will talk with your care giver and make sure this does not happen again. In the meantime, I want to help you feel cared for and not worried about this happening again. Let's talk about what will help right now."*

Essential Functions of Nursing Practice

Following are four essential functions of nursing practice. These functions provide the foundation of Professional Nursing Practice in any care delivery system (Manthey, Felgen & Person, 2003).

Essentials of Practice	Specific Nursing Activities
Assess, plan, implement and evaluate care based on the patient and family needs.	1. Conduct a nursing assessment and determine patient's needs through listening to their personal story, more formalized interviews, and review of records. Identify the patient's #1 concern regarding this episode of care and his or her definition of desired caring behaviors. 2. Develop and implement an individualized plan of nursing care with the patient and family, based on patient and family requests and concerns. 3. Implement the medical plan by assessing medical orders to assure these match the needs and desires of the patient, and by evaluating the effect of the medical orders and taking appropriate action. 4. Continuously assess and take action as needed. 5. Proactively communicate the medical and nursing plans to other team members including assistive staff and multidisciplinary colleagues.

Essentials of Practice	Specific Nursing Activities
Manage and deliver the care required for the patient's condition and individual human response.	1. Establish a therapeutic caring relationship with the patient. 2. Continuously assess, monitor, and prevent complications. 3. Administer and evaluate the effect of medical and nursing treatments. 4. Delegate activities of nursing care appropriately. 5. Revise the nursing diagnoses and plans as the patient's status changes.
Communicate and coordinate care with others who are interacting with the patient.	1. Provide information about the patient in condition reports and care conferences. 2. Conduct creative problem solving to resolve identified issues. 3. Collaborate with interdisciplinary colleagues.
Coordinate the patient transfer or discharge.	1. Teach aspects of care that will need to be carried out upon discharge to the patient and/or family. 2. Communicate care needs and approaches to others who will care for the patient after transfer or discharge. 3. Communicate with case manager or discharge planner as indicated.

Maria O'Rourke's (2003) work on the nurse's professional role and his or her accountability for rigorous decision making practice expands our thinking about the nursing process outlined in the table above. Her work deepens our understanding of the complexity of the nursing process and the depth and breadth of knowledge required to provide nursing services. The O'Rourke Professional Practice Decision Making Process and Stability of the Patient Condition Model© consists of nine dynamically integrated steps as follows:

1. Data collection and data assessment

2. Comprehensive assessment of the patient condition with diagnosis

3. Planning and outcome identification

4. Implementation

5. Evaluation

6. Teaching

7. Dynamic integration of steps 1-6 based on critical thinking

8. Determination of the stability of the patient condition, and breadth and depth of clinical knowledge and experience with the patient condition and patient population. (The patient condition is defined as the maintenance of the physiological functioning combined with psychological and social support as related to the recovery process.)

9. Dynamic integration of the previous eight steps based on critical thinking, substantial scientific knowledge, theory (general and discipline-specific), research findings, determination of appropriate supervision for delegation or assignment of care tasks, and care coordination.*

With this list, Maria O'Rourke brings together the art and science of nursing. She makes explicit that beyond the hands-on ministration of nursing is a depth and breadth of knowledge, scientific findings, research, and theory. O'Rourke recognizes that nursing is not simply providing interventions to improve a patient's condition. Nursing is the blending of scientific, physical, psychological, social, and spiritual knowledge into tangible action on behalf of the patient as a person. Every patient is different. Every health care situation is unique. This list makes the point that the invisible "knowing" of nursing is as important as the visible action.

Delegation of Nursing Functions Supports RBC

Scope of practice among registered nurses (RNs), licensed practical/vocational nurses (LPNs/LVNs), and other care providers is based on professional association standards, state nurse practice acts, regulatory standards, position descriptions, and the role, education, and experience of the care provider. The RN has the responsibility, authority, and accountability for assessing, diagnosing, planning, implementing, and evaluating the patient's nursing care. In a system which embraces RBC, where the nurse-patient relationship is always safeguarded, RNs have the authority to delegate nursing activities to other care providers. This authority promotes continuity of care by allowing RNs to delegate tasks that might otherwise impede continuity of the nurse-patient relationship.

In a system where delegation practices support RBC, LPNs/LVNs provide nursing care under the supervision of an RN or physician and are accountable for providing care within their scope of practice. As the most knowledgeable and skilled of the clinical support staff, LPNs/LVNs are essential partners in caring for high acuity patients and their families. Patients receive optimal care when the care team members are clear about role boundaries and both RNs and LPN/LVNs are functioning at the highest level of their scope of practice.

Four tips for effective delegation by RNs follow:

1. The RN's delegations of responsibility are made based on patient needs, complexity of work, competency of the individual accepting the delegation, and the timing of the work to be done.

2. The RN provides timely information regarding the individual patient, defines specific expectations, clarifies any adaptation of the work in the context of the individual patient situation, and provides guidance and support as needed.

3. The RN retains ultimate accountability for the process and outcomes of care—even those he or she has delegated.

4. The care provider receiving an assignment from an RN accepts responsibility, authority, and accountability for the work assigned.

Items three and four in this list point to an over-lap in responsibility that is an essential part of the successful delegation of nursing functions. In practice, when an RN takes full responsibility for even the processes he or she delegates and the care provider receiving the assignment from the RN takes full responsibility also, both take complete ownership of their work.

Professional Nursing Practice requires ongoing development to sustain proficiency in practice. The boundaries of nursing practice as in all health care disciplines change with the changing needs and requirements of the patients they serve. Furthermore, nursing care is provided by individual nurses at all levels of development and expertise. Therefore, competency levels are determined based on both the individual and the clinical situation. Additionally, effective health care teams have an effective system for assessing competency and assuring ongoing development of all patient care staff. This is fundamental to a safe care delivery system in which nurses and other members of the team thrive in their practice and in which the distribution of responsibility, authority, and accountability is intentional and appropriate.

Developing and Maintaining Competency in Practice

Donna Wright, in her book, *The Ultimate Guide to Competency Assessment in Health Care*, says that *"Competencies are assessed when an individual is hired, during the orientation period, and throughout employment as the requirements of the job and the needs of the organization change"* (Wright, 1998). Wright says further that initial competency assessment is not enough and that *"on-going competency assessment and development reflect the new, changing, high-risk, and problematic aspects of the job as it evolves over time"* (Wright, 1998).

Dorothy del Bueno offered the study of individual growth and development a wonderful frame in which to view competencies. She describes competency for any position, but particularly for nurses, as the successful acquisition of skill in three domains: technical, interpersonal, and critical thinking. We believe there is an essential fourth competency domain—the domain of leadership. In fact, we believe that achievement of

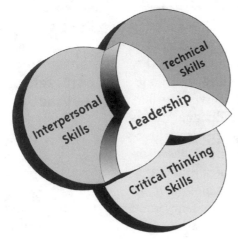

competency in the other three domains creates a springboard for leadership to emerge.

Notice that the intersection of the three intertwining circles representing each of del Bueno's domains makes possible the emergence of this fourth domain, leadership. It is in this leadership domain that nurses demonstrate their individual talents and skills to others as they find professional "voice." Progressing to the leadership domain is the natural result of the nurse's personal integration of technical, interpersonal, and critical thinking skills, and thus serves as the logical next step for a nurse achieving mastery in the original three.

In the American Nursing Association's publication, *The Code of Ethics for Nursing,* the following statement is made regarding the importance of attending to competency:

> Though it has consequences for others, maintenance of competence and ongoing professional growth involves the control of one's own conduct in a way that is self-regarding. Competence affects one's self-respect, self-esteem, professional status, and the meaningfulness of work. Evaluation of one's own performance is a means by which nursing practice can be held to the highest standards (ANA, 1995).

The responsibility and accountability for continuous learning is shared by the nurse and the organization. Nurses are accountable for self-assessment and their own professional growth and development. This means that they are responsible

The extent to which individual nurses engage in the total scope of nursing practice is dependent on their educational preparation, experience, roles, and the nature of the patient populations they serve.

—Nursing's Social Policy Statement 1997

for accessing the knowledge and skills required to attain and maintain proficiency in their practice. The organization is responsible for promoting and supporting continuous learning and providing opportunities for staff development.

Patricia Benner, a prominent nursing professor and scholar in the area of Professional Nursing Practice, has done extensive work in the area of professional nursing and competency development. She describes five levels of competency.

Patricia Benner's Levels of Competency

Stage I. Novice – This is a beginner level and requires clear direction and ongoing supervision.

Stage II. Advanced Beginner – Performance has improved after the novice has considerable experience coping with real situations, learning from this experience, and integrating learning into practice.

Stage III. Competent – After more experience, the number of potentially significant elements of real-world situations the person can recognize may become overwhelming. In this level, people learn to critically analyze and prioritize through instruction, coaching, and mentoring.

There must be a relationship with the patient to know their strengths, weaknesses, hopes and fears. . . our challenge is to balance tasks with relationships.

—Marie Manthey

Stage IV. Proficient – The person has acquired the ability to discriminate between a variety of situations. The proficient clinician taps into intuitive knowing and identifies priorities *in the moment*, without needing to stand back and choose a course of action. Action becomes easier and less stressful as the individual simply sees what needs to be accomplished and then acts accordingly.

Stage V. Expert – The expert knows what needs to be achieved based on mature and practiced situational discrimination, and also knows how to achieve the goal. A more refined and subtle discrimination ability is what distinguishes the expert from the proficient performer.

Caring as the Essence of Nursing Practice

The opportunity to care for patients is what calls many people into the nursing profession. After even minimal time in the field, most nurses respond to the question "What is the essence of nursing?" with one word—*caring*. Kristen Swanson maintains that while the ANA's definition of nursing as *"diagnosing and treating the human response to actual or potential health problems"* clarifies our societal obligation to the public, it does not capture the essence of nursing's values, knowledge, and expertise. Swanson defines nursing as *"informed caring for the well-being of others"* and defines caring as a *"nurturing way of relating to a valued other toward whom one feels a personal sense of commitment and responsibility"* (Swanson, 1993).

She says further:

Making the claim that nursing is informed caring for the well-being of others does not mean that only nurses are caring, and that all nursing practice situations may be characterized as caring. It also does not suggest that nursing is the only profession whose practice involves informed caring. What it does claim is that the therapeutic practices of nurses are grounded in knowledge of nursing, related sciences, and the humanities, as well as personal insight and experiential understanding and that the goal of nurse caring is to enhance the well-being of its recipients (Swanson, 1993).

The ANA's definition and *Social Policy Statement* about nursing was revised in 1995 and represents the emergence of nursing from a profession focused on diagnosis and treatment to one focused on caring and healing.

Since 1980, nursing philosophy and practice have been influenced by a greater elaboration of the science of caring and its integration with the traditional knowledge base for diagnosis and treatment of human responses to health and illness. As such, definitions of nursing more frequently acknowledge four essential features of contemporary nursing practice:

1. *Attention to the full range of human experiences and responses to health and illness without restriction to a problem focused orientation,*
2. *Integration of objective data with knowledge gained to form an understanding of the patient's or group's subjective experience,*
3. *Application of scientific knowledge to the processes of diagnosis and treatment,*
4. *Provision of a caring relationship that facilitates health and healing (ANA, 1995).*

Jean Watson, in her book, *Postmodern Nursing and Beyond,* describes a significant imbalance in modern nursing and medicine. She says that *"within the dominant, modern, Western mindset, the caring-healing practices of nursing have been on the margins—have been repressed and silenced"* (Watson, 1999). It is time for the paradigm to change and for nursing to claim its caring-healing practices. Watson believes that caring calls for a moral commitment toward preserving human dignity rather than reducing a person to the status of an object (Watson, 1990).

A challenge for health care leaders who envision strong Professional Nursing Practice and world class patient care is to find the way to support caring and healing philosophies and practices within institutional settings besieged by complex ethical issues and resource constraints. One large health care system addressed this challenge by incorporating caring as a key ethical principle in their system-wide ethics framework. The organization's leaders sought to be both *"good stewards of limited resources and advocates of a caring and compassionate environment for healing"* (Koloroutis & Thorstenson, 1999). The ethic of caring is defined as follows:

> *Caring involves acts and attitudes of critical thinking and clinical competency, compassion and respect, and listening and acceptance. It is critical in helping people maintain health, affect healing, adapt to stressful experiences, and experience a dignified death (Abbott Northwestern Department of Nursing Philosophy, 1993).*

This health care system defined the ethical principle of caring as emphasizing the organization's commitment to protecting and enhancing the dignity of patients. It incorporated the ethical principle of beneficence—or the "obligation to do good"—and highlighted the organization's mission to serve patients as whole persons with attention paid to their individual circumstances and relationships (Koloroutis & Thorstenson, 1999).

The Voice of the Patient: A Personal Story

The following story exemplifies what happens when care and service are thoughtfully designed and implemented to care for individual patients and families with a focus on what matters most for them. This story took place in the obstetrical department at Abbott Northwestern Hospital in Minneapolis. It demonstrates the power of caring and collaboration among professional nursing staff, physicians, and managers. This story was presented, as The Voice of the Patient, by Cheryl Persigehl, in a plenary session at the 2003 Creative Health Care Management Client Conference in Minneapolis and is used with permission.

Three and a half years ago I became pregnant with our first child. My husband, Jonathan, and I saw the results of the at-home pregnancy test on December 24th, 1998. It was our best Christmas ever.

Like many expectant parents, we began to dream about how this baby would change our lives and bring even more love and joy into our relationship. We walked through the winter and spring together enjoying my "ideal" pregnancy. Then one day, everything changed.

In early May, during our second ultrasound, our perinatologist, Judy, told us she was very concerned about several things she saw on the monitor. She carefully explained the issues and the implications, held my hand, brushed a tear from my cheek, and recommended I have an amniocenteses that day.

Seven days later, my primary OB/GYN physician, Diane, called us at home to share the results of our test. Our son, who was 6 months in utero, had a severe, rare chromosome disorder called Trisomy 18. She informed us that given the diagnosis and the evidence gathered in the ultrasound, our son would not be able to sustain his life outside the womb, and there was a strong possibility I could miscarry within the next few weeks.

We were devastated, dazed, and afraid. My doctor listened to our desperate pleas, comforted us, and after several phone calls that same night, helped us make the most difficult decision of our lives—to induce labor within a few days.

On May 24th, 1999, at 26 weeks gestation, we entered Abbott Northwestern Hospital. Our son, Micah Abram Persigehl-Flak, was alive and moving in my womb that morning—and our precious baby boy was stillborn that same day at 5:50 PM.

There are no words to adequately describe the depth or breadth of the competent, compassionate, respectful care we received from the people who supported us through our diagnosis and delivery, but there are many examples of how our caregivers helped us prepare for and live through that difficult time. A few specific moments (among many) come to mind:

- My OB/GYN doctor said to me shortly after we reached our decision, "I will advocate for you with the hospital staff and help them prepare. You do not need to be concerned about what will happen or how it will happen. We will answer all your questions. We will care for you and your baby. We will be there with you and for you. You are not alone. We will go through this together."

- The hospital's parent infant specialist, Joann, came to our home 2 days before Micah's birth to counsel us and help us prepare, saying, "You are Micah's mother and father. You have been wonderful parents to him for 6 months and you are parenting him now. He is and always will be your son, and you will always be his parents."

- The nursing staff moved quietly, non-intrusively in and out of our hospital room while I was waiting for labor to begin, performing their tasks, always offering a kind word and a gentle touch to my husband and me.

- The anesthesiologist, Judy, came to our room to give me an epidural, and I asked her, "Do you know my situation?" She sat on the edge of the bed for a moment, took my hand, shed a tear with me, and said, "Yes, I do, and I am so sorry."

- Our morning nurse brought us a beautiful little white bassinet before she left her shift, and encouraged us to use it as a place for Micah to rest with us after he was born.

- Our doctor laid Micah on my chest moments after he was born, held me, and cried with me, saying over and over again, "He's at peace. It's all right. He's at peace."

- And at the end of the evening, after we had spent several hours with our son (holding him, bathing him, baptizing him, talking to him, singing to him), and we knew in our hearts it was time to let him go, our nurse came back into the room, offered a gentle word and a touch, and joined hands with my husband, my brother-in-law, my dear friend Mary and me as we offered a prayer of thanks for the miracle and the mystery of Micah's life with us.

Now, I'd like to invite you to fast forward with me 1½ years later. On October 14, 2000, after experiencing an ectopic pregnancy eight months earlier, Jonathan and I learned that we were pregnant for the third time. We were excited, elated, and we *knew* this baby was ready to come in. The following spring, on June 21, 2001, (my due date) we discovered that our little baby girl had moved into a breach position, and so with our doctor's help, we made the decision to give birth via C-section two days later.

Again, from the moment we entered the hospital that morning, our nurses, clinicians, and physicians provided exemplary care:

- As I walked into the prep room that morning, my nurse greeted me with a gentle touch, introduced herself, and said, "I read your birth plan and I am so sorry about the loss of your son....It is a privilege for me to be part of this experience with you. This is going to be a wonderful day.... I want you to know I filled this room with prayer today before you came, and I went into the O.R. a few minutes ago and filled that room with prayer and joy for all of us. This is going to be a wonderful day." I cried tears of joy. She hugged me and cried with me.

- With encouragement from our nurse, we played a CD of our favorite instrumental music in the O.R. during the entire procedure, and we brought a friend into the O.R. with us to videotape and photograph our daughter's birth. When our doctor entered the O.R. she said, "Oh, that's nice music. Let's turn it up a little."

- During the operation, the anesthesiologist, nurse anesthetist, and my doctor provided constant commentary on the procedure, telling my husband and me exactly what was happening, helping us to anticipate what was coming next, and offering gentle words of encouragement with each stage of the operation.

- At 10:36 AM that morning, Chloe Grace Persigehl-Flak, our very healthy 8 lb. 2 oz. daughter, was born. Our doctor pulled her out of my womb and exclaimed, "Oh, Cheryl, she's perfect. She's just perfect," and she held her up for me to see.

- Immediately after her birth, the receiving nurse took Chloe to one side of the O.R. for a few moments to check her vitals and aspirate her. During that time, my husband left my side to hold Chloe's hand. I, of course, was crying great tears of joy, and while my husband was away for one or two minutes, the two men at my head (the anesthesiologist and nurse anesthetist) held my hand and gently dabbed the tears running down my face, saying, "She's just beautiful. She's perfect in every way. You're doing great."

- Just as it was on the day Micah was born, this care was offered in the context of a very welcoming, personal physical environment. My husband and our doula prepared my hospital room prior to Chloe's birth, filling it with personal items we had brought from home—photos, plants, music, memorabilia, pillows, blankets. And Jonathan was not only allowed, but encouraged, to "camp out" with Chloe and me in the room during our entire stay. And he did.

There are many more examples I could share of how the *humanity* of our caring and healing experience was tangible for us. But perhaps, the most important thing to share is that despite the fact that the outcomes of the births of our two children were dramatically different, our experience of care was beautifully consistent. All the clinicians who cared for us at Chloe's birth treated us with the same sensitivity, tenderness, and respect we had experienced at the birth of our son two years earlier.

And today, I know this much is true; the courage, compassion, competence, and humanity of our caregivers is what helped us fully welcome both of our children into this world. That same courage, compassion, competence and humanity helped us move from suffering through healing to joy.

To all of you who care deeply not only about what you do, but also about how you do this work in the world, I say thank you. We are forever grateful. We are forever changed.

Cheryl's story confirms that caring, as the essence of Professional Nursing Practice, deserves organization-wide support and commitment. It deserves to be safeguarded as core to high quality, humane, compassionate patient care. It deserves to be embodied as a leadership principle and to be a visible way of relating among members of the health care team.

Summary of Key Concepts

- Professional Nursing Practice exists within a caring, therapeutic relationship between a nurse and patient.

- Six key roles create a framework for putting the "voice of agency" to the work of nursing care. Nurses play the roles of: sentry, healer, guide, teacher, collaborator, and leader.

- The nurse and patient are mutually responsible for determining the plan of care and the desired outcomes for the patient's stay.

- Professional Nursing Practice is a visible system of responsibility acceptance. The nurse-patient relationship, once formed, is known to the patient, family, physicians caring for the patient, and other members of the health care team. All administrative systems support the continuity of that relationship.

- The registered nurse has the authority to delegate nursing activities to other caregivers. This authority promotes continuity of care by allowing RNs to delegate tasks that might otherwise impede continuity of the nurse-patient relationship.

- The responsibility and accountability for professional growth and development are shared by the nurse and the organization.

- Professional Nursing Practice is the cornerstone of a Relationship-Based Care delivery system.

- Caring is the essence of Professional Nursing Practice and requires ongoing leadership support.

- On a scale of 1-10 (1=very little; 10=very much) how much would you say your organization values its nurses?

- On that same scale, how much would you say your organization demonstrates that level of value daily?

Questions for Self-Assessment

- How well are your nurses able to articulate their scope of practice including delegated, interdependent, and independent realms?

- What are your current areas of excellence within Professional Nursing Practice?

- Is a therapeutic relationship with a specific (primary/attending) nurse established upon admission with each patient?

- Is every patient asked, "What is the number one concern for you regarding this hospitalization or experience?"

- Are families asked, "What is the most valuable thing we can do for you regarding the hospitalization of your loved one?" If so, are the responses to questions regarding the primary concerns of patients and their families clearly documented in the plan of care? Are they discussed during change-of-shift report, or with other key members of the health care team?

- In what ways do RNs proactively communicate pertinent patient/family information to the physician and other members of the health care team?

- Are patients and families given adequate information to enable them to describe the role and responsibilities of their attending/Primary Nurse?

- Are patients and families able to identify their Primary Nurse by name?

- Where are your opportunities for growth in Professional Nursing Practice?

- What will it take to strengthen Professional Nursing Practice within your organization?

Kaleida Health System New York State

Our vision, as individual nurses and as a department of nursing at Kaleida Health, is based on a philosophy of Patient Centered Care (PCC). [Each CHCM client is encouraged to select a name for their care delivery model that best fits their culture. PCC was what Kaleida selected, as its meaning had resonance for their organization. Patient-Centered Care, as its name suggests, is a variation of Relationship-Based Care.] PCC means that we nurses focus all energies on whatever it takes to help patients achieve their goals. It means that we draw together all resources necessary to attain optimal clinical outcomes, and to both increase the nurses' individual time with patients and to improve the effectiveness of that time. PCC strives for satisfaction of patients, families, physicians, and all health care team members.

Patient-Centered Care relies on conscious application of expertise, energy, evidence-based principles of care, and cost-effective utilization of resources. To guide us and to explain this, we have adopted and adapted the patient centered care model conceptualized by Jayne Felgen and illustrated by Brian DeCicco, a graphic designer with Kaleida. We have also used Felgen's I_2E_2 model.

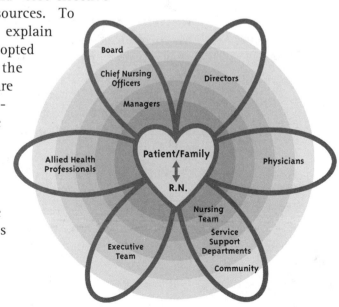

As illustrated here, patient-centered care is both simple and complex. Simply put, the nurse is in close proximity to the patient and family. The complexity is in the interdependent network of the nurse and all other caregivers and resources. When this complex network works, everyone from the unit to the boardroom impacts patient care by assuring that all resources in their control are directed toward meeting patient care needs.

The PCC infrastructure is further supported through our senior nursing team's commitment to the principles of patient centered care. We have set a number ongoing activities in place to move our entire nursing organizations toward a Professional Nursing Practice structure. These activities include a series of inspirational nursing seminars and purposeful educational planning that will contribute to our constantly building professionalism within our staff. While we focus on clinical expertise, we simultaneously promote critical thinking, effective interpersonal relationship skills, and leadership development. Our analysis of the gaps between our idealized structure and the way we were really doing things everyday has helped us to refocus our energies on inspiring and empowering our staff to help them get back the passion and spirit that brought them to nursing in the first place. Our nurses have succeeded in bringing that passion and spirit into a professional practice that is simultaneously autonomous and collaborative.

While staff are refocusing on their practice, our management team has been working on developing their skills for working with an empowered staff. In mid-2003, we introduced a councilor structure, beginning with unit practice councils (UPCs). This was a new challenge for all of us, requiring that we devise, explain, and "sell" the

idea of a shared governance model within a traditional manager-led culture. Initiation of the UPCs
was not entirely smooth; some units embraced the
idea enthusiastically while others established
councils in name only. Our orientation of UPC
members was designed to teach them about
professional practice models and to establish the
boundaries that would define the role of the UPCs.
These boundaries included reference to Professional Nursing scope of practice, fiscal realities,
and contract language that should be considered
in UPC deliberations about how to improve patient
centered care on their units. We are now entering
phase two, in which we are reinforcing effective
councils and redesigning ineffective councils Our
intent is to assure that staff are working effectively with managers and their interdisciplinary
colleagues, and that managers are working effectively with staff and their union leaders in the
interest of positive patient care. We have also been
engaging our interdisciplinary colleagues to assure
that we align all our resources for the benefit of
patients and patient care. To this end we have
begun to establish interdisciplinary Site Practice
Councils (SPCs) that will eventually respond to the
needs of UPCs and also begin to provide them
with some guidance. Our next step will be to
reconfigure our former patient care committee to
a corporation-wide patient centered care council.
In this way we have been working to honor our
past while building our future.

The fourth element in Jayne Felgen's I2E2
model is *evidence.* We thought about evidence
from the earliest days of restructuring. We asked
ourselves: "Where are we going? Where do we
want to take our nursing organization? Where do
nurses fit in the overall organization and delivery
of patient care? And how will we know when we

get there?" We actively pursue quantitative and qualitative data to answer these questions. We use patient satisfaction scores, nursing satisfaction scores, clinical outcomes measures and a positive bottom-line as evidence of the effectiveness of our infrastructure, inspiration, and education efforts.

Our organization is large (five acute care hospitals, several long term care facilities, ambulatory services, and home care) so our effectiveness has been and will remain dependent on how much support we get from our senior executive team. Here we have found that the key is education—when the senior executive team clearly understands the plan, they support it. Because of this support, we are able to enjoin nurses, physicians, and the entire interdisciplinary team (clinical and non-clinical alike) across our organization to get excited about patient care in new and renewed ways. We have several other long-range initiatives, such as mentoring, clinical research, and professional writing, in early stages of development.

Our future opportunities mirror those of the nursing profession as a whole: if we continually strive to make our environment conducive to Professional Practice, we will successfully retain our seasoned nurses and we will continue to recruit the best and the brightest into our profession and into our organization. With Patient-Centered Care as our focus, Kaleida's success is assured.

Eileen Nahigian, RN, DNS, is the Vice President Chief Nursing Officer of Kaleida Health System, New York State.

Children's National Medical Center
Washington, District of Columbia

**A Moment
of Excellence:
Children's
National
Medical
Center**

Children's National Medical Center (CNMC) places a high priority on recruiting and retaining outstanding pediatric nurses. One such program that has transformed our nursing staff is the professional development program which we have implemented in partnership with Creative Health Care Management. CNMC is a 179-bed, non-profit, stand-alone pediatric hospital in the nation's capital, serving children of the District of Columbia, Maryland, and Virginia.

Because of our strong nursing vision, CNMC has become the practice setting of choice for professional pediatric nurses who posses a passion for clinical excellence. Children and families are central to all of our nursing systems and processes. Further, our nursing practice is evidence-based, holistic, and compassionate across the continuum of patient care.

Collaboration in health care begins with a partnership between nurses and families. This relationship is based on respect for patients and families and their stated desire for relationship-based practice. While health care professionals have expertise in a variety of areas, patients and families are the experts on the experience of receiving care. For this reason, *"patients' experience should be the fundamental source of any definition of quality"* (Berwick, 2002).

CNMC implemented its professional development program during an unprecedented shortage of registered nurses—a shortage that was especially severe in specialty institutions such as pediatric hospitals. We found that providing programs that engage employees can be one of the best ways to attract, motivate, and retain talented professional nurses. Prior to the program, staff nurses were becoming increasingly disengaged. Disengagement happens when an individual perceives that his or her job no longer provides growth and a relevant sense of identity (McNeese-Smith, 2002).

Professionals at CNMC found themselves struggling with questions such as, "What happened to caring as the essence of our work?" "Where do patients' and families' needs fit in?" "How do I know I am doing the right thing?" "What is the meaning of my practice?" "How do I provide Professional Nursing Practice with so many complexities around me?" "Where is the joy in my work?" and, " How do I work with my colleagues towards a common goal?"

The main constructs of a Relationship-Based Professional Nursing Practice were articulated through the consultation services of Marie Manthey and Colleen Person as follows:

- A "responsibility relationship" exists between the nurse and the patient.

- The nurse and patient share responsibility for determining the desired outcomes of each episode of care.

- The nurse identifies the amount, degree, and kind of nursing care needed to achieve the desired outcomes.

- Care is given by the nurse and other members of the team.

- The nurse manages the nursing resources to meet those needs.

It is not enough to "talk the talk" of caring in the community; one must "walk the talk" as well. In our organization, nursing leaders were provided with the knowledge and skills to build on the

necessary competencies to provide an environment which supports professional nursing practice. The program *Leading an Empowered
Organization* (*LEO*) provided direction and a philosophical base for the leaders.

Leadership in turn invested in the program
Reigniting the Spirit of Caring as a way of recon-
necting nurses with their original motivation for
having become professional nurses in the first
place. Focusing on communication, relationship-
building, self-care, and both personal and professional integrity freed nurses at CNMC to invest in
themselves and their work in a new way.

Experienced nurse mentors helped the new
graduate nurses and the entire staff to be open to
learning and professional development. Nurses
with less than one year of experience and nurses
with greater than 25 years of experience attended
this program together. Without this opportunity
for collaborating, the community ceases to be a
learning community *or* an innovative and productive unit. The program helps nurses to gain an
understanding of the broad social, cultural,
economic, and political determinants of health care
delivery, and reveals the values, norms, and social
and health concerns of the community, primarily
through the voices of patients and families.

On the second day of the program, patients and
families share their health care experiences, with
particular focus on times they felt cared for versus
the times they did not feel cared for. They talk
about how they felt when they perceived dismis-
sive behaviors related to race, social class, cultural
background, and religious beliefs. This is a strong
emotional experience that touches the hearts and
minds of the nurses. Often we ask care providers
who have been the recipients of care themselves to
share their stories of "being on the other side."

They share their perceptions of what professional nursing "feels" like and "looks" like when they are the recipients of care rather than the providers.

The input from patients and families is not limited to areas of patient care. True caring for patients and families must be evident at all levels of the organization, including decisions related to program evaluation, policy development, quality improvement initiatives, design and planning, and patient safety. The Institute for Family Centered Care advocates that the collaboration between care providers and families touch all levels of the hospital or health system, including the board of trustees, senior administrators, physicians, and all members of staff (Advances in Family Centered Care, Spring 2003).

Changing from a culture of blame to one of improvement and trust, we have integrated the principles of Professional Nursing Practice in our Nursing Practice and Research Council.

Both anecdotal evidence and quantitative data have affirmed the impact of the program on staff engagement and higher quality patient care. We now have vacancy rates and turnover rates below the national average.

CNMC's nurses have experienced so much positive energy from this program that they feel the program could have an impact on the whole field of nursing—to lift up professional practice. CNMC is interested in training more staff to lead conferences at other hospitals and to speak about our experience at health care conferences throughout the country, advancing professional nursing practice.

Mourine Evans, MS, RN, is the Director of Staff Development and Research at Children's National Medical Center, a 280 bed hospital in Washington, District of Columbia.

FIVE
Patient Care Delivery

Colleen Person

The delivery system used is one of the most powerful tools a manager has in creating an environment of stability, with increased predictability and decreased uncertainty being by-products.

—*Marie Manthey*

Overview

A patient care delivery system is an infrastructure for organizing and providing care to patients and families. The patient care delivery system we recommend is one built upon the concepts and values of both Relationship-Based Care and Professional Nursing Practice. Its purpose is to establish a therapeutic relationship between nurses and patients and their families during their episode of care, to accomplish essential nursing interventions, and to maximize collaborative, interdisciplinary practice.

In Relationship-Based Care (RBC), the patient care delivery system provides the structure to support the role of the Professional Nurse, promotes collegial relationships among all members of the team, and provides structures to organize work and effectively utilize resources. In RBC, the human aspect of care drives everything. Relationship-Based Care means that people and relationships matter most—and a commitment to RBC implies a belief in the notion that the most

The patient care delivery system exists to establish a therapeutic relationship between nurses and patients and families during their episode of care.

effective care delivery systems are those designed with the patient always held in the highest regard.

Research on patient satisfaction finds that what matters most to patients are the interpersonal skills and caring behaviors of the hospital staff. It is little wonder nursing care is the most important predictor of overall patient satisfaction with hospital care (Vom Eigen, et al., 1999; Evans, Martin & Winslow, 1998; Varholak & Korwan, 1995).

Although it is arguable that Professional Nursing can exist within any delivery system, if the design of the system does not support Professional Nursing Practice, it is extremely difficult to sustain a commitment to Relationship-Based Care within that system. Fortunately, we are seeing a nation-wide movement from a bureaucratic, task-based view of care delivery to a principles-based, holistic view of care delivery—one that is congruent with Professional Nursing Practice. The table below contrasts bureaucratic and Professional Nursing.

Bureaucratic Nursing	Professional Nursing
Task-based care drives activities.	Knowledge-based care drives interventions.
Cure of disease is the goal.	Healing is the goal.
Nurse focuses on physical, diagnosis-centered care.	Nurse focuses on holistic care—body, mind and spirit.
Policies and procedures drive decision-making.	Professional standards and current research drive decision-making.
Rules, habits, and routines determine nurse's behavior.	Critical thinking and innovation determine nurse's behavior.

Over the past 25 years, we have assisted clients in designing and implementing health care delivery systems that support Relationship-Based Care and thereby strengthen Professional Nursing Practice. We base care delivery design on the following five premises:

1. The purpose of our work is caring for patients and their families.

2. We can most effectively achieve our purpose when we know what matters most to each patient and family.

3. Patients share more information when they feel safe, as within a relationship with a specific registered nurse.

4. Continuity of care improves productivity, efficiency, and patient and staff satisfaction.

5. Clearly defining each of the elements of the care delivery system improves productivity, efficiency, and satisfaction.

Four Elements of Care Delivery Systems

There are four key elements that form the essential building blocks of any care delivery system. The way each element is defined and put into operation distinguishes one system from another. The four elements that define a care delivery system are:

Element 1: Nurse/patient relationship and decision making

This element addresses the role of the registered nurse (RN) and the extent of the nurse's responsibility, authority, and accountability for patient care decisions. This element asks us to look at the length of time a relationship exists between a specific nurse and patient. Does that relationship exist through a single interaction, a shift, an entire length of stay on a unit, or an episode of care across multiple units or settings?

Element 2: Work allocation and/or patient assignments

This element addresses the way in which staff scheduling, patient assignment practices, and delegation of care activities are achieved. Underlying beliefs about the value of continuous nurse-patient relationships determine how work and patient assignments are made.

In any care delivery system the leadership role of the unit manager creates the culture of care, determines the nature of the nurse-patient relationship, and profoundly influences the performance and development of staff.

Element 3: Communication between members of the health care team

Each system of care has specific standards for who communicates with whom about pertinent patient information. Values, beliefs, and group norms contribute to how communication occurs. Communication within the unit team, with physicians, among members of the interdisciplinary team, and with the patient/family all affect the experience of the patient.

Element 4: Management of the unit or environment of care

In any care delivery system the leadership role of the unit manager creates the culture of care, determines the nature of the nurse-patient relationship, and profoundly influences the performance and development of staff.

When these four elements are clearly defined, even a less than ideal care delivery system can function efficiently and effectively. When these four elements are not clearly established, the result may be confusion, inefficiency, frustration, and misuse of resources.

A care delivery system is defined by the way in which each of its four elements is put into operation. Historically there have been four defined care delivery systems. These four care delivery systems, described in sequence of their development are: Functional Nursing, Team Nursing, Total Patient Care, and Primary Nursing (Manthey, 2002; Nelson, 2000). While elements of each system are still in practice today, a review of the four systems reveals the progress that nursing has made over the last half century from a bureaucratic, task-based approach to a professional, relationship-based approach.

Functional Nursing was the most common care delivery system in the 1950s and early 1960s. In this system, tasks are divided among the members of the team by a manager or charge nurse. In the Functional Nursing system, one nurse administered medications to all patients on the unit, another would do all the treatments, and other team members would do daily cares. The focus was on getting the tasks done—not on establishing a therapeutic relationship between a nurse and patient. Functional Nursing was built on an industrial model of care. Some aspects of Functional Nursing exist today, such as delegating to a nursing assistant specific tasks which become a standard part of his or her job description. The nursing assistant may carry out these "assembly line" tasks in lieu of establishing a nurse-patient relationship.

Team Nursing evolved in the mid 1960s to early 1970s. The role of the RN in the team approach was to carry out the most complex tasks herself and to provide supervision and oversight to less prepared care providers on the team. Team Nursing is based on a productivity model of service. While Team Nursing moves clinical decision making closer to the point of care delivery, it does not support the relationship of the patient and

Four Care Delivery Systems Explained

professional nurse over time. In most systems of Team Nursing, continuity of the nurse-patient relationship is easily interrupted by patient location, patient acuity issues, and the accomplishment of tasks within the shift. Team Nursing continues today with a variety of refinements and adaptations.

Total Patient Care began in the late 1960s as a method of care delivery in which the RN provides the majority of direct care to patients. Within this system, nurses are responsible for the nursing care of the patients assigned to them for a specific shift, but do not have overall responsibility for the plan of care for the duration of the patient's stay on the unit. Total Patient Care attempts to provide a more satisfying work environment for the nurse and to enhance patient satisfaction with care by strengthening the nurse-patient relationship. Its move toward relationship-based nursing ends there, however, as a nurse within the Total Patient Care system does not have responsibility for creating or implementing a plan for the continuity of the patient's care over time.

Primary Nursing began at the University of Minnesota in 1969. It is centered on the establishment of a therapeutic relationship between an identified nurse and patient over time. The Primary Nurse is responsible for planning and coordinating the patient's care throughout the patient's stay on that particular unit. Within the Primary Nursing system, continuity of care is highly valued and thus provides the foundation for daily nurse-patient care assignments. Primary Nursing focuses on the nurse-patient relationship, strengthens accountability for care, and facilitates greater involvement of the patient and family in planning and evaluating their care. This care delivery system is recognized as the one most congruent with strong Professional Nursing Practice (Ritter-Teitel, 2002).

Comparison of the Four Care Delivery Systems Applying The Four Elements

Element	Functional Nursing	Team Nursing	Total Patient Care	Primary Nursing
Nurse/ patient relationship and Decision-Making	Decision-making occurs over a single shift; decisions usually made by nurse manager or charge nurse.	Decision-making occurs over a single shift; largely by team leader or nurse manager.	Decision-making occurs over a single shift— either by an RN caring for the patient or by a charge nurse.	RN makes decisions for individual patients based on their therapeutic relationship, which is sustained for the length of stay of the patient on the unit.
Work Allocation and/or Patient Assignments	Nursing assignments are task-based. Nurses are assigned to tasks, rather than to patients.	Nursing assignments are based on level of complexity and commensurate level of expertise; focus is on tasks to be accomplished; assignments change based on patient acuity and work complexity.	Nursing assignments are largely patient-based, with RN providing activities of care. Nursing assignments may vary by shift based on geography and patient acuity, without supporting continuity of care.	Nursing assignments are patient-based to ensure continuity of care. An RN is assigned to a patient and remains that patient's Primary Nurse for as long as the patient remains on the unit (unless circumstances require that a new Primary Nurse is assigned).
Communication between health care team members	Communication is hierarchical; task-completion is documented and communicated to the charge nurse; the charge nurse pulls information together for all patients and communicates with other members of the heath care team.	Communication is hierarchical; the care provider reports to the team leader; the team leader reports to physicians and/or other health care team members.	Communication is direct. However, in some Total Patient Care systems, RNs may be required to communicate with physician and other members of the health care team through a charge nurse.	Communication is direct. Patient information is solicited by the Primary Nurse who communicates directly and proactively with team members, physicians, and other colleagues. The Primary Nurse is responsible for integrating information and coordinating care.
Management of the unit or environment of care	Managers function as overseers, assuring that tasks are accomplished.	Nurse manager supervises the team leader who is responsible for supervising other staff in the delivery of care.	Managers serve as a resource and promote nurses having a stronger role in care decisions.	Managers promote the nurse-patient relationship and the professional role of the nurse. They influence care by creating a healthy work environment and empowering the staff to remove barriers to care.

Primary Nursing and Relationship-Based Care

In Primary Nursing, a therapeutic relationship is established between an RN and an individual patient and his or her family. Within this relationship, the nurse has the responsibility to identify the patient's unique health needs and to communicate and coordinate those needs with other members of the health care team. The relationship is initiated by the nurse and is in effect for the length of the patient's stay in a service or unit. When the patient is transferred from the unit or discharged to another service, the Primary Nurse transfers the relationship and plan of care to care providers in the next setting. One of the hallmarks of the Primary Nursing role is the clarity with which RNs accept responsibility for decision-making regarding the care of the patient. Another hallmark is that once the nurse-patient relationship is established, it is known to the patient, family, physician, and other members of the team.

The Primary Nurse does not provide all of the activities of care. The Primary Nurse determines and prioritizes the needs of the patient and family in order to establish an individualized plan of care, which is communicated to other members of the team. The activities of care may be accomplished by the Primary Nurse or delegated to associate nurses, licensed practical nurses, and nursing assistants. The key is that the Primary Nurse takes the lead in determining priorities with the patient and family and in working collaboratively with other members of the team to meet these priorities.

Partners in Practice is a nurse extending program which espouses a methodology in which an RN and an LPN/LVN or CNA agree to partner with one another in the provision of the activities of care. They choose to work together with a consistent schedule and assignment of patients. In this relationship the care partners come to understand each other's knowledge, skills, and styles, thereby providing a synergy for continuous team development. Nursing decisions match patient needs with care provider skills; delegation is more customized and not limited by typical role descriptions. Further, the relationship with the patient is strengthened by having two care providers who know the patient's needs and preferences. (See appendix A for *Partners in Practice* summary.)

Linda Pullins, Vice President for Patient Care Services at Marion General Hospital in Marion, Ohio describes their experience with *Partners in Practice* and some of the challenges and benefits below:

> *We implemented* Partners in Practice *in the early 1990s as a program to improve our care delivery system, and its basic tenets are still in place today. Members of our nursing staff have said that it is the best thing we've ever done in support of patient care delivery, as it has made everybody better caregivers. The partners may be in teams of two or three. The teams of two consist of a registered nurse and nursing assistant. Teams of three include an RN, LPN/LVN, and NA. Determination of the team size is dependent upon the unit, patients' average length of stay, average daily census, and acuity levels of other patients. The team members are assigned the same shifts and work together on those shifts. The registered nurse is responsible for supporting and developing the knowledge of her team members.*
>
> *We have found the partnered approach particularly helpful with 12-hour shifts. When full time people only work three days*

a week, it really helps ensure continuity and efficiency for them to work with the same people.

We have been at this for over 10 years and find it highly beneficial. The partnered approach has improved both quality and efficiency, as it actually forces the issue of delegation. The registered nurse's confidence in her team members' abilities promotes delegation and helps get past barriers that might otherwise get in the way. Role distinctions between the RN and LPN/LVN continue to be a challenge, but are more likely to be worked out in this model through the continuity of the relationship.

This program is one of many initiatives we have implemented in the past ten years to improve nursing practice and patient satisfaction. The journey has been long and sometimes frustrating, but we are making significant progress. Our nurse recruitment efforts have improved significantly. We have gone from recruiting and hiring 25 RNs/year to this current year successfully recruiting and hiring 66. Our RN turnover rate is running at 1.35%! Most importantly our 2004 first quarter rating for patient satisfaction using the Press Ganey measurement survey was in the 92nd percentile. That reflects a move from the 9th percentile in 2000! (L. Pullins, personal communication, April 30, 2004.)

Whether a model like *Partners in Practice* is in place or not, the number of patients for whom a Primary Nurse is responsible depends upon the acuity of the patient population, the number of RNs available, and the skill mix on the team. The skill mix (mixture of registered nurses, licensed practical nurses, and nursing assistants) should be determined based on patient acuity and overall work volumes and activities. The term *associate nurse* is often used for the nurse who is assigned to care for the patient in the absence of the Primary Nurse. The associate nurse is responsible for following and/or revising the plan of care based on the patient's changing needs and response to care.

RBC has evolved from the basic tenet of Primary Nursing—namely, *a continuous therapeutic relationship of a nurse with an individual patient over time*. The nurse establishes the relationship, involves the patient and family in the care, and uses the patient's and family's input in determining the kind of nursing care the patient will receive for the duration of that nurse's authority. In this system of care delivery, the Primary Nurse experiences the fullness of the Professional Nursing role. In 2002, Marie Manthey wrote, *"Primary Nursing is a delivery system for nursing care at the station level that facilitates Professional Nursing Practice despite the bureaucratic nature of hospitals."*

The following story exemplifies what happens when Primary Nursing works.

> *The University of California-Davis Medical Center in Sacramento, a hospital with Magnet designation, is implementing a Primary Nursing model on all of the units of the hospital. Based in part on feedback from highly satisfied patients and their families on the Pediatric unit (which developed its own Primary Nursing model many years before), nurses throughout the organization are seeking to elevate the level of their practice. In a recent conversation with this*

Relationship-Based Care has evolved from the basic tenet of Primary Nursing— namely a continuous therapeutic relationship of a nurse with an individual patient over time.

author, the Vice President for Patient Care Services, Carol Robinson, stated "Primary Nursing is the best thing that's happening in this organization."

During a recent panel presentation featuring nurses, patients and family members, a nurse introduced herself saying "My name is Ellen, and I'm Cecilia's Primary Nurse." Cecilia responded, "She always takes care of me; she always pushes me to get better. She knows me better than anyone." Cecilia's mother characterized the relationship by saying "It means so much to me to know that Ellen will be there to take care of Cecilia. I can count on Ellen to oversee her care."

According to Ellen, "Primary Nursing has had a tremendous impact on Cecelia's hospitalization. I know her, her medications, what works, what doesn't work. I wish every hospital could do Primary Nursing. I think that's one of the reasons I've been able to work at the bedside for over 20 years...I love it."

Below, Marie Manthey shares the story of the origin of Primary Nursing:

Primary Nursing was implemented in 1968 on Unit 32 at the University of Minnesota Hospital. This radical change in care delivery came about when a colleague, Pat Robertson (nursing supervisor) and I (assistant director of nursing) held an evening meeting with nursing staff and leaders at Pat's home. This was an unprecedented and radical action—to invite staff nurses and leaders to come together to figure out how to improve patient care and the work environment itself. The nurses told stories about attempts to implement Primary Nursing elsewhere in the

United States, and we discussed how it could happen in our organization. Our message to the staff that night was that they have the ability to influence their own practice and how it will look—and step one was that it was okay for them to make patient assignments. The director of nursing was not supportive of Primary Nursing as a model of care. She had difficulty imagining how it could work and worried over things such as "who would supervise the LPNs."

We provided leadership and set about demonstrating how Primary Nursing could work. The intellectual capacity and consistency of values among all those assembled to create Primary Nursing on Unit 32 propelled us into unified action. We agreed on our principles, and they became our guide, while always allowing for individual adaptation and interpretation. We had energy and vision. We knew that a primary relationship between a nurse and patient would improve care, facilitate healing and strengthen accountability. We also knew it was a model of care delivery that would allow nurses to live the values of their practice and ultimately find greater satisfaction and meaning in their work. We became activists for change, and Primary Nursing became a reality.

Despite successes like the those at UC-Davis and the University of Minnesota hospital, many myths and misunderstandings about Primary Nursing persist. Some claim that the implementation of a Primary Nursing model is not even achievable. It is helpful to consider and dispel these myths in order to design and implement a Relationship-Based Care model that includes the element of Primary Nursing.

Myths About Primary Nursing	Facts About Primary Nursing
Primary Nursing requires an all-RN staff.	Primary Nursing can be implemented with the available staff—it does not require special staff, nor does it require an all-RN staff. Licensed practical nurses, nursing assistants, and other team members play vital roles in meeting the needs of the patient and his or her family.
The Primary Nurse does all of the bedside care.	The essence of the Primary Nurse's role is the acceptance of responsibility, authority, and accountability for decisions about patient care. It is not about the Primary Nurse "doing it all."
	It is simply not practical for the Primary Nurse to complete all aspects of care. Obvious barriers to singular care by a Primary Nurse include shortened length of patient stays; escalating patient acuity levels; complex, multifaceted care requirements, and the cyclical nursing shortage. If the Primary Nurse was doing all of the bedside care, he or she would not be able to assume responsibility for planning and coordinating the patient's care.
Primary Nursing eliminates teamwork. Everyone works individually and therefore is not aware of patients other than their own. In a Primary Nurse model, care providers do not help each other.	Teamwork is critical to the Primary Nursing care delivery system. It has been demonstrated that the best utilization of ancillary staff is in relationship with one RN—(at least within a given shift)—not assigned to help many. However, a general culture of "helpfulness" based on a shared commitment to all patients and team members is necessary to achieve consistently safe, quality care.
	Primary Nursing supports collaborative interdisciplinary practice through communication and coordination.
Complex scheduling requirements prohibit continuity of the nurse-patient relationship central to the Primary Nurse model.	Clinical staff report a 25% reduction in work redundancy due to day-to-day continuity of care. They also report a perceived increase in productivity through more consistent co-worker assignments. The key to achieving these results is to find creative methods to schedule nurses with continuity of care as the priority. For example, if a patient's anticipated length of stay is three days, schedule nurses three consecutive days.

We have partnered with numerous clients to design a Relationship-Based Care delivery system that is customized to the needs and intentions of their organizations. The organization identifies key principles in each of the four elements of a care delivery system with emphasis on strengthening all relationships—the relationship of the RN with the patient and family as well as the relationship of care providers with one another, the interdisciplinary team, health care facility administrators, and staff. The principles of RBC provide an overall framework across the organization, with unit groups implementing unit-specific plans.

In a customized RBC delivery system, each organization determines the best terminology with which to clarify what responsibility, authority, and accountability a nurse has for his or her patients. Some organizations are using the term Primary Nurse while others use the terms Professional Nurse, care manager, attending nurse or, simply, registered nurse. Once definitions and terminology are agreed upon, health care organizations can begin implementing the principles of the RBC system in ways that are clear to patients, families, and colleagues.

In a customized Relationship-Based Care delivery system, each organization determines the best terminology with which to clarify the nurse's responsibility, authority, and accountability to the patient.

Implementation of a customized RBC system has been shown to improve the work environment as perceived by staff nurses (Nelson, 2003). In a descriptive study conducted in a 364-bed community hospital in the Midwestern United States, factors of the work environment were rated more positively after RBC was implemented. Target relationships that showed a statistically significant improvement included the nurse-patient and nurse-physician relationships. Other factors of the work environment that showed statistically significant improvements were the nurses' perception of their own autonomy and of the type and number of tasks required of them on the job. All four of these factors have been identified as critical factors for healthy work environments within Magnet hospitals.

The drive for stronger Professional Nursing Practice and patient-centered care delivery systems has intensified due to the latest and most severe crisis in the recruitment and retention of well-qualified nursing staff. Health care consumers are becoming increasingly sophisticated about nursing care and staffing issues. In an article published in the *Reader's Digest* (Pekkanen, 2003), entitled *Condition: Critical...With Nurses Leaving in Droves, a Stay at the Hospital Gets Scarier Every Day*, readers are encouraged to take control over their own health care by taking four actions:

1. **Find out the RN-to-patient ratio.** These ratios, the author says, are directly related to error rates and morbidity and that "if [the ratios] are greater than 1 to 4, you may get sub-par care."

2. **Check also the ratio of RNs to LPNs.** The author differentiates skill from preparation and dispels any public perception that all nurses come to the bedside equally prepared.

3. **Study the facility's "report card."** The author states that these cards rate the quality of hospitals—and, he emphasized, hospitals volunteer to participate.

4. **Locate the nearest Magnet Hospital.** Magnet status is, according to the author, a key indicator of quality nursing care. He says magnet status indicates two things: the hospital provides high quality nursing care and the hospital retains its nurses.

In designing care delivery systems, hospital leaders seek to understand and integrate the characteristics of Magnet hospitals, as such hospitals have demonstrated the ability to retain well-qualified nursing staff, provide higher quality care, decrease error rates, decrease morbidity and mortality, and improve patient and family satisfaction (Aiken, Clarke, Sloane, Sochalski, & Silber, 2002; Ingersoll, Schultz, Hoffart, & Ryan, 1996; Prescott, 1993; Scott et al., 1999). The American Nurse's Credentialing Center (ANCC) was established in 1990 to provide programs and credentialing services to hospitals desiring to achieve Magnet status (ANCC, 2003). The ANCC's *Forces of Magnetism,* shown below, evolved out of a descriptive study conducted by the American Academy of Nursing's Task Force on Nursing Practice in Hospitals, in which 163 hospitals that attracted and retained well-qualified nurses were evaluated.

The categories of the *Forces of Magnetism* are outlined in the following table. All of the standards within these categories are supported by the principles of RBC, and grounded in a therapeutic, continuous relationship between the registered nurse and patient.

Forces of Magnetism

American Nurses Credentialing Center
Forces of Magnetism

- Quality of Nursing Leadership
- Organizational Structure
- Management Style
- Personnel Policies and Programs
- Professional Models of Care
- Quality of Care
- Quality Improvement

- Consultation and Resources
- Autonomy
- Community and Heathcare Organization
- Nurses as Teachers
- Image of Nursing
- Interdisciplinary Relationships
- Professional Development

Health care organizations are designing RBC delivery systems as the infrastructure for providing care that results in improved outcomes; patient, family, physician and staff satisfaction; and more effective and efficient resource management.

Summary of Key Concepts

- Patient care delivery systems provide the organizing framework for accomplishing the activities of patient care.

- RBC has evolved from Primary Nursing.

- Primary Nursing is designed to support Professional Nursing Practice and humane and compassionate care to patients through continuity of nurse-patient relationships.

- Care delivery systems are differentiated by four elements: nurse-patient relationship and decision-making; work allocation and patient assignments; communication between members of the health care team; and management of the environment of care. The way these four elements are designed and implemented determines the nature of care delivery.

- The Primary Nurse has the responsibility and authority to establish a relationship and develop an individualized plan of care with the patient (including discharge planning) and is accountable for the nursing care outcomes.

- An associate nurse is assigned to care for the patient in the absence of the Primary Nurse and is responsible for following or revising the plan of care based on the patient's response to care and changing needs. Other care providers follow the plan and are responsible and accountable for fulfilling their assigned duties within the scope of their positions and licensure.

- The Primary Nurse has full authority for determining the kind and amount of nursing care a patient will receive. The Primary Nurse also determines which work requires his or her own time and attention, and which work can be delegated to other care providers.

- The Primary Nurse proactively provides information to others involved in the care of the patient and seeks information from other members of the health care team.

- As the nurse-patient relationship is established, the Primary Nurse gains insight into what matters most to specific patients, and therefore, can be extremely beneficial in interpreting the patient's need for information.

- The skills, attitudes, and behaviors of the unit manager are key variables to the success of any care delivery system. RBC systems work when managers are skilled in supporting staff in their role as autonomous decision-makers and creative problem-solvers regarding patient care.

- Effective managers focus on the core purpose of their unit—caring for patients and families. They support staff in this purpose by listening, coaching, and teaching, and by resolving issues and removing barriers to care.

- Magnet hospitals are hospitals in which the professional role of the registered nurse is visibly established.

- Hospitals with Magnet status have lower rates of turnover, higher success in recruiting well-qualified nursing staff, and higher quality patient outcomes.

Questions for Self-Assessment

- What elements of Functional Nursing, Team Nursing, Total Patient Care, and Primary Nursing are found in your current care delivery system?

- What does the way activities of care are carried out in your organization reveal about what is valued most in the nurse-patient relationship?

- What do you believe about continuity of care and the nurse-patient relationship? Are your practices consistent with your beliefs?

- How are decisions currently made for patient care? What will you continue doing? What will you change?

- Does your current staffing and scheduling system support the nurse-patient relationship?

- What key values and beliefs drive your staffing and scheduling system? What will you continue doing? What will you change?

- How do you communicate the patient's needs to members of the team?

- In what ways does Professional Nursing Practice currently contribute to individualized patient care through collaborative relationships with other care providers and disciplines?

- What are your expectations of the manager's role? Does your current expectation support Professional Nursing Practice as it is currently defined?

Tufts-New England Medical Center
Boston, Massachusetts

Nurses at Tufts-New England Medical Center (Tufts-NEMC) have practiced Primary Nursing since 1973. Changes in patients' length of stay, reimbursement, staffing patterns, availability of experienced nurses, and a partnership with another health care system necessitated an evaluation of our Primary Nursing care delivery model. Our goals were to improve patient care delivery without compromising the patient care experience across the health care system. The result was a principle-based, customized Primary Nursing model tailored to fit each individual unit.

How We Did It

Tufts-NEMC's Care Delivery Principles were developed by a patient care oversight team with consultation from CHCM. The principles developed by the team created the foundation for our professional practice model and they are as follows:

1. Each patient's nursing care will be the direct responsibility of a Primary Nurse throughout the patient's stay on a unit. This nurse is accountable for coordinating the patient's care and effectively transferring that accountability when the patient leaves the unit. It's expected that patients and families will know the name of the Primary Nurse.

2. The Primary Nurse role will continue to incorporate both care provider and patient care management components.

3. Support staff helping with direct care will be prepared at the appropriate

A Moment of Excellence: Tufts-New England Medical Center

competency level for the patient population's care requirements and within the
context of regulatory requirements.

4. To assure maximum effectiveness of
utilization, support staff assisting with
care will be partnered with an RN.

5. The use of multi-department unit support
staff may be a component of the model.

6. Increased continuity of nurse-patient
relationships will be achieved in acute
care delivery.

7. Increased productivity will be achieved in
care delivery using technology and data.

8. Consistent care teams will be matched
with physicians whenever possible to
ensure coordinated, high-quality, highly
productive standards of Relationship-
Based Care.

The staff on each unit selected a Unit Practice
Committee (UPC). The role of the UPC was to
implement the care delivery principles on their
unit based on input from 100% of the staff. The
role of the unit leaders was to act as a facilitator
and coach for the UPC.

Committee and nursing leadership members
attended leadership, communications, and critical
thinking forums to prepare for their new roles and
responsibilities. UPCs established meeting ground
rules, defined mutual expectations with their
managers, and developed a communication structure to facilitate two-way communication with all
members of the staff. Decisions regarding patient
care delivery were made by consensus with 100%
of the staff participating. Each unit's decisions
about how to implement the care delivery principles became the unit's customized Primary Nursing

Practice model which was tailored to meet the unique needs of their patient populations and staffing patterns.

Unexpected and Welcome Results

Putting care delivery decisions in the hands of those who deliver the care has produced some very satisfying results for patients, families, and staff. In addition to creating and implementing a customized Primary Nursing model for their units, UPCs and staff were able to identify staffing patterns to improve continuity and consistency in care, activities performed by RNs that could be eliminated or performed by other staff, technology to enhance care delivery, current barriers that impact the delivery of care, and clinical protocols that would facilitate care or discharge.

Several UPCs formed work groups with unit staff, leaders, and physicians to develop and implement a variety of evidence-based protocols and standards of care. Some examples of these protocols include: weaning patients from a mechanical ventilator, neuromuscular blockade infusions, and the administration of Lasix by continuous infusion. The work groups continue to review and revise the protocols on a regular basis to incorporate new scientific advances, increase efficiencies, and educate staff. In addition, some UPCs have joined together to resolve patient flow issues and to share practice ideas.

Many other projects surfaced as a result of this initiative. Some examples are the development of a multi-disciplinary cardiac patient discharge teaching class and other patient teaching and informational materials, patient documentation revisions, unit orientation improvements, and unlicensed assistive personnel and charge nurse guidelines.

Where We are Now

Tufts-NEMC initiated the development of its own principles-based Primary Nursing model in 1998. Currently about three quarters of the UPCs remain active (most UPCs have rotated their membership on a regular basis) and continue to monitor the implementation of their customized Primary Nursing Practice models, making revisions as needed. The primary role of the UPCs has become prioritizing and addressing practice issues identified by unit staff, leadership members, and quality improvement data. Work groups continue and the staff continues to feel empowered and in control of their own practice.

Tufts-NEMC currently enjoys a mere 3.4% nurse vacancy rate, versus the average of 11-14%. Recent surveys indicate high patient and employee satisfaction levels.

Sandra Dandrinos-Smith, MEd, RN, a health care education consultant, is former Director of Education and Practice Development and Mary Sullivan Smith, MS, RN, is Clinical Director, Patient Care Services/Nursing at Tufts–New England Medical Center, a 350 bed hospital in Boston, Massachusetts.

SIX
Resource Driven Practice

Marie Manthey and Mary Koloroutis

The greatest achievement of the human spirit is to live up to one's opportunities and make the most of one's resources. Think about the resources that you have in a given day and distribute those resources in a way that makes sense to accomplish the outcomes needed.

—*Vauvenargues*

Overview

Thinking about patient care delivery from a resource, rather than a need perspective, requires for most of us a significant change in mindset about staffing, resource utilization, and patient care. Historically, the mindset about resources for nurses was established in nursing school where grades were linked to the number of patient needs identified. Although the needs could be assessed and found, what was missing in this mindset was the decision-making regarding which needs would be met and which would not be met during a specific episode of care. The mindset was not one of focusing on the resources available and determining common sense ways to distribute them.

Staffing, the connection between workload and resources, is fraught with complex emotions. The intent of this chapter is to put resource realities into a perspective that reduces anxiety about

scarcities and replaces it with a balanced acceptance of the day-to-day realities of staffing and
patient care. And as we all know, two predomi-
nant realities in the world of health care are:

1. There is always more work to do than
   time available.

2. Staff can do little to increase or decrease
   the workload.

Marie has pondered these realities often over
her long career:

*Resource driven
practice focuses on
priorities—what
matters most to
each patient and
family—while bal-
ancing the needs
of the patient
populations as
a whole.*

> I've been in nursing for over forty
> years, from staff nurse to Vice President, to
> President of a consulting company. Staffing
> is always, always the issue. You can have all
> your budgeted positions filled, you can have
> everybody back from a leave of absence, you
> can have everything just perfect and—bam!—
> something happens to knock a hole in it. You
> can do the perfect job of management and—
> bam!—something happens. There you are,
> back in the mess again. Unfortunately, that's
> the nature of our business. We are a twenty-
> four-hours-a-day, seven-days-a-week opera-
> tion. We deal with people. Staffing is always,
> always the issue. So let's take as a given that
> staffing is an issue that won't go away . . .
> I want to change the way you think about
> patient care . . . There's always more work to
> do than time available . . . What we have to
> learn how to do is to decide what NOT to do
> *(Manthey, 2002).*

Resource driven practice is about clinical staff
and managers sharing responsibility, authority,
and accountability (R+A+A) for the resources
required to provide quality patient care. It is a
practical and realistic approach to the provision of

care delivery and it is fundamental to the delivery of Relationship-Based Care (RBC) and to Professional Nursing Practice. Resource driven practice focuses on priorities—what matters most to each patient and family—while balancing the needs of the patient population as a whole. Managers and clinicians who are tuned in to resource needs understand that it is never acceptable to choose between cost and quality; rather, they figure out how to get the highest quality for the lowest cost. The best course is to become effective stewards of our resources so that quality care and service are available to all individuals in need. The most beneficial mindset is one of being conscious of what resources we can use to serve the needs of the whole population while focusing and prioritizing the resources we can use to serve the needs of individuals.

The new mindset requires unit staff to move away from thinking about their work as being driven by tasks and routines to thinking about their work as being driven by prioritized caring.

Because nurses comprise the greatest percentage of direct care providers, their values and beliefs regarding workload and resources determine much of the way care is prioritized and delivered with available resources. A new mindset—one in which resources rather than *needs* drive care—challenges nurses to move away from the belief that since patient needs are endless, there will never be enough time, staff, or resources to effectively provide care. With this old mindset, nurses experience unending frustration and feelings of powerlessness and victimization. The reality is that workload expansions and contractions inevitably occur without commensurate staffing adjustments. Since extra staff cannot be added to cover all such situations, nurses must become adept at deciding which of their patients' needs will be met and which will not. With a clear plan for such decision-making in place, nurses may feel less guilty when all patients do not receive all the care they wish they could provide. Nurses who know and accept this reality are able to engage in an active decision-making process grounded in solid principles of critical thinking.

Moving from the old mindset to a new resource driven mindset requires a shift from passive, needs-driven thinking to active, resource-driven thinking. Shifting the mindset requires a shift in culture and unit norms as well as a shift within each clinician and manager. The new mindset requires unit staff to move away from thinking about their work as being driven by tasks and routines to thinking about their work as being driven by prioritized caring. This requires each clinician to engage in critical thinking, decision-making, and individualization of care within the context of available resources.

This chapter addresses three key beliefs of resource driven practice that impact the experience of patient care for both staff and patients. These three beliefs are:

1. Critical thinking, creative thinking, and reflection help us find new solutions to the challenges of balancing quality and cost.

2. Financial management is an area for mutual commitment among staff, managers, and administration. Mutual commitment is based on the understanding that daily decisions affect long-term financial health and that long-term strategies affect daily decisions.

3. Resource driven care requires a pro-active mindset regarding staffing and scheduling, skill mix, and professional role development for nurses.

Old Mindset: Resource Passive (Victimized)	New Mindset: Resource Driven (Empowered)
I need more help to meet the needs of my patients and their families. It is up to the manager or staffing office to find me that help. If they don't, I don't know how I will get through the shift. If I don't personally meet all the needs of my patients, I am an inadequate clinician.	I will assess and identify the patient's needs and partner with the patient and family to determine what is most essential today as well as what can be addressed later or accomplished by someone else.
I don't want the same patient assignment again. I just need a break from the heavy load.	I will not compromise continuity of care. Even when patient situations are complex, I know it is best for the patient and for efficiency of care to really get to know my patients and their needs.
I hope the schedule meets my needs.	I need to provide my input into the most effective scheduling pattern for our unit. I want my scheduling to safeguard continuity of relationship of care providers and patients and to respect my human needs.
I hope I have a compatible LPN, CNA, or float to work with today. . . quality of care varies so much depending on the team.	I know the members of my care team. We work together consistently, and therefore, efficiently. The relationship makes a huge difference in the way we provide care.
I have to accomplish all the tasks on my list or face the judgment of those on the next shift. This is stressful, because it compromises my ability to meet the priority needs of my patients and their families. Still, I don't want to make my peers mad.	I manage my time (my personal resource) judiciously. I have made an agreement with my patients and their families to help them meet their priorities for today. That takes precedence over unit driven routines. I know and am able to communicate the rationale for my decisions.

Old Mindset: Resource Passive (Victimized)	New Mindset: Resource Driven (Empowered)
I don't have time to orient a new staff member or deal with the questions of floats; they just drain me. I wish they would get up to speed quickly so they can hold their own and lighten the load.	I have a commitment to new staff members—sometimes as their preceptor—but always as a colleague. Each person is a valuable resource and deserves to be supported so they learn how to be successful and want to remain part of this team.
I don't have time to help my team members. If I do, I'll fall behind and not be able to complete my tasks.	I am open and willing to help my team members, and I know they will help me. It is great to know we can count on each other and that we share the common purpose of meeting the priority needs of our patients/families. It lightens the load and things get accomplished so much more quickly and easily.
I need to chart everything and tell the next caregiver all the data.	I will communicate the most critical information (patient progress, impact of interventions) to the next caregiver.
I don't need to know all the financial details. That is the manager's job. My job is to care for my patients.	I want to be informed about our financial status and knowledgeable about what I can do to contribute. Our financial health is the means to providing care to the people we *all* serve.

Critical Thinking, Creative Thinking, & Reflection

We know that health care teams are constantly being challenged to "do more with less." We are pressured by the consumer expectation of high quality within the context of declining reimbursement. The old solution has been to add more staff to do the same work. We know that simply does not work. First, the staff may not be available, and second, the addition of new staff can cause at least a temporary impact on resources. The challenge to do more with less demands creative, principled solutions which focus on making the most of what is available.

One example of a creative, principled solution is to assess the individual contributions of each team member based on the skill mix and then define ways to initiate more targeted collaboration with members of the broader interdisciplinary team. This requires changing the old mindset of having to "do it yourself" to a new mindset of deciding to let go of artificial barriers related to territory and to ask for help and consult with others. This new mindset actually helps us keep RBC in the fore-front, as it can free us to focus on the relationship between the nurse and the patient. Then, the mindset shifts from "taking time" for each patient to "being with" each patient and mutually deter-mining the aspects of care which are most impor-tant, productive, and satisfying to the patient.

The new mindset shifts from "taking time" for each patient to "being with" each patient and mutually determining the aspects of care which are most important, productive, and satisfying.

Critical thinking, creative thinking, and reflec-tion skills help care providers to examine situa-tions, to engage in intelligent prioritization and problem solving, and to determine how to trans-form ineffective ways of thinking about and doing work. Education and ongoing development in the area of critical and creative thinking help clinicians and managers manage resources daily as well as to identify and implement the necessary changes to improve resource utilization in the long term.

Sally Aldrich, Assistant Director of Methodist Alliance Hospice, Memphis, Tennessee (1998) asserts that we have short changed nurses and other clinicians by focusing on "doing" to the extreme—doing tasks, mastering technology, accomplishing procedures—and we have neglected the development of "thinking." She suggests educating people about the mental processes necessary to understand and respond to complex problems such as changing patient conditions and the implications for actions and/or adjustments by the clinical team. Without this understanding, clinicians report feeling overwhelmed by the complexity and amount of the work as well as feeling ill-equipped to think of more effective ways to accomplish it.

Critical thinking is a disciplined, cognitive process based on reasoning. The case review methodology is a familiar process of critical thinking for most clinicians. Although members of all clinical disciplines are schooled in the problem solving process, the discipline of critical thinking takes this process further into sorting complex issues into solvable problems. This certainly applies to the complex issues and questions regarding resource utilization and patient care. The following eight essential elements in critical reasoning are outlined by Dr. Richard Paul of the Center for Critical Thinking at Sonoma State University, Rohnert Park, California (1993) and can be applied to sorting out resource issues and determining solutions:

Reflection is a way for clinicians to gain knowledge and understanding from their own experience.

1. Clarifying purpose—goal

2. Identification of the problem

3. Definition of the point of view—frame of reference or mindset

4. Assimilation of information—available data, evidence

5. Presentation of concepts—theories, principles, rules

6. Working assumptions

7. Discussion of implications

8. Drawing of inferences or conclusions—checking for depth, reasonableness, and consistency.

Creative thinking focuses on the possibility of *many* right answers rather than just one. Effective problem solving includes both critical and creative thinking—they rarely stand alone, and are interdependent processes. While both kinds of thinking are vital to successful problem solving, creative thinking tends to be ignored at the college level, and resurfaces only when people are in the work world trying to find better solutions to complex and persistent problems. Robert Harris (1998), author of *Creative Problem Solving: A Step by Step Approach*, differentiates these two kinds of thinking as follows:

Critical Thinking	Creative Thinking
Analytic	Generative
Convergent	Divergent
Vertical	Lateral
Probability	Possibility
Judgment	Suspended judgment
Focused	Diffuse
Objective	Subjective
The Answer	An answer
Left brain	Right brain
Verbal	Visual
Linear	Associative
Reasoning	Novelty, richness
Yes, but	Yes, and

Harris says creativity is the *"ability to imagine or invent something new"*— to *"generate new ideas by combining, changing, or reapplying existing ideas."* Creative problem solving is what helps us to rethink the way we allocate and utilize resources, encouraging us to create a new mindset or mental model for figuring out how to do what's most important. The solutions are available; the only limitation is our existing mindset.

Reflection is a way for clinicians to gain further knowledge and understanding from their own experience. It is closely related to Aldrich's notion of case review and critical thinking. Guided reflection is a systematic cognitive process designed to help clinicians reflect on their work and to learn from their experiences in order to improve their clinical interactions. "Case conferences" are the most common example of a reflective process.

Guided reflection involves three key elements (Johns, 1993, Johns & Graham, 1994) including:

1. Using a model for structured reflection to guide the inquiry process;

2. Supervision by a colleague, perhaps the clinical manager or another clinical leader; and

3. A structured diary in which to write the significant experiences.

This approach to reflection takes discipline, leadership, encouragement, and support. Christopher Johns, the originator of guided reflection, stresses that reflection is most effective when it is coached or supervised. Supervision can be one-to-one or can be with a group of clinicians. The manager who takes on this type of clinical supervision and support, will create a dynamic culture for purposeful, conscious, fulfilling clinical practice. The supervision process includes a clarification of the model being used for reflection and identification of areas for the structured diary. By writing about and reflecting on the experience in a diary, the clinician is able to reflect on patterns over time, revealing what has emerged as significant in his or her practice. Johns (1993) and Carper (1978) have identified components of effective structured reflection, which we have adapted and outlined below. Each reflection begins with the core question: "What information do I need access to in order to learn through this experience?"

Description of the Experience: What happened? What were the contributing factors? Who was involved?

Reflection: What was I trying to achieve? Why did I intervene as I did? What were the consequences for patient first, then self, then team? How did I feel about it? How did the patient feel? How do I know?

Influencing factors: What internal factors influenced my decision-making? What external factors influenced my decision? What sources of knowledge did I use?

Reflection: How do I now feel about this experience? Could I have dealt better with the situation? What other choices did I have? What would be the consequences of these choices? What impact did my actions have? What would I do the same way next time? What would I do differently?

Learning: What did I learn from this experience? What sense do I make of this experience in light of past and future practice? How has this changed my way of knowing and practice?

Reflection is a key method for meeting the challenges of the complex and constantly changing clinical environment. While reflection may seem like a time-consuming indulgence we cannot afford, it is ultimately a time-*saver*, as it helps us keep from making the same mistake twice. Empowered clinicians who are able to critically evaluate and alter their practice find new solutions to the challenge of delivering high quality care within an environment of decreasing reimbursement and shortage of qualified staff.

Some recommended steps for strengthening managers' and clinical staff's ability to provide leadership in finding solutions include:

- Create an environment in which critical thinking and reflection are consistently modeled and applied to finding practical solutions to difficult situations.

- Provide coaching and supervision for guided reflection.

- Identify and provide education to strengthen and develop people's critical thinking and reflection skills. These may include seminars, workshops and on-line education.

Managing Financial Resources

In the late 1970s to early 1980s, health care organizations began to decentralize financial management to the unit manager level. This was a significant step in creating the conditions under which professional practice could take hold in the hospital setting. Prior to this decentralization, managers, commonly known as head nurses, had little to say about what went into the budget for their unit or how many staff would be allocated to care for their patient population. Chief executive officers, financial officers, and sometimes directors of nursing made those decisions. The decisions were based primarily on historical data and some projections of future volume. The unit managers and their staff were ill-informed and ill-equipped to influence the financial plan or to meet the objectives of the plan creatively and knowledgeably. It established a situation in which the holders of the financial purse strings made decisions which the clinicians had to carry out. This model was extremely parental and created an "us vs. them" mindset between the staff and administration.

When financial management was decentralized to the unit manager level, the unit managers became much more adept at influencing the budget and advocating for the appropriate allocation of resources. At that time, there was significant investment in the education and development of managers in understanding how to effectively manage financial resources. At the staff level, however, a majority of individuals remained distant from the financial working of their health care organizations and, in some cases, adversarial to those in control. With the ever-increasing pressure of decreased reimbursement, there was an ongoing tension between clinicians and managers. The "us vs. them" mindset found another foothold, and misperceptions and distrust about available resources and support of patient care fueled tensions.

In our new era, our new mindset must be an interdependent approach, with each individual taking ownership for financial management.

The mid 1990s became increasingly tumultuous with the advent of consultant redesign teams who were hired by organizations to institute "patient-focused care." Despite its altruistic sounding name, "patient-focused care" was really a mandate to, "find the most inexpensive way to provide care with the least expensive care provider." This created a huge backlash in the industry. Nurses left the profession and schools of nursing found it difficult to recruit new students. As a result, we are faced with a significant staffing crisis in the early years of this century.

In this new era, our mindset supports an interdependent approach, with each individual taking ownership for financial management.

Managers and clinicians jointly own responsibility, authority, and accountability for prudent and judicious management of finite resources. This mindset is grounded in a fundamental ethical principle of safeguarding and managing scarce resources so that health care is available to those who need it.

In order for managers and clinicians to share ownership for the financial management of their work unit, the following conditions must be in place:

- Administrators will assure that managers and clinicians have accurate, relevant financial information available to them in a timely manner. If that happens, the very best real time decisions can be made for resource allocation and conservation.

Effective managers educate their clinical staff, to demystify financial management.

- Managers will educate their clinical staff to demystify financial management. They will institute an efficient and effective process for gaining staff input and have user-friendly financial information available to let staff know whether they are accomplishing their financial goals.

- Clinical staff will take ownership for the financial health of the unit by personally committing to efficient use of time, staffing resources, equipment, and supplies. They will provide thoughtful input based on their understanding of what it takes to provide care and they will engage in critical thinking, creative thinking, and reflection to solve problems and find solutions. This includes taking ownership for redesigning work to efficiently achieve desired outcomes.

- Flexible parameters for decision-making will be identified so that people can work creatively in meeting patient requirements and achieving targeted outcomes.

- Managers take the primary responsibility for procuring resources for their unit. This includes financial resources, staffing, materials, and supplies. Communication and problem solving systems issues are core.

Skill Mix

Over the years, skill mix issues have bedeviled nursing service departments and hospitals. Two elements determine the appropriate mix of staff and the distribution of workload. One is the relationship between acuity and skill mix, and the other is the role of the RN when Professional Nursing is delivered.

If administrators and managers have little confidence in the competence of the nursing staff, the role of the RN will be limited in scope of responsibility, and clinical judgment functions will be severely restricted or not expected at all. Lack of clarity about the essence of Professional Nursing Practice, the role for which only RNs are qualified by license, often creates skill mix and delivery system confusion, and general misunderstanding of *who* is to be doing *what*. When the role of the RN is expressed primarily in terms of task assignment and complexity, role differentiation will be confusing. However, when the role of the RN is developed based on the principles and scope of practice as outlined in the Professional Nursing Practice chapter, role differentiation between RNs and LPN/LVNs is clear.

Task-based assignments truncate whole-patient consciousness.

It is established that in this society, RNs have the license to exercise independent judgment in the delivery of nursing care. This means they have the right to determine the amount, degree, and kind of nursing care to be delivered to a particular patient based on a professional assessment, standards of practice, and established medical protocols. When this function is clearly spelled out in the role description and the means to accomplish it are implemented in the day-to-day operations of the unit, appropriate roles for assistive personnel using good principles of delegation follow fairly naturally. When these principles are applied, staff report that competent LPNs/LVNs are able to effectively perform 65-75% of the nursing work, and CNAs are able to perform 35-65%.

In RBC, patients are always assigned to the registered nurse (as opposed to a nurse of any other licensure). Assistive personnel (i.e. licensed practical nurses, nursing assistants, technicians) are then assigned to the registered nurse. Because effective delegation is essential for reducing staffing stress, if RNs are unwilling or unable to delegate to the full capacity of the assistive staff members capability, the result is frustration for everyone involved. Effective delegation occurs when the RN understands his or her own scope of practice and trusts the competence of the assistive staff on the team. The best way to achieve this trust is through an on-going relationship between a specific RN and a specific assistant or group of assistants over time. Therefore, partnering the RN and assistive personnel is the best way to achieve a high level of effective delegation. Through ongoing relationships, trust is built and work productivity is significantly enhanced.

A logical and financially viable assessment of skill mix is one based on a determination of the volume of work at various levels of complexity. To determine the appropriate skill levels required for any given shift, we look for a match between the complexity of care and the technical competence and clinical judgment of the available staff. The actual staffing plan reflects the volume of work at various skill levels throughout the entire twenty-four hour shift, seven days a week. Using any other basis for determining skill mix (which have historically run from cost cutting as a top priority to "We've always done it this way") will nearly always result in an unmanageable unit and either under- or over-utilization of resources.

Common sense and logic, along with good consensus-based, data driven decision-making provide the basis for a solid and useful scheduling system.

Determining the correct skill mix based on acuity is an administrative decision based on information acquired from the staff of each unit regarding the complexity of work. The work complexity is assessed based on the population of patients and families served and the required knowledge and skills of the care team as well as the volume of work.

Once the skill mix has been determined and the staffing plan established, scheduling and assignments follow. Common sense and logic, along with good consensus-based, data driven decision-making will provide the basis for a solid and useful scheduling system.

Scheduling System

The unit schedule determines a great deal about the way in which patient care is delivered as it determines who will deliver care on any given day. It ultimately determines what combination of skills will be available and whether continuity of nurse-patient relationships is feasible. In essence, the unit schedule is a reflection of the values and beliefs of the unit staff and manager as well as the overall organization.

There are several common approaches to creating a unit schedule, using both computer-based and paper-and-pencil-based technology. By default, many units throughout the country use the 'request' method of scheduling. This simply means that staff members request either days off or days on, and the scheduler (the nurse manager or a designee) fills in the blanks left after requests are filled. While this method is usually fairly acceptable to the staff, it often leaves gaping holes to be filled, results in "multiple shift gymnastics" (unless you are in a part of the country where straight shifts are the norm), and nearly always exacerbates the power struggles that so often surface around scheduling. Unfortunately, the "request" method of scheduling does not support resource driven decision-making or Relationship-Based Care.

There are other scheduling methods that are more systematic and rational. These methods carefully build on an organization's goals for delivering care and are supported by clearly defined parameters and policies. For example, you could design a scheduling system that matches staff members' consecutive days worked with the average length of stay for the unit's patient population. This integrates the value of continuity of care with the schedule design. Two common scheduling methods that support RBC are *self-scheduling* and *cyclical staffing*. Both require sophisticated planning and development.

Self-scheduling works very well when the parameters have been carefully developed and the policies are administered consistently. In this method, staff members "sign up" for their days of work within the framework of the established parameters and individual hospital/unit scheduling policies. In this case, the role of the manager is to define the parameters, establish the policies, and approve each schedule. The staff members are responsible for the critical thinking and creative problem solving often required to meet the parameters and policies.

Cyclical schedules require careful planning and are based on norms, values, and expectations that units establish to support the priorities and vision of the overall organization. Cyclical schedules are established so that staff members have the same schedule pattern throughout the year. The beauty of this system is that staff members have the opportunity to plan their lives months in advance.

Getting staff to accept new scheduling practices is one of the most challenging of all management endeavors, as scheduling has such direct impact on the individual's personal life. For this reason, whenever staffing practices are changed, a great deal of staff input is important. Changes in staffing practice are most widely accepted by all those affected when those implementing the changes educate staff as to how the new system is in better alignment with the values and principles of the organization than the old one was.

Both self-scheduling and cyclical scheduling support the principles of RBC by supporting continuity of care in the nurse-patient relationship, which improves the patient/family perception of their care while increasing productivity. Clinical staff that have participated in CHCM Work Complexity Assessments indicate that they perceive the volume of work to be 25% less when caring for the same patient more than two days in a row. In addition, they perceive an additional 15-25% gain in productivity when working with the same trusted assistive person.

Achieving continuity of care is complex, especially with multiple lengths of shifts and varying skill mixes existing within a 24-hour period. Nevertheless, when schedulers keep the principles

No matter what method of schedule building is used, certain common-sense principles are essential. The first and foremost principle is that continuity of care is of maximum benefit to both patients and nurses.

of Relationship-Based Care in mind when making daily care assignments, it is possible to achieve a fairly high degree of continuity of care during so-called 'normal' staffing periods.

When Primary Nursing is chosen as the care delivery method, implementation includes establishing assignment practices whereby a priority is placed on the Primary Nurse being assigned to his or her patients consistently. When multiple shift lengths are in play (8-10-12 hour shifts), proactive decisions are made about how assignments will be handled when the Primary Nurse arrives for a shift in the middle of another nurse's shift. With an RBC system in place, these decisions will always be based on what best supports the patient's continuity of care.

With this patient-first mindset, it will also be the best decision for the nurses.

It is important to note that although the 8-10-12 hour shift combination offers greater flexibility for staff members, our finding through the Work Complexity Assessment is that multiple shift lengths result in more work in the areas of documentation and change of shift report, and reduce continuity of relationships and subsequent efficiencies in care.

Changing the Nursing Mindset

Old ways of thinking keep nurses trapped in a scarcity mindset. By moving into new ways of thinking about resource allocation and utilization, nurses can experience greater personal and professional empowerment and make a significant difference in the effective distribution of resources for the care of their patients.

Four key mindset changes are:

1. The RN accepts responsibility for deciding how the resource of his or her own time will be spent as he or she cares for assigned patients and families. This acceptance of responsibility can result in some degree of freedom from the sense that everyone else is determining how a nurse's time is spent. In working with assistive staff, it helps if the RN is conscious of the total number of care provider hours that he or she is responsible for distributing in a given shift, for an assigned group of patients. (For example, an RN and an LPN/LVN or nursing assistant working together on an assignment means there are 16 care provider hours available during an 8-hour shift.) With the benefit of this awareness, nurses make better informed decisions about which aspects of care to delegate to support staff.

Knowledge of the support staff members' competency makes effective delegation possible.

Knowledge of the support staff members' competency makes effective delegation possible. This cannot be emphasized strongly enough. The best way to avoid task-based delegation decisions like, "you do all the baths; I'll do all the meds," is to have support staff who are qualified to do up to 75% by volume of the work of the registered nurse. When this is the level of competence of the support staff—and when the RN is aware that this is their level of competence—the RN can make delegation decisions based on a true picture of his or her available staff resources. This is the best way to avoid task-based assignments, which always truncate whole-patient consciousness.

2. **Nurses accept that nursing work is never done until the patient leaves the unit.** As long as a person is a patient on a unit or a client in a clinic, there is nursing work to be done for that person. No one has control over the amount of work called for by a particular set of patients at any point in time. The work of nurses is determined by two factors—doctor's orders and patient acuity. Nurses will never have the authority to tell a physician he cannot order a particular treatment for a patient because the current workload is already appropriate for the amount of staff available. Likewise, we can never tell patients they must maintain their current acuity level as we have exactly the right amount of staff for the amount of work their current acuity requires. Nurses are happier and more productive when they surrender all resistance to the fact that their workload is subject to forces over which they do not now and never will have control. That is the nature of hospital nursing. There is no control over the volume of work, and it is never done.

3. **When the workload exceeds the level of staffing, additional resources may not be the best answer.** The equation "more work = more staff" is tightly held by nurses throughout the country, with the result being that when additional resources are not available, nurses feel undervalued and frustrated. Of course, sustained workload that exceeds staffing is best addressed at the level of resource reallocation (more staffing on that unit). However, the notion that more work than time available always justifies additional

staffing is a myth. It is often this very expectation that causes nurses' frustration and lack of clarity about the RN's clinical judgment authority. When the RN's role is clear regarding his or her authority to determine the amount, degree, and kind of care patients will receive, it is also clear that when there is more work to do than time available, the RN has the responsibility, authority, and accountability to decide what *not* to do.

When there is more work to do than time available, the RN has the responsibility, authority, and accountability to decide what not to do.

4. **Resource allocation decisions proceed from an awareness and understanding of the patients' most urgent needs.** When prioritizing work in excess of staffing, the experienced RN will take many variables into account. An early key step in assessing the variables is to talk with the patient and family. The best way to do this is in a brief beginning-of-shift discussion with patients and families to determine what care is most important to them during the up-coming shift. Armed with this insight, an experienced RN will be able to make the best decisions about what to do and what *not* to do when there is more work than time available. When decisions are made based on what is right for patients, those decisions are easily supported.

Nursing is a twenty-four-hours-a-day, seven-days-a-week operation. We deal with people. It would be very nice if there was some way things could ease up so we weren't always under pressure, but it isn't going to happen. The best we can do is to have effective, well-defined systems in place to deal with whatever variables come our way. In fact, the ever-changing nature of nursing is part of what drives us to create the very best systems feasible to maximize continuity of care and appropriate division of work and responsibilities, while promoting clear responsibility and authority for decision-making within the nursing care team.

Summary of Key Concepts

- Resource driven practice means that clinical staff and managers share responsibility for the resources required to provide quality patient care.

- Our new mindset asks us to think about care as being "resource driven" rather than "needs driven."

- Shifting to a new mindset requires a shift in culture and unit norms as well as a new commitment from each clinician and manager.

- Critical thinking, creative thinking, and reflection skills facilitate the ability to effectively examine situations, to engage in intelligent prioritization and problem solving, and to determine how to transform ineffective ways of thinking about and doing work.

- We can refine and nurture nurses' problem solving skills and teach them how to apply those skills to sorting complex issues and finding resolutions.

- Effective resource allocation and financial management requires the commitment of administrators, managers, and unit staff.

- Managers support the clinical staff's understanding and commitment to resource driven practice by providing education and timely financial information.

- Clinical staff takes ownership for the financial health of the unit by taking responsibility for understanding the financial information and by efficient use of their time, staff resources, equipment, and supplies.

- There are two scheduling approaches that are rational and systematic enough to support RBC. They are self-scheduling and cyclical scheduling.

- Continuity of care promotes increased productivity and patient safety.

- Resource decisions are best made by applying the principle of common sense: determine what is best for the patient. This includes assessing what must be done and what can be left undone.

- Continuity of daily assignments and effective delegation within carefully planned and well-executed staff scheduling systems provide the foundation for resource driven practice.

- In what ways do our current skill mix, staffing, and scheduling practices meet our patient needs within the context of available resources?

- How do we plan our annual budgets? How is the staff involved? What is the manager's role?

- What are our values and beliefs about staffing and scheduling? What consider-

**Questions
for Self-
Assessment**

ation do we give patients when staffing? What consideration do we give staff?

- What is the average length of stay for patients on our units? What do we know about the cycles, patterns, and trends of patient admissions and transfers onto our unit?

- How are decisions made for patient care assignments? What is most important to us? What is least important? What do we desire to continue doing? What do we desire to change?

- Are the roles and responsibilities of each member of the care team clearly defined?

- What do we believe about delegation? What is working currently? What do we desire to change?

- What is our current mindset about resource allocation and utilization? What do we want to build on? What do we want to change?

- What will it take for administration, managers, and staff to work together to most effectively manage resources in the best interests of patients?

- What can I do to make the most of available resources?

- How can I advocate for resources on behalf of patients?

- How do staff reflect on their practice? Are multidisciplinary clinical caring conferences held to learn and share what made a difference for the patient and family?

Allina Hospitals and Clinics
Minneapolis/St. Paul, Minnesota

A Moment of Excellence: Allina Hospitals and Clinics

I have been the manager of OB Homecare at Allina Hospitals and Clinics since 1984. From the beginning, I have involved staff members in decisions affecting resource utilization. Prior to 1984, we had all worked in traditional inpatient units. Homecare was a new service, and I knew it was important to set a standard of mutual ownership for all aspects of our service from the very beginning. I also knew that in order for our service to survive and thrive, we needed to share ownership in both the quality of our care for patients and the financial health of our department.

After 20 years, the principle of shared ownership continues, along with the most important rule for how I lead daily—the Golden Rule—"Do unto others as you would have others do unto you." I believe that if a leader treats others like he or she would like to be treated, and communicates the intent to do so, then the manager-staff relationship becomes what it is intended to be—a truly collegial relationship. We are all interdependent. I expect effective professional nursing and non-clinical staff to do their best and to provide leadership for patient care and service, and they expect me to be an effective manager and to do my best to create a positive environment for care.

Several years ago I led the merger of two homecare programs. The purpose for the merger was twofold. We wanted to expand our breadth and depth of service to patients in the area, and we wanted to gain efficiencies that would help us more effectively utilize resources. Our merger was a textbook example of resource driven decision-making. We knew what we wanted to accomplish and we knew that we could make the most of our available resources by merging the two departments.

Here's a brief outline of the steps we took to merge the programs:

- The senior executive team asked me to determine the risks and benefits of merging the two programs, expected outcomes, and my recommendations on whether to merge or remain separate. I worked with the assistants from both programs to pull both quality and financial data together.

- We shared an overview of this data with staff members from both programs so both staffs knew the question of whether to merge the programs had been raised as well as what we were doing to address it. Their insights regarding the data were solicited and helped us in our preparation for the executive team. This process took several months and I maintained ongoing communication with the staff to provide them with updates as often as possible.

- Once the decision to merge was made by the senior leadership of the two organizations, the assistants from both programs and I met to make the plans for the next steps and to design the structure of the merged organization. We also had one union involved and had meetings with the union during this process. We openly shared our findings including the benefits to patients and staff and to the greater financial viability of our service.

- We then met with each of the original staffs separately and gave them the chance to again review the data and have their questions answered. They were also all given the chance to choose not to merge with the new program and to move to different jobs within our organization. All staff members chose to become staff members in the newly merged program.

- We had staff members from each unit help plan for the merger and the new program. We had joint meetings to discuss merger issues and how patient care was to transition during this time. Staff members provided valuable input to all aspects of the transition.

- Once the merger happened, it was expected that both teams be respectful of each other's experience and feelings and to resolve problems in the newly merged program together. This resulted in a successful merger with the result of a stronger team.

I have successfully managed the challenges of merging two programs, streamlining the use of existing resources, growing the programs, and maintaining high standards of productivity. I hold a core value that knowledge is power and believe that:

- People function best when they know and understand how their work fits into the big picture.

- Staff members feel shared ownership in the success of the program when they have input into setting strategic goals for the department and receive reports on their progress toward those goals.

- Staff members must understand financial goals, costs of conducting the business, and productivity indicators. When they are given a chance to understand the financial picture, have input into the productivity targets, and their opinions are sought and valued regarding ongoing resource utilization, they know how to contribute and make the best use of resources.

A key factor in our successful merger was skillful resource management. Staff took ownership for the stewardship of their time and managed their own productivity and I provided them with ongoing information and feedback.

- About five years ago, two other home care programs similar to ours closed in our community. At the time of their closing, I called the leaders of those programs to find out why they were closing and shared my findings with the staff. The discussion itself proved tremendously valuable to us. We identified the problems and failures of the closing programs that were common to us, and I asked for staff volunteers to help me look at these common issues and to come up with solutions for our program to overcome them.

- One main issue was the amount of time each home visit required. Our staff looked at how to set mutual goals with the patients and families for their home visits so the time was used to more efficiently meet their needs and goals. Additionally, we identified changes in documentation which significantly streamlined the process. These changes decreased the time spent on both the visit and follow up. The goal setting element helped care providers improve the quality of time spent with the patient and family, while improving the use of the invaluable resource of their own time as well.

- We collected data on the various types of patients' home visits and the amount of time they required. We divided patients into three types and then staff assisted with determining daily productivity based upon the types of patients the nurse was seeing each day. This gave us a staffing tool to help us structure productivity.

- Based on this mutually determined pro-ductivity process, we were able to increase the number of visits per day for some nurses without decreasing our patient satisfaction or quality outcomes.

For all of the nuts-and-bolts practicality of resource driven practice, I believe it still leaves room for a "people first" approach. Like any change, the implementation of resource driven practice has the best chance of success if it is presented in a way that inspires a commitment to a common purpose. The patient comes first, and the way we manage our resources determines how we provide care.

The merger of our two programs, like so many examples of changes that support resource driven care, helped refine our infrastructure to better support our purpose.

By establishing a clear and efficient mechanism for ongoing communication, problem-solving, and conflict resolution, we ultimately support professional practice as well. Throughout the merger, we made communication a high priority, educating all staff members throughout all steps of the process, sharing information and promoting a culture of continuous learning.

Finally, we shared evidence of our progress. We continue to regularly provide data that tracks how we are achieving our purpose. Our merger was, and continues to be, a great success. We have much to celebrate.

Nancy Dahlberg-Reiners, MS, RN, is a Patient Care Manager with the OB Homecare program, Allina Hospitals and Clinics, which serves patients in the Greater Minneapolis/St. Paul Metropolitan Area, Minnesota.

SEVEN
Outcomes Measurement

Leah Kinnaird and Sharon Dingman

"In attempting to arrive at the truth, I have applied everywhere for information, but in scarcely an instance have I been able to obtain hospital records fit for any purpose of comparison. If they could be obtained they would enable us to decide many other questions besides the one alluded to. They would show the subscribers how their money was being spent, what good was really being done with it, or whether the money was not doing mischief rather than good."

—*Florence Nightingale, 1860*

Overview

We know in our hearts that Relationship-Based Care (RBC) has a positive impact on outcomes; the challenge is to create a meaningful representation of that reality on paper. Our purpose for this chapter is to present a simple, practical process for collecting and measuring outcomes to elevate standards and enhance the value of Relationship-Based Care in your organization. We'll address practical processes to collect, analyze, and report valid, reliable data so that all members of the organization trust it, own it, and become willing to refine their practice based on its findings.

We measure many things in health care; however, the data we collect may not always be useful. A basic premise of effective outcomes measurement is that data need not only be meaningful, but also to be motivating for leaders and practitioners to improve the way they work. Consider how reports can age, sometimes arriving to end-users after they are no longer relevant. Sometimes reports have little effect even when they are timely. When the data indicate that what's being measured is functioning well, leaders can become complacent. On the other hand, when the data are undesirable, some may become defensive or make excuses such as, "It was a really bad month all around" or "There must be something wrong with the numbers." To be truly motivating, data and measurement processes must be seen as trustworthy, tangible, and useful—relevant from the point of care to the boardroom.

Health care organizations are data-rich environments with electronic databanks and off-site warehousing of volumes of documents to deal with the exponential growth of their information systems. In the world of health care, enormous attention is being given to how information is collected and used. As Tim Porter-O'Grady states, *"The information infrastructure is becoming the new architecture for health care. The system will build its future around the construction of the information system and the infrastructure necessary to sustain it and the work of health care"* (1999). In spite of the availability of data and information, measuring outcomes can be a complex, "low-luster," and, at times, painful undertaking for an organization.

In this chapter, the development of a meaningful outcomes measurement system is framed in the I_2E_2 conceptualization of *Inspiring* both leaders and staff, creating the *Infrastructure* for effective outcomes measurement, *Educating* all involved, and identifying and evaluating *Evidence* of progress through outcomes measurement.

In the *Inspiration* section you will learn how measuring outcomes related to Relationship-Based Care helps to inspire care givers and organizational leaders. The outcomes measurement process begins with articulating the vision of the organization and the uniqueness of the work areas for which measurement data are collected. The vision for care delivery serves as a springboard for the process and keeps it aligned with the organization's mission. You will also see that further inspiration comes from defining— *with the input of those who will be using the data*—the indicators by which outcomes will be measured. We will also introduce a practical tool—the Generic Outcomes Grid—for defining and collecting clinical, financial, and/or satisfaction information. The grid serves as a tool for selecting indicators recognized by the ANCC Magnet Recognition Program™, the National Center for Nursing Quality (NCNQ), National Quality Forum, and The Joint Commission.

The *Infrastructure* section challenges readers to assess their current systems and processes for collecting, analyzing, and reporting. Like any other element of care giving, outcomes measurement requires an infrastructure of well-defined responsibility, authority, and accountability. The report format is an aspect of the infrastructure that must be determined upfront, rather than after the data are collected.

The *Education* section includes a discussion of "numerators and denominators," as well as how to evaluate the validity and reliability of the instruments used to collect data. While it is obvious that data managers and administrators must have a clear picture of what data they are tracking and how well those data correlate to what they ultimately want to measure, the *perception* of the validity and reliability of the outcomes measurement process by everyone in the organization will affect its ability to stimulate change. The education section also includes the notion of using outcomes data to determine what changes to make to improve patient/family care and service.

In the *Evaluation* section, we look at how our findings might best influence our practice. By engaging staff at all levels in the organization in tracking and trending *data they trust,* we see increased investment by those closest to the point of care, reducing error potential and improving care and service. For this reason, the most enjoyable aspect of evaluation is celebrating the improvements. We believe that every story of even the smallest improvement is cause for celebration. Celebration enhances the likelihood of doing more of what is working well.

Inspiration

Many people enter health care professions for the expressed purpose of helping others. In describing the change in nursing practice that has resulted from the decreased length of stay and the increase in patient acuity, an experienced nurse lamented the loss of reward that comes from having a "two-way" relationship with the patient:

> ...there isn't time to give a piece of yourself anymore...It's a one-way relationship now. It used to be a give and take. You'd sit on the bed with a ninety-year-old man and say, 'So what did you do to live so long. What's your secret?' I don't have time to do that anymore (Weinberg, 2003).

The shortened stay has not only reduced time nurses see patients; it has also created a situation in which patients leave hospitals sicker, leaving the nurse to wonder if the family can manage and how the patient will fare. Unless they can see the value of their work (the outcomes of their practice), individuals can question why they work so hard and may become more focused on simply carrying out the tasks rather than establishing relationships. Once task-based, rather than relationship-based work permeates the culture, those new to the staff are socialized to do the same, perpetuating the demise of a therapeutic relationship with *"no referent for a high-quality care"* (Weinberg, 2003). Clearly, we need data that will test the quality of care in environments that provide Relationship-Based Care. If the indicators that are measured support task-based, assembly-line work, one might reasonably predict that error rates will continue to increase, as will the nursing shortage.

We believe that people at all levels of the organization can benefit from inspiration. Leadership must be inspired to seek ways to measure the degree to which Relationship-Based Care is measured. The link between Relationship-Based Care and clinical outcomes must be clearly established in the measurement process. Staff need to be inspired to change the way they work so they can confidently develop and deliver Relationship-Based Care. A healthy dose of inspiration is required to shift from a task-based to a relationship-based practice.

Clearly, we need data that will test the quality of care in environments that provide Relationship-Based Care.

Articulating the Vision of Relationship-Based Care

If the vision for the organization is that care will be delivered in accordance with the principles of RBC, what RBC *is* and is *not* must be clearly defined at the outset. The definition must be both narrative, including accounts of RBC successes, and analytical, including the measurable improvements in clinical, financial, and or service outcomes that come with the implementation of a Relationship-Based Care model. It is the analytical aspect of RBC implementation that we address in this chapter.

The foundation of an effective data measurement system is based on the question, "What are we really trying to achieve?" If the answer for your organization is, "We want Relationship-Based Care," then the next question to ask is "What will

Relationship-Based Care 'look like' in our organization?" Once we have a clear vision of what RBC will look like, we can choose to measure data that pertains to exactly what it is we wish to see happen in the organization. For example, if an organization's vision of RBC includes nurses interacting for a set amount of time with patients upon admission, then we'll choose indicators like "number of minutes nurses spend interacting with patients upon admission," as well as "Patient/family perception of the admissions experience."

It may be necessary to ask, "What will Relationship-Based Care 'look like' in our organization?" over and over until individuals can truly grasp RBC, avoiding the rush to indicator selection until a deeper understanding of RBC is established.

For instance, RBC involves both the words *relationship* and *care*. Jean Watson (2002) indicates that caring-based models positively affect costs and outcomes as well as improve care environments for practitioners and patients alike. The measurement of those models is designed in response to the questions: "How can we measure caring and its relationship to patient outcomes?" "What are the indicators of quality caring?" and "How can we measure the subtlest or most common elements of caring—those that are often taken for granted or dismissed?" The outcomes we deem desirable for RBC can be measured with indicators taken directly from patient and family perceptions; the indicators themselves can validate caring in everyday practice. Survey tools exist with data points that represent the real experience of patients and families. In fact, some of our most inspiring data have come from our measurement of patient satisfaction.

Relationship can be measured from the perspective of the patient and family, from the nurse, and from the manager. Most organizations use patient satisfaction surveys to measure the patient's and family's perception of the relationship. Questions on such surveys include indicators such as: care providers communicate effectively, treat me as a person, spend the right amount of time with me, answer my questions, keep me informed, calm my fears, answer my call light, and treat me with respect. The leader may wish to know more about the extent to which a therapeutic relationship has been established between the nurse and patient and family, and may ask a similar set of questions to a sample of patients on a routine basis or determine staff perceptions through another measurement tool.

John Nelson (2001) has developed a psychometrically tested tool for evaluating the role of the professional nurse—part of what he refers to as the *Professional Nurse Index* (PNI). By posing questions to staff nurses, he measures the degree to which nurses have established relationships with patients and families, the extent to which nurses build trust with patients and families, and the degree to which the nurse develops and facilitates a plan of care for the period of time the patient is on the unit. Questions like these address Relationship-Based Care specifically, and can serve as indicators of the RBC environment for practice, while supporting the vision for providing care that incorporates a therapeutic relationship between nurses and patients/families.

Defining the Indicators

Generally speaking, indicators are reference points that add meaning to experience. Let's say we want to measure the quality of a summer day. Some of the indicators we might use are temperature, humidity, and total number of sunny daylight hours. We would measure these three indicators with measurement tools including a thermometer, a humidity gage, and observation. To make meaning of our measurements we'd compare how our indicators change—what their averages are over a period of time, perhaps even how they are perceived by the people who experience them. Once all of our data are collected, measured, and compared, we would draw conclusions about our findings.

Health care indicators work the same way. They serve as reference points to measure a wide variety of situations. Categorizing indicators helps us to sort whether an indicator measures a true outcome or something that is *related* to the outcome. In 1966, Avedis Donabedian developed three categories of health care indicators that have been widely used ever since in healthcare outcomes measurement (Millenson, 1997). Donabedian's three categories were used to group nursing quality indicators in the 1995 *Nursing Report Card for Acute Care:*

1. **Structure of Care Indicators**—these measure staffing patterns including ratio of registered nurses to total nursing staff, registered nurse staff qualifications, ratio of total nursing staff to patients, total nursing care hours provided per patient, staff continuity, registered nurse overtime, and nurse staff injury rate.

2. **Process of Care Indicators**—These measure how care is delivered and may provide information on nurse satisfaction, assessment and implementation of patient care requirements, pain management, maintenance of skin integrity, patient education, discharge planning, assurance of patient safety, and responsiveness to unplanned patient care needs.

3. **Outcome Indicators**—these measure how patients and their conditions are affected by their interaction with nursing staff and include mortality rate, length of stay, adverse incidents, complications, patient/

family satisfaction with nursing care, and adherence to discharge plan (Adapted from ANA, 2004).

These categorizations and descriptions have been a part of the ongoing identification of nursing-sensitive indicators. Nursing-Sensitive Quality Indicators are defined in *Nursing Facts* as *"those indicators that capture care or its outcomes most affected by nursing care"* (American Nurses Association, 2004). Since the above-mentioned indicators were categorized, they continue to be discussed and refined. In fact, all applicants to the Magnet Recognition Program™ must now collect data and participate in a national database such as the National Center for Nursing Quality (NCNQ) database (ANCC, 2003). Organizations applying for Magnet status must submit unit-level data for the following:

1. Patient/resident/client falls;

2. Pressure ulcers;

3. Patient/resident/client satisfaction (with overall nursing care, nursing care, patient/resident/client education and pain management);

4. Nursing staff satisfaction;

5. Skill mix of RN, LPN/LVN and unlicensed staff; and

6. Nursing care hours per patient/res-ident/ client day (ANCC, 2003, p. 20).

The Magnet process also requires that applicants select additional indicators such as "length of stay" and "nursing-sensitive clinical outcomes." The work of Linda Aiken, PhD, RN, and her colleagues, whose studies are listed in the Magnet manual (ANCC, 2003, pp. 14-15) indicates that hospitals that have attained Magnet status have characteristics that lead to improved patient outcomes and better circumstances for nursing staff, including higher levels of autonomy and control over practice.

On January 30, 2004, the National Quality Forum (NQF) released a statement on nursing-sensitive performance measures with this statement from Kenneth Kizer, M.D., President and CEO of the NQF. *"These measures recognize the importance of nursing in achieving positive healthcare outcomes... The role of nursing hasn't historically received the attention it deserves as a contributor to the quality of care" (Kizer, 2004)* The list of fifteen NQF indicators include adverse incidents, restraint prevalence, smoking cessation counseling, nurse staffing indicators, and voluntary turnover.

Other regulatory and professional organizations are creating requirements for use of indicators that are in some way related to RBC. The Joint Commission (2004) requires that *"hospitals use data on clinical service screening indicators in combination with human resource screening indicators to assess staffing effectiveness"*. The step of correlating indicators recognizes that structure, process, and outcome indicators are all related. Structure and process indicators that can be *correlated* with outcome indicators will describe RBC.

Selection of indicators brings up again the question of responsibility, authority, and accountability for process, practice, and results. In outcomes measurement, accountability rises all the way to the board level, but the board cannot reasonably take responsibility for carrying out the work, and instead must pursue evidence that the work is being carried out in a way that supports the vision of the organization. The organizational leaders may feel compelled to single-handedly establish the plan, the goal, and the methods for outcomes measurement, overlooking that their task is to provide the direction, not the details. The closer the accountability for outcomes—and specifically, indicator selection—can be moved to the point of care, the more effective the outcomes measurement plan will be. Therefore, the design of the process (from creating a vision through selecting indicators, to review of the data—including evidence of the indicators in real-life practice) belongs in the hands of those who provide care. Mutual accountability for a common outcome is the primary factor that pulls a team of people together to exceed their own expectations and those of the people they serve. If RBC is to be successful, the team at the point of care will always have an active role in designing the process for measuring outcomes.

The Generic Outcomes Grid

We have found that the use of a Generic Outcomes Grid helps the successful implementation and maintenance of an RBC system because it aids our understanding of the meaning of indicators and their link to the practice of the unit. The grid serves as a simple tool to engage a team of *individuals who are close to the work* to establish what the group wants to measure as well as how and from where they will collect the data. Perhaps most importantly, the grid helps team members relate their work to the vision of the organization.

Our approach is to teach the leader of a work group how to use the grid before involving team members. The grid can be used throughout the organization, beginning with the executive level deciding how they want to measure the vision they have for the organization. All departments, both clinical and non-clinical, can use the grid to determine what they want to measure.

For example, executives who are interested in improving morale or being the "employer of choice" want to see a low voluntary turnover rate out of the organization; therefore, they may select turnover as an indicator to track over a period of time. Turnover has been talked about, benchmarked, and reported at length; however, the definition of turnover varies. ASHHRA (the human resources affiliate of the American Hospital Association) in their 2004 survey defined voluntary turnover *as "... all employees who left voluntarily EXCEPT those who retired or were transferred to other locations within the organization"* (Hosler, 2003).

Voluntary turnover out of the organization also attracts attention because of the nursing shortage and difficulty in filling nurse vacancies. The boardroom interest in turnover may be related to both morale and replacement costs. While voluntary turnover from the organization may be low, staff providing patient care may discount turnover data because it may not reflect their experience. *All turnover* off a nursing unit (voluntary or not) is data of interest to the nursing staff. High turnover off the unit, regardless of the reason, creates more work for the remaining staff and ultimately reduces time that could be spent creating relationships with patients and families.

There is no magic to using the grid; it is simply a chart that focuses users on the key elements related to an indicator. It is a tool for individuals or groups to determine what they want to achieve and how they want to measure those achievements. When regulatory bodies, professional groups, or the organization have prescribed a certain indicator be measured, it helps to fill in the columns of the grid in order to make sure the pre-selected indicator is fully understood and can be applied in the situation. Response to using the grid at the unit level has been encouraging, as managers and staff members find it simple to use and immediately meaningful. The grid can serve as a reference tool when questions are raised about the relevance of indicators.

Generic Outcomes Grid

What to collect		Source of data and who will collect			How to evaluate and trend/track			Celebration
Indicator	Definition	Method	Source	Report Format	Numerator Denominator	Validity Reliability	Target	
RN turnover off the unit.	Indicator is defined as all RN turnover (voluntary and otherwise) whereby staff leave the unit or even reduce their work agreement to the extent that they are replaced (change of status). This includes resignations, terminations, retirements, and change of status to per diem.	Manual collection until electronic database is available.	Unit employment records retained by the unit manager.	Quarterly report to director and wall chart in staff lounge.	The numerator is the total # of separations from unit of full-time and part-time RNs during the quarter—over the denominator, total # of full-time and part-time RNs at beginning of the quarter. (Note: this is # of RNs, not FTEs)	Validity: Match data with personnel records. Review data with staff to determine their perception of accuracy. Reliability: Have the nurse manager and additional person collect data independently and compare results periodically.	Set a reasonable target, driven by current realities. Target to be determined after two quarters of data collection. Track data until the target is stable and sustained.	Link the data to the real meaning and value of work, so that staff not only can celebrate the changes on paper, but can also be excited about what they know are real changes in practice. Do this in small ways daily, and in larger gatherings periodically.

Using the grid, a team of staff from the nursing unit can discuss what turnover off the unit means and how they and RBC are potentially impacted by turnover. Arriving at a meaningful definition of the indicator requires some research. If an indicator is one for which comparisons are going to be made outside the organization, definitions may be available from the outcomes literature and government/professional organizations that are nationally and (if possible) internationally recognized. Only when indicators are defined in standardized ways can data be aggregated and information obtained that has accuracy for benchmarking.

Check the definition of your indicators against the following graphic to determine whether your definition will have meaning beyond a specific unit or geographical region.

International Comparison Indicators
National Comparison Indicators
State/Province Comparison Indicators
Organization Indicators
Unit-level Indicators
Individual Indicators

While it is not essential that every indicator be universally defined, it is essential to be aware of how your definitions compare to the definitions of the comparison data. If you intend to use your data in comparisons beyond your own organization, we recommend defining your indicators in as close alignment as possible with national and international definitions—while remaining careful not to sacrifice your organization's commitment to measuring indicators that relate as directly as possible to RBC.

Infrastructure

The second aspect of the outcomes measurement plan is to create an infrastructure that can be sustained over changes in leadership and that has the flexibility to shift with the changing needs of the organization. Infrastructure exists at the patient, unit, departmental, and organizational levels of operation. Outcomes measurement infrastructure addresses the question: "What are your sources of data and who will collect them?" The report format must be considered early in the planning stages in order to assure that the data are provided in a meaningful way.

Establishing and Sustaining the Outcomes Measurement Process

To illustrate the infrastructure of an outcomes measurement process, we will use the example of an outcomes measurement plan for a patient care unit. In this case, the leader or manager first works with a subset of the unit team to determine the vision they have for carrying out the unique mission of their unit. One of the first steps to undertake is for the group to describe the uniqueness of their unit, including, but not limited to their patient population, the unit's layout, the relationships with other providers, and their resources. The Nursing Management Minimum Data Set, NMMDS© (Huber & Delaney, 1999) is a tool that organizes 17 core data variables into three categories:

1. **Environmental data elements**–including characteristics of the patient population, capacity, and volume.

2. **Nurse resource data elements**–including leader and staff characteristics.

3. **Financial resource data elements**– including budget and/or payor type.

Collecting a full NMMDS© (or "data set") provides a baseline against which the manager, staff, and interested parties can measure changes that occur in the unit. This information is recorded on a document or electronically to be sustained through changes in leadership. By collecting the NMMDS©, the staff on the unit see that they are being recognized for what is unique about their unit, so that they can compare their own practice and performance over time rather than being compared with dissimilar units.

Let's use the example of patient satisfaction as an outcome that has had sustainability over the past decade. Virtually all health care organizations collect patient satisfaction data as a set of scaled responses, and patient satisfaction with nursing care is recognized as a nursing-sensitive indicator. Frequently the patient survey process is provided by an outside vendor with access to data that can be benchmarked with other organizations. It is surprising how little information clinicians at the point of care may have or understand about the patient satisfaction survey tool. They don't always know what questions are asked of patients, what questions pertain to care, the way the data are recorded, or when and how the data are collected. (This information is often found in the background information provided by the patient satisfaction survey vendor.) Even though collecting patient satisfaction data is a well-established practice, if clinicians are not convinced of the accuracy and relevance of the information collected, the data will do little to motivate improvements in practice.

When coupled with the NMMDS©, patient satisfaction data can have more meaning to leadership and staff. For instance, on units where there is high patient turnover (such as a telemetry unit), it may be that the opportunity for RBC is less than on units where patients have a longer length of stay (as on an oncology or rehabilitation unit). In such a case, recognizing the difficulty in creating RBC on units with short lengths of stay allows the staff of those units to look just at their data—

without comparisons to units where patients have longer stays—until they begin to trust that the data represent their work. Once they trust in the validity of their own data, they can begin to work on ways to make improvements that make sense for *them*, rather than to think they will not be able to achieve what comes more easily for other units. Part of the job of creating infrastructure is creating the baseline, giving staff the responsibility for understanding and making improvements to their own practice.

Again, we'll use the Generic Outcomes Grid to illustrate the adaptation of an indicator. This time, focus specifically on the way the grid helps to establish the infrastructure of the measurement process (see next page).

Report Format

An important, yet often overlooked aspect of outcomes measurement is the reporting process. While many creators of outcomes measurement infrastructures are inclined to leave the step of determining the report format for the end of the process, its early establishment can actually help move along the outcomes measurement process. Reporting is a critical element of the process, for unless the information gets to the people concerned quickly, the likelihood of that information inspiring real change is diminished. If the intent of tracking data is to make improvements, then the people who are expected to improve must get the information fast and in a format that makes sense to them. If there is too much information and the information comes too often, there is little real opportunity to change. In truth, the reporting format you choose will lead to either defensiveness or acceptance, frustration or curiosity, resistance or improvement.

Generic Outcomes Grid

What to collect		Source of data and who will collect			How to evaluate and trend/track			Celebration
Indicator	*Definition*	*Method*	*Source*	*Report Format*	*Numerator Denominator*	*Validity Reliability*	*Target*	
Patient Satisfaction with Overall Care. (This is a macro indicator related to the organization's vision to be the Provider of Choice.)	Indicator is defined as patient opinion of care during a health center encounter as determined by specific questions asked on a vendor-supplied survey as a set of scaled responses (from 1–5).	Vendor survey sent to randomly-selected patient four weeks post discharge.	Patient relations department coordinates survey process internally. Data summarized by vendor.	Data collected monthly; reported quarterly; reports sent to executives and department directors and managers simultaneously.	Numerator is the number of patients who reported at the level of "strongly agree" on the set of scaled responses (level 4) on a scale of 1–5) over the denominator of the total number of patients responding to the survey questions.	Vendor provides validity and reliability data in background information describing the instrument.	An improvement in the responses from the "agree" (level 3) to "strongly agree" (level 4) by 2% on the identified questions. Track the data until the target is stable and sustained. Trend line kept in common area for staff to discuss ways to continue to improve.	Reward and recognition for improving is determined by staff and managers who are accountable for the change.

In large organizations, getting reports to end-users who have the responsibility for making changes requires a communication plan. Report distribution is often a top-down approach, with executives and directors getting first copies. Sometimes these people are responsible in turn for distributing copies. The larger the organization, the more cumbersome and political this process can be.

One system which has proven effective is to create a reporting tree that is managed by an individual with access to personnel and/or cost center information. This person is accountable for creating and maintaining (or pruning) a communication tree that can be retraced to see when and how reports are distributed. It may be that executives want reports first; however, our experience is that the sooner managers who are accountable for the outcomes of care in their work areas get the information to staff, the better. Thus, individual reports can be sent to units at the same time that the summary report is sent to the executives. The executives need not have any responsibility for distributing reports. The more the managers are accountable for reviewing, verifying, and communicating their unit's data, the more effective the outcomes measurement process will be.

Maintaining an effective communication tree is not an easy task. Managers change positions enough that it can be difficult to keep the names and cost centers current in the database. The tree requires monthly attention in order to get reports quickly into the appropriate hands. If a manager changes positions, the correction must always be made in the communication tree before reports arc sent.

The report format must be such that managers are not distracted by the data from other areas, but instead can concentrate on their own. Lately we've noticed an encouraging trend—that organizations are reporting data in such a way that managers are given virtually no data besides their own. This practice avoids placing managers in embarrassing circumstances whereby their data are compared with others whose circumstances are appreciably different. Reports are most valuable when they focus on the individual unit's performance. Once managers and team members come to trust the data, they may eventually want to compare their work with similar units, data likely to be found in other organizations.

Education

What do we learn by measuring outcomes? We learn how to improve practice. This is quite different from the case study method—the way that medical and health care practice were formerly developed, when one learned by practice rather than data collected over various circumstances. We live in an age in which data are readily available, and we are learning more about how to apply and use the information. The intent in this section is to keep the concepts of numerators, denominators, validity and reliability *practical* enough for staff to want to participate in the outcomes measurement process.

Numerators and Denominators

The only way data can be compared meaningfully is if they are grouped from a common denominator, or starting point. Knowing the number of falls that occur from month to month is not enough to be able to say that the staff are doing a better (or worse) job of managing patients who are at risk for falls. Instead the number of patient falls must be presented as a percentage of the volume of patient activity. Since falls don't occur that often, the denominator recommended by the ANA is reported as a rate—specifically "the rate per 1,000 patient days at which patients fall and incur physical injury (unrelated to a surgical or diagnostic procedure) during the course of their hospital stay" (ANA, 1996, p. 15). The denominator, as illustrated below, is "total number of patient days."

By stating the occurrence of falls this way, the measurement can be compared and trended.

$$\frac{\text{Total Number of Patient Falls Leading to Injury}}{\text{Total Number of Patient Days}} \times 1,000$$

Simply counting numbers of incidents provides no information for staff to learn how to improve; hash marks give us no way of comparing. Selecting an accurate and meaningful numerator and denominator will allow "percent of change" to be tracked and trended. This step validates that comparative data (internal or external) can be used reliably to benchmark.

Let's say that a unit had a very high number of patient falls during a particular quarter. On first glance, if there is no denominator, it can appear that care has been neglectful. If we consider, however, that the number of patient days was very high for the same quarter, we may find that the rate of falls was even *lower* than the previous quarter when patient days were much lower. Staff cannot know how they are performing unless there is a denominator for comparison purposes. Only then can they learn what to improve and what are best practices.

Validity and Reliability

Validity is a statement of the truth of a measurement; valid data measure what they *intend* to measure. For example, if the topic of research is *job satisfaction of staff nurses,* it is important to measure what really does contribute to a nurse's job satisfaction, such as the RN/patient relationship, workload, rewards in the job, etc. There are over 300 variables that have been measured in nurses' job satisfaction, and selecting the items that contribute *most* consistently to job satisfaction is essential if the results are to have any validity (Nelson, 2003). John Nelson (2003) has identified 14 factors of job satisfaction for staff nurses by utilizing the plethora of research conducted in this domain. Combined, the 14 factors of job satisfaction represent over 70% of what makes up job satisfaction for staff nurses. If this careful analysis of how well our chosen indicators measure what we actually wish to measure is not conducted prior to measurement, the model will not be valid because it will not be compiling or measuring the data most closely related to the topic of our research. It will be what statisticians call a misspecified model—it is measuring items that don't relate directly to the area of interest.

Validity can be acquired a number of ways. Using the pre-existing work of established experts is one way to establish validity. If experts concur that an existing measure captures content that is relevant, we can say that face validity has been established. Another method of establishing validity is to use an additional instrument to measure the same content and then evaluate how well the two measures correlate. If the results from both measures are highly correlated, we can assert that the measure has been evaluated for criterion validity. If validity is not established prior to use of the instrument, the researcher risks putting time, energy, and resources into a misspecified model. If data from an invalid study are utilized, the time, energy, and resource drain continues.

One of the criteria for Magnet designation includes the use of internal validation studies

(ANCC, 2003). Internal validity requires continued monitoring of outcomes as they are collected and analyzed.

Reliability, on the other hand, addresses consistency. Reliability refers to the degree of consistency with which an instrument measures the attribute of interest (Polit & Hungler, 1999). For the measure to be reliable, it must be worded so that the responder to the measure understands it the same way each time. For example, a researcher asks a responder to state if they "agree" or "disagree" to the following question: "The organization I work within supports me in what I do." The first time, responders may interpret "support" as professional support. In subsequent measurement, the responder may interpret "support" as personal support. If the research was seeking an understanding of professional support, the resulting correlation will be .50. With a resulting correlation this low, one might as well flip a coin, as it is easier than conducting actual research, and the same results will be obtained.

The reliability of purchased instruments (such as patient satisfaction surveys) is reported in the instrument's background explanations. Staff and managers may have questions about reliability and may not be interested in the statistical significance. What they will want to know is what the instrument's reliability means in practical terms so that they can trust the data being reported for their units.

A systematic approach to interpretation of the data and its ongoing analysis allows us to accurately measure our intended outcomes. To continually measure and collect data without a systematic approach to interpretation, contributes to the staff's (and others') fully justified mistrust of the data. The intent is for staff to learn from their data so that they can take actions to make improvements.

Evaluation

Evaluation of the evidence, the fourth aspect of the I_2E_2 process, provides the opportunity to review outcomes and to determine next steps. Data collection and data analysis are action-oriented activities. Interpretation of data includes examining evidence, forming conclusions, considering implications, exploring the significance of the data, generalizing the findings, and suggesting further action. Effective data gathering, reliable findings, and the application of those findings to everyday practice are all essential for successful implementation and maintenance of RBC.

Tracking and Trending

Tracking and trending data requires creating a picture—a graphic picture that represents reality. The more visual the image, the more meaning the data will have for those who are expected to make improvements in practice.

RN Turnover Rate at Marion General Hospital

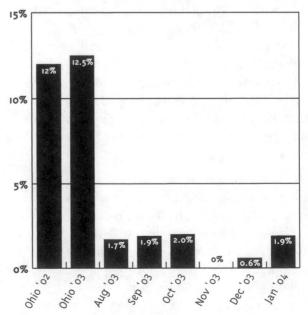

Well displayed data show staff what to attend to. Unit report cards that can be visible in areas where staff have access, but where information can be kept private from public groups, help staff to see how they are doing. Having software that can display data in a customized way for the uniqueness of each unit is a useful tool for the manager to review in staff meetings and with groups that have accountability for improvements.

In the previous graphic, "RN Turnover" refers to voluntary separations from Marion General Hospital in Marion, Ohio. This graph is inspirational to the staff because they have made an effort to improve their professional practice through designing and implementing a coaching model. At Marion General Hospital, a professional coach works side-by-side with experienced staff to help them improve their practice—including how they relate to each other and involve patients in their own care. Although at Marion General turnover data is not available prior to August, 2003, it was known turnover was a problem. Since professional coaching, staff are able to see Marion General's turnover rates are lower than the state average. As of spring 2004, Marion General has more applicants for nursing positions than they have open positions. The improvement is dramatic and a cause for celebration within the full organization.

Linking outcomes measurement to the RBC model requires continuous education about the way in which indicators of quality patient care can help us improve practice. It requires linking how we evaluate and trend/track data to the real-world practices of RBC in order to establish meaningful outcome comparisons. For example, in the case of patient satisfaction, there is what one might call the "being ignored factor." Patients can feel that they are being ignored if it takes too long for their call lights to be answered or if they don't have a nurse to talk with when they are lonely. *"For patients, not having nurses respond to calls for help in a timely manner could prolong pain or discomfort or could engender fear that no one would rescue them should something really be wrong"* (Weinberg, 2003). If staffing limitations increase the perceived lack of responsiveness by nurses, there can be a direct impact on patient satisfaction outcomes.

Celebration

The topic of celebration can best be conveyed by a parable:

Once upon a time there was a data manager who had the job of collecting all kinds of data for the World's Best Hospital. This job meant that the data manager spent countless hours in an office with a large desk, computer, and huge trash can that was always full of reams of paper that had been printed off the computer. The data manager could hardly find his way to the door after a long day of collecting data, analyzing it, sending it to other important people, and thinking of new data to collect.

The data manager received many emails from people who were higher in the organizational hierarchy. These people had questions about departments, incident reports, staffing ratios, core measurements, finances, where reports were being sent, and the actions that were being taken to prevent problems from recurring. The data manager worked very hard and met all the requirements of these people.

Every year, in July, the head of the World's Best Hospital came to town from the World's Best System of Hospitals to attend the data meeting. At that time the data manager would give a Power-Point presentation with all the organization's data on slide after slide of graphs, tables, and numbers.

The head of the World's Best Hospital enjoyed the meeting and seeing the improvements the World's Best Hospital was making.

The other people who were invited to the meeting didn't enjoy the PowerPoint presentation as much as the Head of the World's Best Hospital. When the lights were down, they sometimes took quick naps before racing back to make more improvements on the units of the World's Best Hospital. They wanted so much to tell the Head of the World's Best Hospital how they had saved lives, how they had made a difference one person at a time. They had story after story that could bring the PowerPoint presentation to life.

So the data manager got a bright idea. He had the authority to create a meeting *before* the July meeting to which he asked all the hard working improvement people to enter their stories into a book of stories that the World's Best Hospital would publish annually. The stories could not take more than one written page, and the presentation could take no more than five minutes. The stories had to be submitted in advance so that the data manager could plan the meeting.

So in June, the hard working people gathered to hear each other's stories. The room was abuzz with excitement. Pride welled up in the hard-working improvement people as they talked about the care they provided. They inspired each other to do what they thought was impossible on their own units. Word got out to the Head of the World's Best Hospital about the story telling meeting. He was genuinely moved by the messages he heard and thought it would be a good idea to include some stories with the PowerPoint presentation in July. In addition, he decided to read the group some patient letters about exceptional care experiences. The data manager was happy because he could see pride and respect grow for both the Head of the World's Best Hospital and in the hard working improvement people. He sat back and enjoyed watching the celebration.

It doesn't take much to turn this parable into reality. A wise data manager will recognize his or her accountability for closing the feedback loop between data collection and improvement in performance and practice. The most effective rewards come from the work itself—when people *see* that they have made a difference and that their work is valued.

Collecting stories along the way is a way of marking the change in the culture; the legacy we leave is captured in the data.

The incentive is inherent in the outcomes—but only in the outcomes we see and understand. If *any* resources are to be put into celebrating the accomplishments measured by the outcome measurement process, we'll want to consider very carefully, where those resources will do the most good. Some team members will be more inspired by stories while others will respond to data comparisons. Collecting stories along the way is a way of marking the change in the culture; the legacy we leave is captured in the data. Conversely, aggregated data help us to understand how the outcomes measure our improvement. Stories of our successes help us to see how the outcomes are a reflection of what's real and tangible in our day-to-day experience.

Summary of Key Concepts

- In the practice of outcomes measurement, useful data are those which are not only meaningful, but motivating—those that inspire leaders and practitioners to improve the way they work.

- Data and measurement processes must be trusted, tangible, and useful—relevant from the point of care to the boardroom.

- The vision of an organization determines what indicators to measure. Selecting indicators based on organizational vision links outcomes to daily practice, ultimately inspiring the people who are charged with delivery of services.

- If the Relationship-Based Care model is to be successful, the team at the point of care will be involved in selecting the indicators to be measured.

- Evaluation of the effectiveness and quality of outcomes is still ultimately subject to the clinical judgment of those most closely associated with the care or service being rendered.

- If indicators are defined consistently and in standardized ways with national and international standards, data can be used for national and international comparison.

- Creating an infrastructure that can remain constant through changes in leadership, and has the flexibility to shift with the changing needs of the organization sustains the outcomes measurement plan.

- The closer the accountability for outcomes is moved to the point of care, the more effective the outcomes measurement is.

- Mutual accountability for a common outcome pulls a team of people together to exceed their own expectations and the expectations of those they serve.

- Reporting is a critical element of the process. Unless information gets to the people involved in a timely way, the value of the information for inspiring real change is undermined.

- The only way data can be meaningfully compared is if they are grouped from a common denominator or starting point. Selecting a meaningful numerator and denominator will allow "percent of change" to be tracked and trended.

- Valid data measures exactly what it intends to measure—nothing more, nothing less.

- Reliability refers to how consistent a finding is in different situations or conditions.

- Data collection and data analysis are action-oriented activities. Interpretation of data includes examining evidence, drawing conclusions, considering implications, exploring the significance of findings, generalizing the findings, and suggesting further action.

- Measurement helps to create a supportive environment when expectations are clear and people get recognition for improvement.

- Celebration of positive outcomes helps build unity within an organization.

Questions for Self-Assessment

- What are the current attitudes within your organization about outcomes measurement?

- Is your current process for collecting and analyzing data meaningful? How do you know?

- What are your key indicators?

- What will Relationship-Based Care "look like" in your organization? How will your indicators reflect your vision for RBC?

- Does your current outcomes measure- ment system measure what you want measured most?

- Is your measurement process motivating individuals and groups within your organization to improve practice?

St. Francis Health Center
Topeka, Kansas

St. Francis Health Center participated in a descriptive study to evaluate the effectiveness of an organizational intervention called *Kindness Connects,* beginning in January of 2003. Baseline data were gathered in October of 2002. Four nursing units were included in the study; one unit in wave one, one unit in wave two, and two units in wave three. The units in wave three served as the "control" units since they had not experienced most of the organizational interventions intended to improve the work environment.

Results from the study indicated that following a ten month period of education, training, and organizational support for the initiative there was generalized improvement of the work environ- ment. The most substantive changes were found in the unit that participated in wave one of the study. We concluded that the consistent improvement in wave one was due to the units having had time to adjust to the training over ten months time. In contrast, the groups from wave two and the control group were still adjusting to the changes when outcomes were measured, so they did not show as consistent improvement in their perceptions of the work environment.

A Moment Of Excellence: St. Francis Health Center

Kindness Connects was designed to reduce the concerns of patients and family members through improvements in nurse-patient relationships and conversation, and through random acts of courtesy by nurses. The initiative was introduced as an enhancement to St. Francis Health Center's existing commitment to excellence.

Kindness Connects values are:

- Kindness Connects us with patients, families, and each other.

- We take responsibility for the success of our mission.

- We appreciate each other and the value of our work.

Its primary goals for the organization are:

- To build on current excellence

- To become the employer of choice in northeast Kansas

- To become the health center of choice for employees

Specific indicators measured in the work environment as perceived by the nurses included:

- Relationships with colleagues:
  - Registered Nurses
  - Physicians

- Relationships with patients and their families

- Relationships with Clinical Coordinators

- Job satisfaction

- Organizational commitment:
  - Identification with the organization
  - Intent to stay within the organization

- Disposition of the nurse

- Perception of autonomy

- Task requirements (both type and number of tasks)

- Rewards (including pay)

The work environment of the nurse has been evaluated using a nurse work environment survey (Honeyguide©). The indicators we measured in the work environment of the nurses consistently represent over 67.6% of what nurse job satisfaction includes.

Figure 1: Six of the nine indicators we measured showed statistically significant improvements.

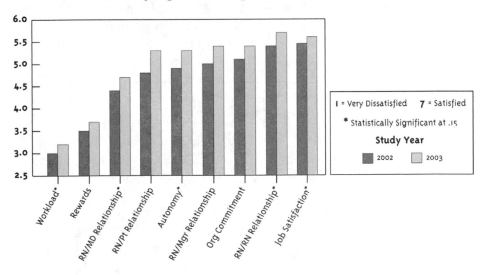

It should be noted that this measurement of the nursing environment is the second in a series of three evaluations. Each measurement has been separated by a time period of 10 months, with the final of the three measurements yet to be taken. Measurement was taken in a series of three in order to evaluate the change in the environment over time, as the *Kindness Connects* initiative becomes fully integrated into culture at St. Francis Health Center.

Initiatives like *Kindness Connects* are costly in terms of staff time and other organizational resources. In order for health care organizations to justify the implementation and continuation of such models, they must often prove to leaders in every level of the organization that such expenditures are beneficial—that they improve both the financial bottom line *and* the organization's ability to provide the highest quality of care possible. For this reason it is essential that every initiative implemented is accompanied by valid, reliable outcomes measurement.

At St. Francis Heath Center, *Kindness Connects* is proving its worth. Improvement in nurse job satisfaction was only one of many indicators measured. Other improvements were found in physician job satisfaction, employees job satisfaction, patient satisfaction, patient outcomes, and financial indicators.

Health care organizations are often data rich and information poor. At St. Francis, however, data are broken down by demographic—with information specific to individual units, and even individual *shifts* within a unit provided for all those involved—so that individuals working at the point of care can help administration interpret the data and apply it meaningfully. Data becomes information when people make it meaningful.

John W. Nelson, MS, RN, is a health care consultant and President of Healthcare Environment, Inc., Minneapolis, Minnesota.

Afterword

by Mary Koloroutis

True healers provide the space for patients to heal themselves. We provide that space by embodying caring as individuals; we provide that space in behaviors that demonstrate caring; we provide that space by our deliberate creation of a physical environment that promotes healing; and we provide that space by creating care delivery systems that support and promote relationships. Relationship-Based Care challenges all of us to practice healing every day.

This book is a guide for transforming practice. But ultimately it is the transformation of people that changes an organization. In order for RBC to thrive, individuals within the organization must learn the values and principles of Relationship-Based Care, commit to putting them into action, own their own practice, and eventually embody these values in *all* of their relationships.

But team members will sign on for this transformation only if they feel as if they've chosen it. Earlier in this book we addressed the notion that RBC will *not* be successfully implemented by way of dictates like, "From this day forward, we will be operating according to a Relationship-Based Care model." It is not compliance we are looking for; it is agreement, and agreement requires partnership.

A basic premise of this book is that each practitioner can be inspired and educated—and then *empowered* to fulfill his or her role well. Further, we have stated that individuals from all levels of the organization can emerge as leaders. We have great faith in people—in their ability to do their jobs well, and in their desire to be part of something good.

While the RBC model is built around the nurse-patient relationship, in an RBC culture—as in any culture—*every* relationship ultimately shapes the culture. People relate to each other, to their practice, and to their environment—and people relate to information. The RBC model is new information that aims to transform practitioners, practice, and physical space. And that can be threatening to some. How individuals relate to this information will have much to do with how the information is conveyed to them.

We recommend that you approach dissemination of this information with a healthy mix of caution and optimism. Transformation happens from the inside out. Substantive change comes from within each individual, and as individuals *own* the change to Relationship-Based Care, the work culture begins to transform into a community of people devoted to caring relationships. Such a community is built on shared learning and mutual commitment. The role of leaders within this community is to inspire a shared vision and lead the way to achieving it; to help design an infrastructure which will support the new ways of working so that success can happen; to provide support and education so that people within the community gain competence and confidence in their capacity to work within the RBC model; and finally, to provide evidence of progress so that all members of the team can see the benefits of their work and know that they are moving toward the vision they all desire.

Throughout this book we have presented "Moments of Excellence"—stories about organizations that made great changes and realized success. But it is important to recognize that every organization's success is made one person at a time. It isn't that an organization "turns itself around;" it's that individuals within an organization make personal decisions to be better, and *they* turn the organization around. In health care, we get opportunities for personal moments of excellence every day. The story of one such moment follows:

It was a busy day, but what day wasn't? Yet, today felt like the day. Steven was dying.

He had been lingering on the edge of death for several days. His wife, Julia, had remained at his side constantly over the past difficult weeks. She shared their story with me through many interactions. Although they were in their sixties, they had only been married for eight years. There was a great deal of pain and estrangement in their families, and they found themselves with only each other at this important time. She had wanted to care for him at home, but had been unable to manage. They had only each other, and soon, she would be alone. It terrified her to lose him, and yet she wanted him to let go. She knew it was time for him to release the pain and struggle. She said she thought he was holding on because he was worried about her—about her being left behind and alone.

Everyone on the unit was aware of their story and of Steven's imminent death. We had a quick team consult and decided that it was important for me to support them through this shift. We looked at how we could redistribute some of the workload so that I could be with them. I felt immense gratitude that I worked with colleagues who "got it."

That day I served as guide and witness. I learned about love, fear, and letting go. I guided Julia through these hours knowing that there would never be a second chance.

I encouraged her to talk with Steven—to not let anything that was important go unsaid. She shared many stories with me. She cried and she laughed and she wondered. I encouraged her to let him know that he could go, and to share any thoughts or feelings she wanted him to know in this life. With her permission, I invited our hospital chaplain to join us. She led us in prayer, and Julia shared more stories about Steven and their life together. I encouraged her to hold him, to lie with him in his bed, and to say goodbye.

The experience of being with people through such powerful and intimate times is beyond explanation. There are few professions that gift individuals with the privilege of such trust. Steven had only one opportunity to die with dignity. Julia had only one opportunity to make his death as comfortable as possible. And I had only one opportunity to be fully present for both of them. It takes all of us to make the whole story come to be. The care provider at the bedside can only be present in such important moments when they are supported by their team members behind the scenes—from those at the point of direct service, to those indirect departments that make it all work, to the board room. In exercising our human capacity to extend beyond ourselves, to touch the lives of others and help facilitate their healing; we become part of a privileged community of healers, and in the process we heal and enrich ourselves.

Please accept our admiration and gratitude for those who have served in *any* way—and for those who will now commit to finding the very best in themselves as they practice Relationship-Based Care.

Appendix A

Partners-In-Practice Overview

Partners-in-Practice is a nurse extender program which partners an experienced RN (Senior Partner) with another care provider (Practice Partner). The Practice Partners select one another, work the same shift, and share a patient assignment greater than the two could handle separately. After very little time, the partnership promotes a synergy between the two care providers (usually an RN and LPN or CNA).

Many hospitals are discontinuing the ill-advised system of task-based care that emerged during care delivery consultations in the 1990s. Leaders are embracing systems that support the RN's authority to determine the kind and amount of care to be provided.

Within a Partners-in-Practice program, each patient is assigned to *both* individuals in the partnership. The pairing ensures that each patient, even in a facility facing a shortage of nurses, has the benefit of the evaluative assessment and judgment of an RN. The partnership means that work is no longer divided up by task or by geography, but by a commitment to matching nursing behaviors with each care provider's skills. The RN is free to delegate tasks without the constriction of conventional role descriptions.

The Partners-in-Practice program helps solve the recurring problem of nursing shortages by placing care providers in partnerships that promote synergistic collaborations which increase efficiency, and, by natural extension, productivity. This program conserves our most vital resource—the nursing staff providing care, and the skills and knowledge they bring to their practice—while strengthening and enhancing the value of Professional Nursing Practice.

Characteristics of Partnerships:

- Senior Partners (RN) and Practice Partners (LPN or CNA) select each other and sign an understanding of the terms of their relationship.

- Partners work together on the same shift, sharing the patient assignments and allowing a synergy to evolve between them.

- Every patient assigned to the partnership has his or her care directed by an RN.

- The Senior Partner is given the authority to determine appropriate work for the Practice Partner. This delegation is not limited by departmental role descriptions for either partner. The primary determiners of work allocation are the knowledge and skill level of the Practice Partner, the state's Nurse Practice Act, and standards from The Joint Commission.

- The Senior Partner assesses the Practice Partner's competency level and defines a plan with the Practice Partner to develop the appropriate skill and knowledge. Within the Partners-in-Practice system, Practice Partners may be taught to perform activities of a highly technical nature.

Advantages of Partnership:

- There is more flexibility and efficiency in caring for patients because of the Partners' ability to negotiate completion of care tasks, and the trust that grows with knowing each other.

- Improved relationships within and outside the partnerships. Staff report that, because of increased efficiency (up to 25%), they're more likely to proactively assist others on the unit.

- Senior Partners learn leadership and mentoring skills.

- Senior Partners know the competency level of their partners and can delegate more effectively and confidently.

- The Practice Partner works consistently with one RN who uses the Partner's demonstrated knowledge and skill instead of relying on generic expectations that place limits on the Practice Partner. Each partnership is unique.

- Practice Partners develop skill and knowledge faster by working consistently with the same RN and RNs advance their own clinical knowledge through the stimulation of interacting with a partner.

- Experienced LPN Practice Partners receive recognition for their unique contributions. Nursing assistants and technicians have a relationship framework for advancing their skills.

- Patients identify improved communication, coordination of care, and increased availability of care providers.

Appendix B

Commitment to My Co-worker©
Healthy Team Assessment Survey

Read each statement below and rate it on a scale of 1-7
based on how often it is true for you (column 1) and for your
team as a whole, (column 2):

1 = Almost never; 2 = Rarely; 3 = Once in a while;
4 = Frequently; 5 = Quite often; 6 = Usually
7 = Almost always

Self   Team

_____ _____ A.   I believe that it is less important that I "like" my colleagues and more important for us to be committed to the same purpose and goals.

(My team believes that it is less important that we "like" each other and more important for us to be committed to the same purpose.)

_____ _____ B.   I accept responsibility for establishing and maintaining healthy interpersonal relationships with my work team members.

_____ _____ C.   I speak directly and promptly with the person involved in a conflict or problem.

_____ _____ D.   I trust my co-workers to do the job they are required and prepared to do.

_____ _____ E.   I address the situation directly and constructively whenever I see a problem in the quality of work.

_____ _____ F.   I respect my colleagues without consideration to titles, education or job position.

_____ _____ G. I require my colleagues to treat me with respect.

_____ _____ H. I address any behavior I perceive as disrespectful or abusive to others or to myself.

_____ _____ I. I avoid engaging in the "3 Bs": bickering, back-biting and blaming.

_____ _____ J. I practice the "3 Cs" in my colleague relationships: caring, commitment and collaboration.

_____ _____ K. I affirm and recognize my colleagues for quality work.

_____ _____ L. I avoid complaining about my colleagues; if I have a complaint I address it with the person.

_____ _____ M. I avoid gossip.

_____ _____ N. If I hear someone complaining about another, I will ask that person to speak directly to the person.

_____ _____ O. I accept others and myself as imperfect... a work (masterpiece) in progress!

_____ _____ **TOTAL SCORE**

_____ _____ **AVERAGE SCORE (Total/15)**

1. I believe our team excels at: _____

2. I would like to see us build on our already excellent ability to:

   _____

   _____

   I think we can accomplish this by: _____

   _____

3. I think we need to strengthen in the area(s) of: _____

   _____

   I think we can accomplish this by:_____

   _____

   _____

(Koloroutis, 2002)

References

Abbott Northwestern Hospital. (1993). *Department of Nursing Philosophy.* Minneapolis: Author.

Aiken L., et al. (2002). Hospital nurse staffing and patient mortality, nurse burnout, and job dissatisfaction. *Journal of the American Medical Association, 288*(16),1987–93.

Aiken L., and Slocane, D. (1997). Effects of organizational innovations in AIDS care on burnout among urban hospital nurses. *Work and Occupation, 24*(4), 453–77.

Aiken, L., et al. (1997). Hospital nurses' occupational exposure to blood: prospective, retrospective, and institutional reports. *American Journal of Public Health, 87*(1), 103–7.

Aiken, L., et al. (1994). Lower Medicare mortality among a set of hospitals known for good nursing care. *Medical Care, 32*(8), 771–87.

Albert, H., et al. (1992). 7 Gryzmish: toward an understanding of collaboration. *The Nursing Clinics of North America, 27,* 47–59.

Aldrich, H. (1998). Critical thinking. In Price, S., Koch, M. and Bassett, S (Eds.), *Health care resource management: Present and future challenges.* St. Louis, MO: Mosby

American Nurses Association (1991). *Nursing quality indicators: Definitions and implications.* Washington, DC: Author.

American Nurses Association. (2003). *Nursing: A social policy statement.* Washington, DC: American Nurses Publishing.

American Nurses Association. (2004). *Nursing-sensitive quality indicators for acute care settings and ANA's safety & quality initiative.* Retrieved March 04, 2004, from the American Nurses Association Website: www.nursingworld.org.

American Nurses Credentialing Center. (2003). *The Magnet Recognition Program health care organization application manual.* Washington, DC: Author.

Aroskar, M. (1998). Ethical working relationships in patient care: challenges and possibilities. *Nursing Clinics of North America, 33,* 313–324.

Barrere, C. and Ellis, P. (2002). Changing attitudes among nurses and physicians: a step toward collaboration. *Journal for Healthcare Quality, 24*(3), 9–15.

Benner, P., & Wrubel, J. (1989). *The primacy of caring: Stress and coping in health and illness.* Boston, MA: Addison–Wesley.

Benner, P., Tanner, C., and Chelsea, C. (1996). *Expertise in nursing practice: Caring, clinical judgment, and ethics.* New York, NY: Springer Publishing Company.

Bilchik, G. (2002). A better place to heal. *Health Forum Journal, 45*(4), 10–15.

Bopp, J., et al. (1990). *Sacred tree: Reflections on Native American spirituality.* Twin Lakes, WI: Lotus Press.

Buresch, B., Gordon, S., and Jeans, M. (2000). *From silence to voice: What nurses know and must communicate to the public.* Ithaca, NY: Cornell University Press.

Carper, B. (1978). Fundamental ways of knowing in nursing. *Advances in Nursing Science. 1*(1): 13–23.

Clarke S., et al. (2002). Needlestick injuries to nurses, in context. *LDI Issue Brief 8*(1),1–4.

Collaborating with patients and families to improve quality and patient safety. (2003, Spring) *Advances in Family Centered Care. 9*:1.

Cousins, N. (1979). *Anatomy of an illness.* New York, NY: W. W. Norton.

Creative Health Care Management. (2003). *Leading an empowered organization: Participant manual.* Minneapolis, MN: Author.

Culhane-Pera, K., et al. Eds. (2003). *Healing by heart: Clinical and ethical case stories of Hmong families and western providers.* Nashville: Vanderbilt University Press.

Curtin, L. (2003). An integrated analysis of nurse staffing and related variables: Effects on patient outcomes. Retrieved March 15, 2004, from *Online Journal of Issues in Nursing* Website: www.nursingworld.org.

Darbyshire, P. (1987). Doctors and nurses: The burden of history. *Nursing Times, January 28. 83*(4), 32–34.

D'Aunno, T., Alexander, J., and Laughlin, C. (1996). Business as usual? Changes in health care's workforce and organization of work. *Hospital and Health Services Administration, 28*(3), 20–27.

Dingman, S., et al. (1999). Implementing a caring model to improve patient satisfaction. *Journal of Nursing Administration, 29*(12), 30–37.

Eisenberg, D., et al. (1998). Trends in alternative medicine uses in the United States, 1990–1997; Results of a follow-up national survey. *Journal of the American Medical Association, 280*(18),1569–1575.

Evans, M., Martin, M., and Winslow, E. (1998). Nursing care and patient satisfaction. *American Journal of Nursing, 98*(12), 57–9.

Felgen, J. (2001). ICN 2001: A Celebration of nursing and a call to action. *CHCM News, 5*(5), 1–3.

Felgen, J. (2000). The patient as CEO: Passion in practice. *Journal of Nursing Administration, 30*(10), 453–456.

Flexner, A. (1910). *Medical education in the United States and Canada.* Stanford, CA: Carnegie Foundation for the Advancement of Teaching.

Gatto, R. (2002). *The smart manager's FAQ guide: A survival handbook for today's workplace.* San Francisco, CA: Jossey-Bass.

Gerteis, M. et al. eds. (1993). *Through the patient's eyes: Understanding and promoting patient centered care.* San Francisco, CA: Jossey-Bass.

Glouberman, S., and Zimmerman, B. (2002). Complicated and simple systems: What would successful reform of Medicare look like? Discussion paper #8, *Commission of the Future of Health Care in Canada.* July 2002.

Goleman, D. (1997). *Emotional intelligence.* New York, NY: Bantam Books

Harris, R. (1998). *Introduction to creative thinking.* Retrieved on March 10, 2004, from VirtualSalt. July1, 1998.
Website: http://www.virtualsalt.com/crebook1.htm.

Health Resources and Services Administration. (April 20, 2001). HHS study finds strong link between patient outcomes and nurse staffing in hospitals. *Health Resources and Services Administration Press release.* Rockville, MD.

Hosler, S. (2003). *Leveraging healthcare human resources benchmarks: metrics tell the story.* Retrieved on April 14, 2004, from Session materials at the MHA annual convention.
Website: http://www.mtha.org/annual/sessPDF/D31.pdf

Huber, D. and Delaney, C. (1999). Nursing Management Minimum Data Set NMMDS Research Team, (available from delaney@umn.edu).

Ingersoll, G., et al. (1996). The effect of a professional practice model on staff nurse perception of work groups and nurse leaders. *Journal of Nursing Administration, 26*(5):52–60.

Johns, C, and Graham, J. (1994). The growth of management connoisseurship through reflective practice. *Journal of Nursing Management, 2*(6):253–60.

Johns, C. (1990). Autonomy of primary nurses: the need to both facilitate and limit autonomy in practice. *Journal of Advanced Nursing, 15*(8), 886–894.

Joint Commission, The. (2004). *Hospital accreditation standards: Accreditation, policies, standards, and elements of performance.* Oakbrook Terrace, IL: Joint Commission Resources.

Katenback, J., and Smith, D. (1993). *The wisdom of teams: Creating the high-performance organization.* Boston, MA: Harvard Business School Press.

Kizer, K. (January 30, 2004). Nursing-sensitive performance measures. National Quality Forum press release. Washington, DC.

Knaus, W., et al. (1986). An evaluation of outcome from intensive care in major medical centers, *Annals of Internal Medicine, 104*(3), 410–8.

Kohn, L., Corrigan, J. and Donaldson, M., eds. (2000). *To err is human: Building a safer health system.* Washington, DC: National Academy Press.

Koloroutis, M. (2002). *Reigniting the spirit of caring journal.* Minneapolis, MN: Creative Health Care Management.

Koloroutis, M. and Miller, T. (1997). Intentional caring: An intervention essential for healing. *Medical Journal of Allina, 5*(4).

Koloroutis, M., and Thorstenson, T. (1999). An ethics framework for organizational change. *Nursing Administration Quarterly, 23*(2):9–18.

Kouzes, J. and Posner, B. (1995). *The leadership challenge.* San Francisco, CA: Jossey-Bass.

Kouzes, J. and Posner, B. (2003). *Encouraging the heart: A leader's guide to rewarding and recognizing others.* San Francisco, CA: Jossey-Bass.

Kreitzer M., et al. (2002). Attitudes towards complementary and alternative medicine in medical, nursing and pharmacy faculty and students: A comparative analysis. *Alternative Therapies in Health and Medicine, 8*(6):44–53.

Larisey, M. (1996). Socialization to professional nursing. In Cresia, J. and Parker, B. (Eds.) *Conceptual foundations of professional nursing practice.* St. Louis, MO: Mosby.

Manion, J., Lorimer, W., and Leander, W., (1996). *Team-based health care organizations: Blueprint for success.* Sudbury, MA: Jones and Bartlett.

Leider, Richard. (1997). *The power of purpose.* San Francisco, CA: Berrett-Koehler.

Leininger, M. (1994). *Transcultural nursing: Concepts, theories and practices.* New York, NY: McGraw-Hill.

Malkin, J. (1992). *Hospital interior architecture.* Hoboken, NJ: John Wiley and Sons.

Manthey, M (2002). *Staffing: Changing the way we think.* Minneapolis, MN: Creative Health Care Management.

Manthey, M. (2002). *The practice of primary nursing,* second edition. Minneapolis, MN: Creative Health Care Management.

Manthey, M., Felgen, J., and Person, C. (2003). *The four essential elements of nursing practice.* Unpublished document, Creative Health Care Management.

McNeese-Smith, D. (2002). Jobs stages of entry, mastery, and disengagement among nurses. *Journal of Nursing Administration, 30*(3), 140–147.

Millenson, M. (1997). *Demanding medical excellence: Doctors and accountability in the information age.* Chicago, IL: The University of Chicago Press.

Murphy, E. (1995). [unpublished data]

National Center for Nursing Quality. (2004). Retrieved March 4, 2004. Website: www.nursingquality.org.

Needleman, J., et al. (2001). *Nurse staffing and patient outcomes in hospitals.* Health Resources and Services Administration.

Nelson, J. (2000). Models of nursing care: A century of facilitation. *Journal of Nursing Administration, 20*(4), 156, 184.

Nelson, J. (2001). *A professional nursing care model and satisfaction of the staff nurse.* Unpublished master's thesis, University of Minnesota, Minneapolis, MN.

Nelson, J. (2003). *Nurse Environment Survey Results.* Retrieved April 21, 2004, from Healthcare Environment, Inc. Website: http://www.hcenvironment.com/contactus.html

Nightingale, F. (1859). *Notes on nursing: What it is and what it is not.* London: Harrison & Sons.

O'Rourke, M.(2003). Rebuilding a professional practice model: The return of role-based practice accountability. *Nursing Administration Quarterly, 27*(2), 95-105.

Ornish, D. (1999). *Love and survival: 8 pathways to intimacy and health.* New York, NY: HarperCollins.

Paul, R. (1995). *Critical thinking: How to prepare students for a rapidly changing world.* Santa Rosa, CA: Foundation for Critical Thinking.

Pekkanen, J. (September, 2003). Condition: Critical. *Reader's Digest.*

Peplau, H. E. (1952). *Interpersonal relations in nursing: A conceptual frame of reference for psychodynamic nursing.* Itasca, Il: Putnam.

Person, C. and Marsh, B. (2002). Creating and enhancing healthy work environments. *CHCM News, 6*(2), 1,3.

Plsek, P. (2003). *Complexity and the adoption of innovation in health care.* Paper prepared for Accelerating Quality Improvement in Health Care: Strategies to Speed the Diffusion of Evidence-Based Innovations, convened by the National Institute for Health Care Management Foundation, Washington, DC.

Polit, D. and Hungler, B. (1999). *Nursing research.* 6th ed. Philadelphia, PA: Lippencott.

Porter-O'Grady, T. (1987). Shared governance and new organizational models. *Nursing Economics, 5*(6), 281-287.

Porter-O'Grady, T. (1999). Sustainable partnerships: The journey toward health care integration. In E. Cohen & V. De Back (Eds.), *The outcomes mandate: Case management in health care today.* St. Louis, MO: Mosby.

Prescott, P. (1993). Nursing: An important component of hospital survival under a reformed health care system. *Nursing Economics, 11*(4):192-9.

Prescott, P. (1993). RN care is key component to hospital competitiveness. *Nev RNformation, 2*(4):18.

Press-Ganey Associates. (1997). One million patients have spoken: Who will listen? Press-Ganey Associates Press release. South Bend, IN.

Ritter-Teitel, J. (2002). The impact of restructuring on professional nursing practice. *Journal of Nursing Administration, 32*(1), 31-41.

Roberts, C. (1994). *Reinventing relationships: Leverage for dissolving barriers to collaboration.* In P Senge, *The fifth discipline fieldbook (pp 69-73).* New York, NY: Doubleday/Currency.

Rosenstein, A. (2002). Nurse-physician relationships: Impact on nurse satisfaction and retention. *American Journal of Nursing, 102*(6), 26-34.

Savett, L. (2000). Keeping nursing human: A roundtable discussion. *Creative Nursing Journal 6*(3), 4-10, 14-15.

Scheller, Mary D. (1990). *Building partnerships in hospital care: Empowering patients, families, and professionals.* Boulder, CO: Bull Publishing Company.

Scott, J., Sochalski, J., and Aiken, L. (1999). Review of magnet hospital research: Findings and implications for professional nursing practice. *Journal of Nursing Administration, 29*(1), 9-19.

Senge, P., et al. (1994). *The fifth discipline fieldbook.* New York, NY: Doubleday/ Currency.

Shortell, S., et al. (1994). The performance of intensive care units: Does good management make a difference? *Medical Care, 32*(5):508-25.

Stein, L. (1967). The doctor-nurse game. *Archives of General Psychiatry. 16*(6), 699–703.

Stein, L., Watts., D, and Howell, T. (1990). The doctor-nurse game revisited. *New England Journal of Medicine, 322*(8), 546-549.

Swanson, K. (1993). Nursing as informed caring for the well-being of others. *Journal of Nursing Scholarship, 25*(4), 352-357.

The National Quality Forum. (2004). *National Quality Forum endorses national voluntary consensus standards for nursing-sensitive performance measures and endorses two additional nursing home performance measures.* Retrieved February 3, 2004, from the National Quality Forum Website: www. qualityforum.org.

Thomas, S. (1998). *Transforming nurses' anger and pain.* New York, NY: Springer Publishing Company.

Tresolini, C. and the Pew–Fetzer Task Force. (1994). *Health professions education and relationship-centered care.* San Francisco, CA: Pew Health Professions Commission.

Ulrich, B. (1992). *Leadership and management according to Florence Nightingale.* Norwalk, CT: Appleton & Lange.

Ulrich, R. (1984). View through a window may influence recovery from surgery. *Science, 224*(4647), 420-421.

Varholak, D., and Korwan, R. (1995). The patient's perceptions of quality: implications for nurse managers in long-term care. *Seminars for Nurse Managers, 3*(3),152-6.

Vom Eigen, K., et al. (1999). Carepartner experiences with hospital care. *Medical Care, 37*(1), 33-8.

Watson, J. (1988). *Nursing: Human science and human care.* New York, NY: National League for Nursing.

Watson, J. (1988). New dimensions of human caring theory. *Nursing Science Quarterly, 1*(4), 75-181.

Watson, J. (1990). Transpersonal caring: A transcendent view of the person, health, and healing. In M. Parker (Ed), *Nursing theories in practice.* New York, NY: National League for Nursing.

Watson, J. (1999). *Postmodern nursing and beyond.* Edinburgh: Churchill Livingstone.

Watson, J. (2002). *Assessing and measuring caring in nursing and health science.* New York, NY: Springer.

Webster, D. (1985). Medical students' view of the nurse. *Nursing Research, 34*(5) 313-317.

Weinberg, D. (2003). *Code green: Money-driven hospitals and the dismantling of nursing.* Ithaca, NY: Cornell University Press.

Williams, S. (1993). The relationship of patients' perceptions to improve quality care. *Journal of Nursing Care Quarterly, 7*(2), 42-51.

Wolf, G., Boland, S., and Aukerman, M. (1994). A transformational model for the practice of professional nursing. *Journal of Nursing Administration, 24*(4), 51-57.

Wright, D. (1998). *The ultimate guide to competency assessment in healthcare,* second edition. Eau Claire, WI: PESI HealthCare.

Wright, S and Sayre-Adams, J. (2000). *Sacred space: Right relationship and spirituality in healthcare.* Edinburgh: Churchill Livingstone.

Index

A

Administrative Model of shared governance, 75

Aiken, Linda
    Magnet Designation and patient outcomes, 118–119
    Nursing-Sensitive Clinical Outcomes, 223–224

Aldrich, Sally
    and "doing" vs. "thinking," 189–190

Allina Hospitals and Clinics, Mineapolis, MN Exemplar:
    Resource Driven Practice Chapter,
        209–214

alternative medicine, 40

American Nurse Credentialing Center (ANCC)
    common characteristics of Magnet Hospitals, 118
    Forces of Magnetism, in Nurse Retention,175–176

American Nurses Association (ANA)
    and "The Code of Ethics for Nursing," 138
    and definition of Nursing, 140
    and Professional Nursing Practice, conceptual frame-
    work, 125–128
    Nursing-Sensitive Quality Indicators
        and RBC Outcomes Measurement, 223
    Social Policy Statement
        and Professional Nursing Practice, 140–141
        and the science of caring, 140–141

articulating expectations and team building, 100

B

Benner, Patricia
    levels of competency in professional practice, 139–140

Bethune, Golden
    Examplar, Leadership Chapter, 84–89

Bilchik, Gloria
    stress reduction through control of environment, 41–42

boundaries
    and Professional Nursing Practice, 125–128, 137

bureaucratic nursing practice
    contrasted to professional nursing practice, 160
Buresh, Bernice
    Voice of Agency, 128

C

Captain of the Ship
    and physician role paradigm, 107–108
care delivery - see Patient Care Delivery
care environment in RBC
    and indicator selection in outcomes measurement, 221
    and nurse-patient relationship, 117
care practice innovations
    in response to care priorities, 24
care provider-patient relationship, 4, 5
care provider-self relationship, 4, 5
caring
    dimensions of, (St. Francis Health Center, Topeka, KS),
    81–84
    ethic of, 142
    incorporated into Nursing as ethical principle, 142
    Leininger's Five Theoretical Assumptions on, 34
    Swanson's Middle Range Theory of, 140
caring actions
    "universal" characteristics, 23–24
Caring Connection
    Relationship-Based Care model at Parma Community
    General Hospital, Parma, OH, 47–50
caring leaders
    and caring processes, Swanson, 57
    and transformation
        Reigniting the Spirit of Caring, 55–56
    attributes of, 56
    behaviors of, 57
    Kouzes, James & Pozner, Barry, 58–59
    Transformational Leadership Cycle, 60–66
    vs. "victim leader" mentality, 60
Caring Model™; Dingman
    and Professional Nursing Practice model, 83
    introduction, 24
Caring Processes, five; Swanson
    and caring leader attributes, 57
    introduction, 22

caring-healing consciousness; Watson, 31–32
    and self awareness, 32
    and self care, 32
    integrated with nursing process, 30–32

celebration
    and Outcomes Management Evaluation, 240–242
    and Resource Driven Practice, example, 214

Centra Health, Lynchburg, VA
    Examplar, Leadership Chapter, 84–89

Children's National Medical Center, Washington, DC
    Exemplar, Professional Nursing Practice Chapter, 155–158

CNA - see Nursing Assistant

Code of Ethics for Nursing, The American Nurses
    Association (ANA), 138

collaborative practice
    between nurses and physicians, 108–112
    interdisciplinary, in Primary Nursing, 172

collaborator role
    and Voice of Agency
        in Professional Nursing Practice, 128–132

colleagues
    within Relationship-Based Care, concept of, 106
    within relationship-based culture, 110

Commitment to my Co-worker
    and use of in Team-Building, 102–103

communication
    and "transparent environment," 116
    between team members
        element of Patient Care Delivery System,
        161–162
    in nurse-physician relationship
        and collaborative practice, 110
    tree
        in Outcomes Measurement Reporting Structure, 233
    with team members
        comparison of across Patient Care Delivery
        Models, 165
    in Primary Nursing, 166–174

competency
    and domains, 137–138
    and Professional Nursing Practice, 137–140
    levels of, 139–140

complementary medicine, 40

conditions facilitating change
    5 C's: Clarity, Collaboration, Commitment,
        Competency, Confidence, 9–10

Congressional Model
    of Shared Governance, 75

continuity of care
    and American Nurse Credentialing Center (ANCC) Forces
    of Magnetism, 175–176
    and Primary Nursing, 172
    and Resource Driven Practice, 198
    foundation of Primary Nursing, 164

Continuous Quality Improvement (CQI)
    and Team-Building exemplified, Rice Memorial
        Hospital, Willmar, MN, 115–116

core
    and Professional Nursing Practice, 125–128

Councilor Model
    of Shared Governance, 75

creative thinking
    and Resource Driven Practice, 191–192

critical thinking
    and Resource Driven Practice, 190–192

cultural care universality and diversity; Leininger, 22

culturally-sensitive care, 24

Culture of Care
    and leadership, 54

cyclical staffing
    within resource driven practice, 200–202

D

Dahlberg-Reiners, Nancy
    Exemplar: Resource Driven Practice Chapter, 209–214

Dandrinos-Smith, Sandra
    Exemplar, Patient Care Delivery Chapter, 179–182

Data Measurement System
    utility, 215

decentralization
    and Shared Governance, 74–76
    effect on patient care, 78
    Infrastructure for Relationship-Based Care, 72–78
    myths about, 76–78

decision-making
    and Responsiblity, Authority and Accountability
    (RAA), 74

by RN, element of Patient Care Delivery System, 161–162

comparison of across Patient Care Delivery Models, 165

del Bueno, Dorothy

competency in terms of skills acquisition, 137–138

delegated practice

realm of Professional Nursing Practice, 124

delegation of tasks

by RN, and skill mix, 198–199

in functional nursing, 163

in Primary Nursing, 166–174

scope of practice

and Professional Nursing Practice, 135–136

Denominator and Education, in Outcomes Measurement, 234–235

deprofessionalization of nursing, 117

dimensions

and Professional Nursing Practice, 125–128

Dimensions of Caring (Five), 83

Dingman, Sharon

Outcomes Measurement (Chapter Seven), 218–248

disengagement and nurse job satisfaction, 156–158

doctor-nurse game

nurse-physician role socialization, 107

domains (and competency)

and Professional Nursing Practice, 138

Donabedian, Avedis

categories of health care indicators, 222–223

E

Education (in I₂E₂)

and Outcomes Management, 216, 217, 234–237

and Outcomes Measurement, 234–238

and Patient Centered Care Exemplar: Kaleida Hospital, NY, 151–154

and Resource Driven Practice, example, 212–214

definition, 6, 8–9

element of transformation, 6, 8–9

Eisenberg, John

nursing staffing and quality of care, 119–120

Elkjer, Joyce

Exemplar, Teamwork Chapter, 114–116

Environment of Care

and caring-healing consciousness, 28–37

caring and healing, defined, 24

element of Patient Care Delivery System, 161–162
influence of on care provided, 28

environmental data elements
Nursing Management Minimum Data Set (NMMDS)
Outcomes Measurement, 229–231

Evaluation
and Outcomes Management, 238–240
and Resource Driven Practice, example, 212–214

Evaluation (in I_2E_2)

Outcomes Measurement, 216, 217–218, 238–240

Evans, Mourine

Exemplar, Professional Nursing Practice Chapter, 155–158

Evidence (in I_2E_2)
and Patient Centered Care Exemplar: Kaleida
Hospital, NY, 151–154
definition, 6, 9
element of transformation, 6, 9

F

Felgen, Jayne
and I_2E_2 Model, 6–10
Caring and Healing Environment (Chapter Two), 23–52
elements for transformation of care environment (I_2E_2), 6
Example of I_2E_2 Kaleida Health, Buffalo, NY, 151–154
Patient-Centered Care Model - graphic, 151

financial resource data elements
Nursing Management Minimum Data Set (NMMDS)
Outcomes Measurement, 229–231

Five Dimensions of Caring
see Caring, Dimensions of

Flexner, Abraham
definition of profession, 122–123

Functional Nursing
comparison to other Patient Care Delivery System, 165
historical analysis of, 163

functions of nursing practice, five essential, 132–133

G

Generic Outcomes Grid
Introduction, 217
Usage of, in RBC
infrastructure example, 231–232
initial example, 225–228

Gordon, Suzanne
  Voice of Agency, 128
Guide role and Voice of Agency
      in Professional Nursing Practice, 128–132

H

Harris, Robert
  Creative Thinking vs. Critical Thinking, 191–192
Healer role
  and Voice of Agency
      in Professional Nursing Practice, 128–132
health care team members relationship, 4, 5–6
Heintz, Shirley
  Exemplar, Leadership Chapter, 81–84
Housekeeping Staff
  and teamwork, 98

I

I_2E_2; Felgen
  and Outcomes Management, 216–240
  and Patient Centered Care Exemplar: Kaleida Hospital, NY, 151–154
  and Resource Driven Practice, example, 212–214
Independent Practice
  realm of Professional Nursing Practice, 124–125
indicators
  categories of, 222–223
  correlation of, 224
  defined, 221–222
  quality care, 220
  selection
      and RBC care environment, 222–225
      Responsibility, Authority and Accountability (RAA), 224–225
Infrastructure
  and Resource Driven Practice, example, 212–214
Infrastructure (in I_2E_2)
  and Outcomes Management, 111
  and Patient Centered Care Exemplar: Kaleida Hospital, NY, 151–154
  definition, 6, 7–8
  element of transformation, 6, 7 8
  Patient Care Delivery System, 159
Infrastructure for Relationship-Based Care
  decision-making, 72–78

Inspiration
   and Resource Driven Practice, example, 212–214
Inspiration (in I_2E_2)
   and Outcomes Management, 216–217, 218–228
   and Patient Centered Care Example, Kaleida
      Hospital, NY, 151–154
   definition, 6, 7
   element of transformation, 6, 7–8
Institute of Medicine
   and nurse-patient relationship, 107
interdependent practice
   and nurse-physician practice, 111
   realm of Professional Nursing Practice, 125
interdisciplinary team
   and awareness of Independent Realm of Nursing
      Practice, 125
   and Collaborative Practice
      in Primary Nursing, 172
   and Site Practice Councils, 153
   and teamwork, 98–99
   nurse-physician relationship
      role socialization, 107
intersection - health care team
   and Professional Nursing Practice, 125–128

J

Johns, Christopher
   Guided Reflection, 192–193
Joint Commission, The
      and leadership, Centra Health, Lynchburg,
      VA, 84–85
      Generic Outcomes Grid, 217

K

Kaleida Health, Buffalo, NY
   Exemplar, Professional Nursing Practice Chapter, 151–154
Katzenbach, Jon
   work groups vs. teams, 91
Kellerman, Teresa
   Exemplar, Leadership Chapter, 81–84
Kindness Connects
   and outcome measurement, 246
   organizational initiative at St. Francis Health Center,
      Topeka, KS, 83

Kinnaird, Leah
    Outcomes Measurement (Chapter Seven), 215–248
Kizer, Kenneth
    and importance of nursing in quality of care, 224
    National Quality Forum, 224
Koloroutis, Mary
    and ethic of caring, 142
    and team members as colleagues, 106
    Leadership (Chapter Two), 53–89
    Professional Nursing Practice (Chapter Four), 117–158
    Relationship-Based Care, Introduction to (Chapter One),
        101–116
    Resource Driven Practice (Chapter Six), 183–214
    Six Practice Roles, 60–66
    Transformational Leadership Cycle, 60–66
Kouzes, James
    and caring leadership, 58–59
Kreitzer, Mary Jo
    Exemplar, Caring and Healing Environment Chapter, 50–52

L

Larisey, Marian
    profession vs. occupation, 122–123
Leader role
    and Voice of Agency
        in Professional Nursing Practice, 128–132
leadership
    and transformation, 74
    caring leader behaviors, 57
    Kouzes, James and Pozer, Barry, 58–59
    Reigniting the Spirit of Caring, 55–56
    Transformational Leadership Cycle, 60–66
Leading an Empowered Organization
    and Leadership, Exemplar, 87
Leininger, Madeline
    Cultural Care Diversity and Universality, 34–35
    Five Theoretical Assumptions on Caring, 35
Licensed Practical Nurse (LPN)
    and Primary Nursing, 166–174
    and skill mix, 197–198
    and teamwork, 97
Licensed Practical Nurses (LPN)
    Scope of Practice
        and Professional Nursing Practice, 135–136
Licensed Vocational Nurse (LVN)
    and teamwork, 97

Licensed Vocational Nurses (LVN)
  Scope of Practice
    and Professional Nursing Practice, 135–136
LPN - see Licensed Practical Nurse

M

Magnet
  designation
    and patient outcomes, 118–119
    example of, at University of California-Davis Medical
    Center in Sacramento, 169–170
    four common characteristics, 118
    internal validation studies, 236–237
healthy work environments within
  critical factors, 173–174
public awareness of, 174
recognition program requirements
  Nurse-Sensitive Quality Indicators, 223
Malkin, Jain
  the relationship between the environment and healing, 42–43
management
  comparison of across Patient Care Delivery Models, 165
Manthey, Marie
  and "Commitment to my Co-worker," 102
  on origin of Primary Nursing, 170–171
  Resource Driven Practice (Chapter Six), 183–214
Marion General Hospital, Marion, OH
  and coaching for retention, 239
Marsh, Bonnie
  new leadership model, 59–60
mindset, new
  contrasted to old mindset, 186–188
  key changes, in resource driven practice, 202–206
  resource driven practice, away from needs
  driven, 186–188
mindset, old
  needs-driven thinking
    contrasted to resource-driven thinking, 183
    resource-driven thinking, shifting away from, 183
misspecified model
  and Education, in Outcomes Measurement, 236
myths
  of decentralization, 76–78
  of Primary Nursing, 171–172

N

Nahigian, Eileen
    Exemplar, Professional Nursing Practice Chapter, 151–154

National Center for Complementary and Alternative Medicine (NCCAM)
    Therapeutic Relationship of Nursing, 40

National Center for Nursing Quality (NCNQ)
    Generic Outcomes Grid, 217
    Nurse-Sensitive Quality Indicators
        Magnet Recognition Program Requirements, 223

National Quality Forum
    Generic Outcomes Grid, 217

National Quality Forum (NQF)
    Nursing Sensitive performance measures, 224

needs-driven thinking
    contrasted to resource-driven, 183
    resource driven practice, and shifting away from, 183

Nelson John
    and outcomes measuring tools regarding the role of the professional nurse and the PNI, 221
    Exemplar, Outcomes Management Chapter, 245–248
    fourteen factors of nurses' job satisfaction, 236

Nightingale, Florence, 40, 801
    holistic, integrated pursuit of Nursing, 40

Numerator
    and Education, in Outcomes Measurement, 234–235

Nurse Executive
    Role in transformational organization, 85–86

Nurse Leadership Development Program
    at Centra Health, Lynchburg, VA, 86–87

nurse resource data elements
    Nursing Management Minimum Data Set (NMMDS)
        Outcomes Measurement, 229–231

nurse-patient relationship
    and care environment, 117
    and Professional Nursing Practice, 118
    and Relationship-Based Culture, 69
    element of Patient Care Delivery System, 161–162
        Tufts-NEMC's Care Delivery Principles, 179–182
    focus of Primary Nursing, 164–174

nurse-physician relationship
    "doctor-nurse game," 107
    Collaborative Practice, 108–112
    role socialization, 107
    strategies for improvement, 111–112

nurses
  job satisfaction
    and disengagement, 156–158
    Nurse-Sensitive Quality Indicators - Magnet
    Recognition Program, 223
Nursing
  autonomy
    and boundaries, scope of practice, 125–128
  definition of, 140
  processes
    integrated with caring-healing consciousness, 22
    professional practice - see Professional
      Nursing Practice
  retention
    Forces of Magnetism (ANCC), 175–176
  social responsibility of, 124–125
Nursing Assistant (N.A.)
  and functional nursing, 163
  and Primary Nursing, 166–174
  and skill mix, 197–198
  and teamwork, 97
Nursing Management Minimum Data Set (NMMDS)
  and Outcomes Measurement in RBC, 229–231
Nursing Report Card for Acute Care (1999), Donabedian and
  nursing quality indicator groupings, 222–223
Nursing Unit
  Unit Manager
    Responsibilities of, 68–72
  Unit Practice Councils
    Example of, at Kaleida Health, Buffalo, NY, 152–153
  Unit Schedule
    and resource driven practice, 199–202
Unit Staff
  Responsibilities of, 68–72
Nursing-Sensitive Quality Indicators
  and RBC Outcomes Measurement, 223
    Example of, 230

O

O'Rourke, Maria
  and Professional Nursing Practice, 132–135
Outcome Indicators
  and Magnet Designation, 118–119
  and RBC Outcomes Measurement, 222–223
  and staffing mix, 119–120

Outcomes Measurement
    Articulating the Vision, 219–221
    celebration, 240–242
    data, 215–216
    Education, 216, 217, 234–237
    Education - improving practice, 234–238
    Evaluation, 216, 217–218, 238–240
    Evaluation - review and next steps, 238–240
    Generic Outcomes Grid, 225–232
    I_2E_2, 216–240
    indicators, 221–225
    Infrastructure - longevity & flexibility, 216, 217, 228–234
    Inspiration, 216–217, 218–228
    report format, 233–234
    Responsibility, Authority and Accountability
        (RAA), 224–225
    Tracking and Trending, 238–240
    Validity, 235–237

P

Parma Community General Hospital, Parma, OH
    Exemplar, Caring and Healing Environment Chapter, 47–50
Partners-in-Practice
    and LPN / LVN staffing, 97
    and Primary Nursing, experience with, 166–169
patient
    satisfaction, 155
Patient Care Delivery System
    and Professional Nursing Practice, 159
    and therapeutic relationship, 159
    defined, 159
    design of, premises, 161
    elements, 161–162
    four historical configurations of
        analysis, 163–165
        comparisons between, 165
    Primary Nursing Model - Tufts-NEMC's, 179–182
Patient Centered Care
    Exemplar: Kaleida Health, Buffalo, NY, 151–154
Paul, Richard
    essential elements in critical thinking, 190–191
Person, Colleen
    and disengagement, Nurse Job Satisfaction, 156
    functions of nursing practice, 132
    new leadership model, 59–60
    Patient Care Delivery (Chapter Five), 159–182

Phoenix Group
    and transformation, St. Francis Health Center, Topeka,
        KS, 81–83
physical layout, 41–42
physician-nurse relationship
    and teamwork, within Relationship-Based Care model, 95
point of care
    caring and healing relationships at, 7
    outcomes measurement, 225
Porter O'Grady, Tim
    conditions necessary for professional practice environ-
        ment, 75
    information systems and health care structures, 216
Pozner, Barry
    and caring leadership, 58–59
Primary Nursing
    and Relationship-Based Care, 166–174
    and Responsibility, Authority and Accountability (RAA), 172
    and transformation example, 83
    comparison to other Patient Care Delivery
        System, 165
    historical analysis of, 163–165
    Myths and Misunderstandings, 171–172
    Tufts-New England Medical Center's Care
        Delivery Principles, 179–182
productivity
    focus on, in Team Nursing, 163–164
Professional Nurse Index (PNI)
    and use in indicator selection for RBC Outcomes
        Measurement, 221
Professional Nursing Practice
    and Patient Care Delivery System, 159
    and Primary Nursing, 164
    and transformation, at St. Francis Health Center, Topeka,
        KS, 83
    boundaries, 125–128
    characteristics of, 122
    conceptual framework, 125–128
    contrasted to bureaucratic nursing practice, 160
    functions of, 132–133
    nurse-patient relationship, 118
    public awareness of, 174
    realms of, defined, 124–125
    Responsibility, Authority And Accountability (RAA)
        Resource Driven Practice, 184

Professional Practice Decision Making Process and Stability
of Patient Condition Model™
O'Rourke, Maria
and Professional Nursing Practice, 132–135
Pullins, Linda
and Partners-in-Practice example, 167

Q

quality of care
and American Nurse Credentialing Center
(ANCC) Forces of Magnetism, 175–176
and staffing patterns/skill mix, 119–120
process of care Indicators
and RBC Outcomes Measurement, 222

R

recruiting
and Professional Nursing Practice
public awareness of, 174
positive factors, 168
reflection skills
and Resource Driven Practice, 192–194
Registered Nurse (RN)
and decision-making, element of Patient Care Delivery
System, 161–162
and staffing, skill mix
determinations, 197–199
effect on adverse outcomes, 118
and teamwork, 96
role of, in Primary Nursing, 166–174
role of, in Team Nursing, 163–164
role of, in Total Patient Care, 164
scope of practice
and Professional Nursing Practice, 135–136
Reigniting the Spirit of Caring
and caring in leadership, 55–56
patient and family perspectives on caring, 55–56
Relationship-Based Care model
and "Caring Connection," Parma Community General
Hospital, Parma, OH, 47–50
and correlation of indicators, 224
and decentralized decision-making, 72 74
and nurse-patient relationship, 117
and outcomes measurement, 215
and physician-nurse relationship, 24
and teamwork, 95

and the therapeutic relationship, 4
and work process improvements, 24
defined, three crucial relationships, 11–14, 106–109
diagram of, 15
fundamental principles, 69
introduction, 4
Responsibility, Authority and Accountability (RAA), 94
reliability
and Education, in Outcomes Measurement, 235–237
report format
implementation in Outcomes Measurement, 233–234
resource allocation
and Resource Driven Practice, example, 209–214
I_2E_2, 212–214
resource driven practice
and staffing,
at Allina Hospitals and Clinics, Mineapolis, MN, 209–214
scarcity, 183–184
skill mix, 197–199
key beliefs, 186–202
Responsibility, Authority And Accountability, 184
Responsibility, Authority and Accountability (RAA)
and boundaries, in Professional Nursing Practice, 125–128
and contrasts between teams and work groups, 91–92
and decentralization, 74
and decision-making
and infrastructure of Relationship-Based Care, 74
element of Patient Care Delivery System, 161–162
and delegated realm of practice, 124
and indicator selection in outcomes measurement, 224–225
and Primary Nursing, 164, 172
and teamwork, 92
resource driven practice, 184
retention
and nurse-physician relationship, 111–112
and Professional Nursing Practice
public awareness of, 174
Forces of Magnetism, ANCC, 175–176
specialist, at Centra Health, Lynchburg, VA, 88–89
Rice Memorial Hospital, Willmar, MN
Exemplar, Teamwork Chapter, 114–116
RN - see Registered Nurse
Roberts, Charlotte
transforming the work environment, 67
role socialization
and nurse-physician relationship, 107

Rosenstein, Alan
    nurse-physician relationship, 111–112

S

Scope of Practice
    and Professional Nursing Practice, 135–136
    and skill mix, in resource driven practice, 198
self awareness, and caring-healing environments, 22
self care
    in caring-healing environments, 22
    overview, in relationship-based care, 4
self-knowing, 4
self-scheduling
    within resource driven practice, 200–202
sentry role
    and Voice of Agency
        in Professional Nursing Practice, 128–132
Shared Governance
    five necessary conditions of, 75
    in practice, at Centra Health, Lynchburg, VA, 88
    in practice, at Kaleida Hospital, Buffalo, NY, 152–153
    in practice, at Rice Memorial Hospital, Willmar, MN, 115
    three models, 75
shared ownership
    resource allocation, example, 209–214
skill mix
    and resource driven care, 186
    optimal determinants, 197–199
    public awareness of, 174
Smith, Douglas
    work groups vs. teams, 91
Social Policy Statement
    and Professional Nursing Practice, 123–124
social responsibility of Nursing, 124–125
Sorbello, Susan
    Exemplar, Caring and Healing Environment Chapter,
    47–50
St. Francis Health Center, Topeka, KS
    and Leadership - recapturing the essence of Nursing, 81–84
    Exemplar, Leadership Chapter, 81–84
    Exemplar, Outcomes Management Chapter, 245–248
staffing
    patterns - and skill mix
        and Outcome Indicators, 118–119

and quality of care, 119
and RBC Resource Driven Practice, 197–199
public awareness of, 174
patterns - structure of care Indicators
and RBC Outcomes Measurement, 222

Stein, Leonard
nurse-physician relationships, 107–110

structure of care indicators - staffing patterns
and RBC Outcomes Measurement, 222

success
and multiple measures of it, 6

Swanson's Middle Range Theory of Caring
and definition of Nursing, 140

Swanson, Kristen
5 caring processes, 33–34
and definition of Nursing, 140

T

teacher role
and Voice of Agency
in Professional Nursing Practice, 128–132

Team Nursing
comparison to other Patient Care Delivery System, 165
historical analysis of, 163–165

Team-Building
and "transparent Environment" level of communication, 116
and articulated expectations, 100
and use of "Commitment to my Co-worker" statements,
102–105

Teams
contrasted to Work Groups, 91–92

Teamwork
characteristics of healthy teams, 101
essential functions in Professional Nursing Practice, 132–133
in high quality patient care delivery systems, 92
in Primary Nursing, 172
necessary skills, 93
Responsibility, Authority and Accountability (RAA), 92
tools for achieving goals of, 93
within the Relationship-Based Care model, 94–95

therapeutic relationship
and American Nurse Credentialing Center (ANCC) Forces
of Magnetism, 175–176
and indicator selection in RBC outcomes measurement, 221

essential functions in Professional Nursing Practice, 132–133
established, in Primary Nursing, 164, 166–169
in Patient Care Delivery System, 159
optimal, within relationship-based care, 23

Thomas, Sandra
and deprofessionalization, 118

Total Patient Care
comparison to other Patient Care Delivery System, 165
historical analysis of, 163–165

tracking
and Outcomes Management Evaluation, 238–240

transformation
and leadership, 74
main elements of (within environment of care), 6
role of clinical manager within, 68
within Relationship-Based Care model, 6

Transformational Leadership Cycle; Koloroutis
and caring leaders, 60–66

transparent environment
and communication in team-building, 116

trending
and Outcomes Management Evaluation, 238–240

Tufts-New England Medical Center
Care Delivery Principles
Primary Nursing Model, 179–182
Exemplar, Patient Care Delivery Chapter, 179–182

U

Ulrich, Roger
"supportive design" in health care, 41–42

Unit - see Nursing Unit

University of Minnesota
and beginnings of Primary Nursing, 1969, 164
Center for Spirituality and Healing
Exemplar, Caring and Healing Environment Chapter,
50–52

V

Validity
and Education, in Outcomes Measurement, 235–237

Voice of Agency
and Professional Nursing Practice, 128–132

W

Watson, Jean
    Forward to Relationship-Based Care, vii–x
    and caring-healing practices of nursing, 141
    and effect of caring-based models on outcomes and
        environments, 220
    Transpersonal Caring-Healing Framework, 30–32
work allocation
    comparison of across Patient Care Delivery Models, 165
    element of Patient Care Delivery System, 161–164
work complexity assessment
    and continuity of care, 201–202
    and skill mix, in resource driven practice, 198
work groups
    contrasted to teams, 91-92
work process improvements
    and continuity of care with relationship-based care, 39
Wright, Donna
    competency assessments, 137
    Teamwork (Chapter Three), 91-116
    tools for goal attainment by teams, 93-94

About the Authors

Sharon Dingman, MS, RN, has worked in health care for over 20 years with experience in staff and leadership roles in a variety of health care settings. Sharon has conducted research confirming the positive impact interpersonal behaviors and caring interactions of caregivers can have on the patients' perceptions, expectations, and outcomes. Her work with care delivery design, leadership development and organizational infrastructure support, and patient/family satisfaction is part of initiatives in the United Kingdom, Denmark and the United States. Sharon has developed The Caring Model™, a practical tool to improve patient, employee, and physician satisfaction and loyalty which has been implemented successfully in numerous hospitals.

Jayne Felgen, MPA, RN, is a specialist in organizational management and work redesign with a patient outcomes orientation. Her experience includes 35 years in virtually every area of health care as a clinician, educator, and executive. She works with executives, physicians, trustees, nurses, allied health professionals and teams using her unique ability to inspire and galvanize individuals to focus on common goals and structure their work to achieve measurable objectives. Most recently, her work has involved strengthening Relationship-Based Care in Canada, the United Kingdom and the United States. Jayne is the President of Creative Health Care Management.

Leah Kinnaird, EdD, RN, is the developer of a wide range of innovative educational programs. She has taught at the University of Miami and at Miami-Dade Community College Schools of Nursing and has been a Magnet consultant with the Institute for Education, Research, and Consultation of the American Nurses Credentialing Center. Leah is the recipient of many awards in the field of education, including the Distinguished Achievement Award through the American Society for Education and Training. Governor Jeb Bush recently appointed her to the Board of the Florida Center for Nursing.

Mary Koloroutis, MS, RN, has over 20 years experience in health care in a variety of settings. She taught nursing leadership at the University of North Dakota and was a community faculty member at the University of Minnesota and Metro State University in Minneapolis. As director for Clinical and Professional Development for Abbott-Northwestern/Allina Hospital (Minneapolis, MN), she emphasized caring and healing in the acute care setting and led the design and implementation of a Professional Nursing Practice model. Mary created the curriculum for Reigniting the Spirit of Caring (RSC), Transformational Leadership, and other holistic approaches.

Marie Manthey, MNA, FRCN, FAAN, has held positions in every level of nursing, from staff nurse to Vice President for Patient Services, as well as Associate Professor at the University of Connecticut, Associate Clinical Professor at Yale University School of Nursing, and Assistant Professor in the University of MN School of Public Health. Her interest in the delivery of hospital services began in the 1960s when she provided leadership for the development of Primary Nursing.

Since that time she has designed and implemented Primary Nursing systems for numerous hospitals and authored *The Practice of Primary Nursing.* Marie is President Emeritus of Creative Health Care Management.

Colleen Person, MMA, RN, provides facilitation, consultation and education services to health care facilities in leadership, team and personal development, healthy work environments, professional nursing practice and health care delivery systems. She brings extensive clinical and administrative experience to her work with client health organizations. She is known for her practical orientation to the challenges and change processes in today's health care environment. Colleen Person is adjunct faculty of Creative Health Care Management.

Donna Wright, MS, RN, has published and lectured across the nation on topics such as creative educational strategies, self-directed learning, competency assessment and validation, creative approaches to mandatory training, creating a healthy work environment, and implementing shared governance. Donna is the current president of the National Nursing Staff Development Organization and is a 1995 recipient of their Promoting Excellence in Consultation Award. She has vast experience in both staff and leadership roles in a variety of health care settings and is the author of *The Ultimate Guide to Competency Assessment in Health Care.*

Components of a
Relationship-Based Care Delivery System

The central focus of Relationship-Based Care is the Patient and Family.
All care practices and priorities are organized around
the needs and priorities of patients and families.
Care is experienced when one human being connects with another.

Leaders know the vision, act with purpose, remove barriers, and consistently hold patients, families and staff as their highest priority.

Teamwork requires a group of diverse members from all disciplines and departments to define and embrace a shared purpose and to work together to fulfill that purpose.

Achieving quality outcomes requires planning, precision and perseverance. It begins with defining specific, attainable and measurable outcomes and uses outcome data to continuously enhance performance.

Professional practice integrates compassionate care with clinical knowledge and expertise. Professional nurses work collaboratively with all caregivers, disciplines and departments in the interest of patient care.

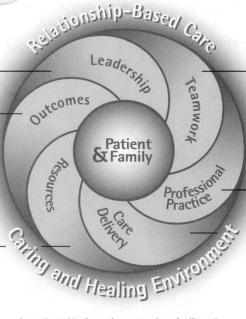

A resource driven practice is one which maximizes all available resources, staff, time, equipment, systems and budget.

The patient care delivery system is the infrastructure for organizing and providing care to patients and families. The system determines the way in which the activities of care are accomplished and is built upon the concepts and values of professional nursing practice.

In a caring and healing environment patients, families and colleagues experience care that is attentive to body, mind, and spirit. Caring theory and science informs intentional actions that support self-care, therapeutic relationships with patients, families and healthy peer relationships. Operational practices and physical settings reinforce this commitment to a caring culture.

Consulting Services from Creative Health Care Management:
A Critical Step in a Successful Relationship-Based Care Implementation

Relationship-Based Care

(RBC) is an adaptation of Primary Nursing for the current state of health care with short-term patients, part-time nurses, and 12-hour shifts. Relationship-Based Care provides the map and highlights the most direct routes to achieve world-class care and service to patients and families in your organization. Organizations who have implemented this model report an increase in patient satisfaction and loyalty, an increase in staff and physician satisfaction and a more resource conscious and efficient work environment.

Here are some of the ways we can help you implement Relationship-Based Care:

- **Education Session**. How does Relationship-Based Care work on individual units and system wide?
  What outcomes can be expected? (Half day or one day)

- **Design Day**. A customized design for your organization and the infrastructure needed to support the implementation of the Relationship-Based Care model. (One day)

- **Appreciative Inquiry Organizational Assessment**. Identifies organizational strengths and desired outcomes. (One to two days)

- **Reigniting the Spirit of Caring**. An inspirational/educational experience to enhance awareness about the different dimensions of caring: caring for self, colleagues, patients and their families. (Three days)

- **Leadership at the Point of Care**. Provides clinical leaders the knowledge and skills to create a healing environment for participants and colleagues. (Three days)

- **Relationship-Based Care Practicum**. A practical five day intensive to provide Relationship-Based Care Project Leaders with the clarity and competence essential for assembling a collaborative team of change leaders. Also a chance to share strategies, ideas and challenges with others implementing Relationship-Based Care. (Five days)

The Relationship-Based Care Practicum

Training for Leaders and Team Members

Sharing the Relationship-Based Care concept with peers and employees, helping managers understand its benefits, and making it a success in your organization is a true challenge. Implementing what matters most in a complex environment requires persistence and strategic knowledge and skills. We know these skills and knowledge can be taught, learned, and applied to any organizational environment. Whether you're a new or experienced Relationship-Based Care Leader, this program will help give you the direction you need to make Relationship-Based Care succeed at your organization. Join us in taking Relationship-Based Care to another level. Enjoy learning and sharing ideas and strategies with other Relationship-Based Care participant teams throughout the country.

The Relationship-Based Care Practicum has been developed specifically to help with the challenges you face in implementing Relationship-Based Care. This practical five day course will provide Relationship-Based Care Leaders with the clarity and competence essential for assembling a collaborative team of change leaders. The program blends a variety of experiential methodologies to develop competencies, integrate learning relative to Relationship-Based Care, and design customized strategies and outcomes in your individual organizations. The experiential methodologies such as dialogue, circle and reflection, appreciative inquiry, and action learning will ensure that participants are actively involved in the experience and apply their learning through presentations and group discussions.

For more information visit:
www.relationshipbasedcare.com

Leading Lasting Change: The Relationship-Based Care Journey
Resource Package

Welcome to the growing community of courageous leaders who have embraced Relationship-Based Care as the means and method for transforming point-of-care and service experiences for patients, families, physicians and staff. This knowledge transfer package has been designed to assist you in engaging leaders from all levels of your organization in understanding the vital and unique roles they play in transforming dreams into reality. Individually, each of us can make an important impact. Collectively, we can create the most desirable environments of care we can imagine!

This ground-breaking resource gives you timely tools to inspire the culture change necessary to implement Relationship-Based Care. In this package, we have bundled award-winning products with expert faculty coaching and education—providing you a virtual consulting experience.

Each Leading Lasting Change Resource Package includes:

Consultation Support • *Your choice of one of the following:*

- Three hours of expert phone consultation with a Creative Health Care Management faculty member, or
- One complimentary tuition for the five-day Relationship-Based Care Leader Practicum

Leading Lasting Change: The Relationship-Based Care Journey DVD Series • 5 copies of the Leading Lasting Change DVD Series including handout. Each copy includes:

1. The C-Suite Journey (54 min.)
2. The Executive Sponsor and RBC Implementation Leader Journey (41 min.)
3. The Results Council Journey (58 min.)
4. The Unit/Department Manager Journey (51 min.)
5. The Unit/Department Staff Journey (63 min.)

Award-winning Books • Five copies each of *Relationship-Based Care*, *I₂E₂: Leading Lasting Change*, *The Practice of Primary Nursing* and one copy of the *Relationship-Based Care Field Guide*.

For more information call: **800.728.7766 or 952.854.9015**

Relationship-Based Care Field Guide: Visions, Strategies, Tools and Exemplars for Transforming Practice

Mary Koloroutis, Jayne Felgen, Colleen Person, Susan Wessel; Editors

This follow-up title to the award winning, national bestseller *Relationship-Based Care: A Model for Transforming Practice*, shows readers how Relationship-Based Care transforms the culture of care delivery – organization wide and at the bedside. Written as a field guide, this book will inspire those who are working on the critical relationships that deliver superior patient care.

Using a unique framework centered around inspiration, infrastructure, education and evidence (I_2E_2), the editors compile stories and experiences of real executives, managers, and frontline care givers implementing Relationship-Based Care nation wide and around the world. *Relationship-Based Care Field Guide: Visions, Strategies, Tools and Exemplars for Transforming Practice* is an essential resource for anyone wanting to implement Relationship-Based Care.

Softcover, 740 pages. (2007) $99.00
ISBN 13: 978-1-886624-23-8

I_2E_2: Leading Lasting Change
Jayne Felgen

In *I_2E_2: Leading Lasting Change*, Jayne Felgen shares her in-depth, practical and elegantly simple formula for inspiring and leading real change at all levels of any organization. *I_2E_2* is not a step-by-step guide to re-creating the ne west business model; rather, it is a new way of embracing change. Leaders learn to organize the whole process, from shared vision to detailed changes in infrastructure. I_2E_2 is a simple and elegant formula for initiating and sustaining lasting change over time.

Softcover, 181 pages. (2007) $24.95
ISBN 13: 978-1-886624-12-2

For more information visit:
www.relationshipbasedcare.com

ORDER FORM

1. Call toll-free 800.728.7766 x111 and use your Visa, Mastercard or Discover or a company purchase order

2. Fax your order to: 952.854.1866

3. Mail your order with pre-payment or company purchase order to:

   Creative Health Care Management
   5610 Rowland Road, Suite 100
   Minneapolis, MN 55343-8905
   Attn: Resources Department

4. Order Online at: www.chcm.com

CREATIVE

HEALTH CARE

MANAGEMENT

5610 Rowland Road, Suite 100

Product	Price	Quantity	Subtotal	TOTAL
B510 – Relationship-Based Care: A Model for Transforming Practice	$34.95			
B650 – See Me as a Person Book	$39.95			
B600 – Relationship-Based Care Field Guide	$99.00			
B560 – I_2E_2: Leading Lasting Change	$24.95			
B651 – Advancing Professional Nursing Practice	$42.95			
M501 – Commitment to My Co-worker Cards (pack of 25)	$15.00			
Shipping Costs: 1 item = $6.00, 2–9 = $8.00, 10 or more = $10.00 Call for express rates				
Order TOTAL				

Need more than one copy? We have quantity discounts available.

Quantity Discounts (Books Only)		
10–49 = 10% off	50–99 = 20% off	100 or more = 30% off

Payment Methods: ☐ Credit Card   ☐ Check   ☐ Purchase Order PO# _____

Credit Card	Number	Expiration	AVS# (3 digit)
Visa / Mastercard / Discover	– – –	/	
Cardholder address (if different from below):	Signature:		

Customer Information	
Name:	
Title:	
Company:	
Address:	
City, State, Zip:	
Daytime Phone:	
Email:	

Satisfaction guarantee: If you are not satisfied with your purchase, simply return the products within 30 days for a full refund.
For a free catalog of all our products, visit www.chcm.com or call 800.728.7766 x111.